MW01138131

Hölderlin's Hymns
"Germania" and "The Rhine"

Studies in Continental Thought

Martin Heidegger

Hölderlin's Hymns "Germania" and "The Rhine"

Translated by
William McNeill
and
Julia Ireland

Indiana University Press
Bloomington and Indianapolis

This book is a publication of

Indiana University Press
Office of Scholarly Publishing
Herman B Wells Library 350
1320 East 10th Street
Bloomington, Indiana 47405 USA

iupress.indiana.edu

Telephone   800-842-6796
Fax   812-855-7931

Published in German as Martin Heidegger, *Gesamtausgabe 39: Hölderlins Hymnen "Germanien" und "Der Rhein,"* ed. Susanne Ziegler
© 1980 by Vittorio Klostermann, Frankfurt am Main

English translation © 2014 by Indiana University Press

Manufactured in the United States of America

Library of Congress Cataloging-in-Publication Data

Heidegger, Martin, 1889–1976.
    [Hölderlins Hymnen "Germanien" und "Der Rhein". English]
Hölderlin's Hymns "Germania" and "The Rhine" / Martin Heidegger ; translated by William McNeill and Julia Ireland.
        pages cm. — (Studies in Continental Thought)
ISBN 978-0-253-01421-4 (cloth : alk. paper) — ISBN 978-0-253-01430-6 (ebook)
1. Hölderlin, Friedrich, 1770–1843. Germanien. 2. Hölderlin, Friedrich, 1770–1843. Rhein. I. McNeill, William Hardy, [date] translator. II. Ireland, Julia, translator.
III. Title.
    PT2359.H2A7433713   2014
    831'.6—dc23

                                                        2014006761

1 2 3 4 5   19 18 17 16 15 14

CONTENTS

Chapter Two
The Fundamental Attunement of Poetizing
and the Historicality of Dasein

PART TWO
"THE RHINE"   133

Chapter One
The Demigods as Mediating Middle between Gods and
Humans. The Fundamental Attunement of the Poem. The
Beyng of the Demigods and the Calling of the Poet

Chapter Two
A More Incisive Review. Poetizing and Historical Dasein

Chapter Three
That Which Has Purely Sprung Forth as Strife in the Middle of Beyng

Translators' Foreword

This text makes available an English translation of Martin Heidegger's first lecture course on Hölderlin's poetry, devoted to an interpretation of the hymns "Germania" and "The Rhine." Delivered in Freiburg in the winter semester of 1934–35, this course marks Heidegger's first sustained engagement with Hölderlin's poetizing, and is particularly important for understanding the works of Heidegger that follow in the mid- to late 1930s and beyond. Key works such as the *Introduction to Metaphysics* (1935), "The Origin of the Work of Art" (1936), and the *Contributions to Philosophy (Of the Event)* (1936–38) receive essential illumination from the first Hölderlin course, as does the 1936 essay "Hölderlin and the Essence of Poetry." Prominent themes of the lecture course include not only the turn to language and poetic dwelling, as well as an engagement with the Hölderlinian themes of the Earth and of the flight of the gods, but also issues of politics and national identity. The scope and significance of the course are thus by no means limited to Heidegger's encounter with a poet.

The lecture course on "Germania" and "The Rhine" was the first of three major lecture courses that Heidegger devoted to Hölderlin, the other two being a course on the hymn "Remembrance," delivered in winter semester 1941–42, and a course on "The Ister" directly following in summer semester 1942.[1] In addition, Heidegger published a collection of essays entitled *Elucidations of Hölderlin's Poetry,* a volume that originally appeared in 1944. Its current, expanded edition contains essays written between 1936 and 1968.[2] The course on "Germania" and "The Rhine" was first published in 1980 as volume 39 of the *Gesamtausgabe* or Complete Edition of Heidegger's works, and subsequently

---

1. The three lecture courses are published as Gesamtausgabe Bd. 39. *Hölderlins Hymnen "Germanien" und "Der Rhein,"* Frankfurt: Klostermann, 1980; Bd. 52. *Hölderlins Hymne "Andenken,"* Frankfurt: Klostermann, 1982; and Bd. 53. *Hölderlins Hymne "Der Ister,"* Frankfurt: Klostermann, 1984. An English translation of the third lecture course has been published as *Hölderlin's Hymn "The Ister,"* translated by William McNeill and Julia Davis, Bloomington: Indiana University Press, 1996. For an overview of the three lecture courses, see William McNeill, "The Hölderlin Lectures," in *The Bloomsbury Companion to Heidegger,* edited by François Raffoul and Eric S. Nelson, New York: Bloomsbury, 2013, 223–35.

2. See Gesamtausgabe Bd. 4. *Erläuterungen zu Hölderlins Dichtung (1936–1968),* Frankfurt: Klostermann, 1981. Translated as *Elucidations of Hölderlin's Poetry* by Keith Hoeller, Amherst, New York: Humanity Books, 2000.

in a second, slightly revised edition in 1989. A third, unaltered edition was published in 1999. The translation presented here takes into account the minor revisions of the second edition.

Translating Heidegger's lectures on Hölderlin is especially challenging, given the fact that his interpretations themselves constitute a unique and original "translation" of Hölderlin, an emergent and ongoing dialogue of the thinker with the poet. Thus, Heidegger's interpretations placed certain constraints on the translation of Hölderlin's poetry and prose, frequently requiring a somewhat more literal rendition of the German than might otherwise be ventured. In our attempts to render Hölderlin's work into English in a manner befitting Heidegger's readings, we have consulted and greatly benefited from the existing translations of Hölderlin by Michael Hamburger, adopting or adapting certain of his solutions on occasion.[3] Also of great assistance has been the French translation of Heidegger's lecture course by François Fédier and Julien Hervier.[4]

Of the particular translation difficulties posed by Heidegger's text, two merit special attention at the outset. First is the use of the German *Seyn*, an archaic form of *Sein* ("being") that was used by Hölderlin and that Heidegger appropriates to mark a non-metaphysical sense of being.[5] Fortunately, English also preserves a parallel archaic form of *being* in the word *beyng*. Thus, in the present volume we have rendered *Seyn* as *beyng* and *Sein* as *being* throughout; the few instances of *das Seyende* we have rendered as *beyngs*, retaining *beings* for *das Seiende*. A second and greater challenge is posed by Hölderlin's use of the word *Innigkeit* and the associated adjective or adverb *innig*, a central and key term of Hölderlin's thinking and poetizing. There appears little choice but to translate this word as "intimacy," which *Innigkeit* typically conveys in everyday German, and this is, for the most part, the solution we have opted for in the present translation.[6] But it needs to be underscored that for Hölderlin this word is not meant to convey an

---

3. Hamburger's translations have appeared in a number of different editions. Those we have consulted are: *Friedrich Hölderlin: Poems and Fragments*, New York: Cambridge University Press, 1980; and *Friedrich Hölderlin: Selected Poems and Fragments*, Penguin Classics Edition, London: Penguin Books, 1998.

4. *Les hymnes de Hölderlin: La Germanie et Le Rhin*. Paris: Éditions Gallimard, 1988.

5. Nevertheless, as the German editor notes, it appears that Heidegger was not always consistent in his marking of this distinction. See the Editor's Epilogue for details.

6. For an exception, see the passage from Hölderlin's essay "On the Operations of the Poetic Spirit" in §8, where it seemed more appropriate to render *innig* as "collected."

interiority of feeling, nor indeed a form of human relationship at all, but rather a certain tension and intensity within beyng itself. For Heidegger's own discussion of Hölderlinian *Innigkeit,* see especially §10 of the present volume.

Throughout the lecture course, Heidegger's focus is on the essence of poetic *Sagen,* a word that we have rendered as both "saying" and "telling," depending on context. According to Heidegger, understanding Hölderlin's poetry entails the task of *mitsagen,* which we have translated as the task of "following the telling" of the poetry. The word "poetry" generally translates the German *Dichtung,* which has also been rendered on occasion as "poetic work," but for the most part as "poetizing," since Heidegger's attentiveness is to the inner movement and flow of the poetic telling. It should be kept in mind that *Dichtung* in ordinary usage refers not simply to the narrow sense of the poetic, of poetry as poesy (*Poësie*), but to literature and the composition of literary works quite generally. See §4(b) for Heidegger's discussion of this.

Since the term *Dasein,* referring to the being of humans, has a rigorously defined and by now well-known meaning in the early Heidegger, we have for the most part followed convention and left it untranslated. In those places where it appears to convey a more general sense of "existence," we have indicated the German in brackets. Consistent with our translation of the "Ister" course, the word "people" translates *das Volk,* a term that has a specific political resonance in the Third Reich, yet also a broader spectrum of meaning that extends back to Hölderlin's poetry and beyond.

Finally, it should be noted that the noun *Bestimmung,* which we have rendered as "vocation," implies "determination" in the sense of that to which something is by its essence or nature determined or "called." For Heidegger, such *Bestimmung* is fundamentally related to the *Stimme,* the "voice," and to the *Stimmung,* the "attunement" of Hölderlin's poetic telling. See especially §8 for details.

References to Hölderlin are to the von Hellingrath edition used by Heidegger. Translators' notes are indicated in square brackets and provided at the end of the volume. Regarding the use of single versus double quotation marks, see the Editor's Epilogue. A German–English and English–German Glossary indicating the translation of key terms are also provided.

The translators would like to thank David Farrell Krell and Mathias Warnes for their assistance and helpful suggestions regarding earlier versions of the translation. We are especially grateful to Ian Alexander Moore of DePaul University for his thorough review of the entire manuscript, which resulted in many improvements, and to Lara Mehling of Whitman College for her suggestions on an early draft of Part

One of the lecture course. The translators thank our readers Charles Bambach and Christopher Fynsk for their careful review of the manuscript and helpful suggestions. We are further grateful to Andrew Mitchell for his input on the translation. William McNeill would like to thank DePaul University for a University Research Council grant that funded the review of the translation, as well as the College of Liberal Arts and Social Sciences for a summer research grant that enabled completion of the translation. Julia Ireland would like to thank Whitman College for the Louis B. Perry Summer Research Grant, and the Alexander von Humboldt Foundation for a summer research grant that enabled her to review Heidegger's original manuscripts at the Deutsches Literaturarchiv in Marbach am Neckar, Germany. We owe special thanks to our copy-editor, Dawn McIlvain Stahl, for her careful work on a difficult manuscript. Last, and not least, we are grateful to Senior Sponsoring Editor Dee Mortensen and to our project manager/editor, Michelle Sybert, at Indiana University Press for their enduring patience with what has been a longer than anticipated project.

Hölderlin's Hymns
"Germania" and "The Rhine"

PRELIMINARY REMARK

Hölderlin

A silence must be maintained around him for a long time to come, especially now, when 'interest' in him is thriving and 'literary history' is seeking new 'themes.' People write now about 'Hölderlin and his gods.' That is surely the most extreme misinterpretation whereby this poet, who still lies ahead of the Germans, is conclusively stifled and made ineffectual under the illusion of now finally doing 'justice' to him. As if his work needed such a thing, especially on the part of the bad judges running around today. One treats Hölderlin 'historiographically' and fails to recognize the singular, essential point that his work, still without time or space, has already surpassed our historiographical rummagings and has grounded the commencement of another history: that history that starts with the struggle over the decision concerning the arrival or flight of the God.

INTRODUCTION

Was bleibet aber, stiften die Dichter.

Yet what remains, the poets found.
("Remembrance," IV, 63, line 59)

The work that we are attempting demands that Hölderlin himself begin and determine it. We shall first listen to the poem that is entitled "Germania."

§ 1. Outline of the Beginning, Manner of Proceeding, and Approach of the Lecture Course

Before we do so, some brief mention should be made of three things: (a) concerning the nature of the beginning of our lecture course, (b) concerning our manner of proceeding in general, and (c) concerning our particular approach.

a) Concerning the Nature of Our Beginning. Commencement and Beginning

What is the significance of our beginning with the poem "Germania," and what does it not mean? A 'beginning' [*Beginn*] is something other than a 'commencement' [*Anfang*]. A new weather pattern, for example, begins with a storm. Its commencement, however, is the complete change in air conditions that brings it about in advance. A beginning is the onset of something; a commencement is that from which something arises or springs forth. The World War had its commencement centuries ago in the political and spiritual history of the Western world. The World War began with skirmishes at the outposts. The beginning is immediately left behind; it vanishes as an event proceeds. The commencement—the origin—by contrast, first appears and comes to the fore in the course of an event and is fully there only at its end. Whoever begins many things often never attains a commencement. Of course, we human beings can never commence with the commencement—only a god can do that. Rather, we must begin with—that is, set out from—something that will first lead into or point to the origin. Such is the nature of our beginning in this lecture course.

We place the poem "Germania" at the beginning in order to point ahead to the commencement. That means: This poem points toward the origin—to what is most remote and most difficult, to that which we ultimately encounter under the name Hölderlin. A word of Hölderlin's passed down to us as a fragment from a late poem tells us where the poem "Germania" belongs, and provides a pointer with which we may begin:

Vom Höchsten will ich schweigen.
Verbotene Frucht, wie der Lorbeer, ist aber
Am meisten das Vaterland. Die aber kost'
Ein jeder zulezt.

Concerning what is highest, I will be silent.
Forbidden fruit, like the laurel, is, however,
Above all the fatherland. Such, however, each
Shall taste last.

(Fragment 17, IV, 249, lines 4ff.)

The fatherland, our fatherland Germania—most forbidden, withdrawn from the haste of the everyday and the bustle of activity. The highest and therefore most difficult, that which comes last, because fundamentally first—the origin withheld in silence. This also tells us what our beginning with "Germania" does not mean. It is not our intention to offer something useful or practicable for the needs of the day or even to recommend the lecture course by so doing, thereby giving rise to the pernicious view that we wish to bring Hölderlin into line with the times. We have no desire to bring Hölderlin into line with our times. On the contrary: We wish to bring ourselves, and those who are to come, under the measure of the poet.

b) Concerning Our Manner of Proceeding in General. Poetizing and Thinking

When we turn to Hölderlin in the context of a lecture course, it remains inevitable that we must *speak* of this poet and of his poetic work. However—to 'talk' 'about' poetry is always in bad taste, since of necessity a poem surely says on its own whatever it has to say. Talking it to death only destroys our 'aesthetic pleasure.' So people say, and thereby imply that our fundamental relationship to a work of art is one of 'enjoyment': the savoring of 'stirrings in the soul' and dabbling in nice feelings. Yet if this orientation toward 'aesthetic pleasure' is in fact a misunderstanding of art, and if we cannot use the criterion of enjoyment with regard to poetry, then there is nothing there that could in all seriousness be talked to death or endangered by such talk. And this quite apart from the fact that in the end there can be a discourse concerning poetry, and that such a thing is not only appropriate, but indeed demanded by poetry. Perhaps we can talk *poetically* concerning poetry, which certainly does not mean we should talk in verses and rhymes. Thus a discourse that takes its lead from a poetic work need not necessarily be an idle talking 'around' or 'about' poems.

There is something else, however, that is more problematic and suspect: that *philosophy* should now launch an assault upon a poetic work. The weapon and defense of philosophy is, after all—or at least ought to be—the icy boldness of the concept. In place of the danger of talking something to death there now arises the danger of thinking it to death, to say nothing of the fact that it appears as though thinking could shortly be abolished altogether. There arises the danger of our dissecting the poetic work into concepts, of our examining a poem merely for the poet's philosophical views or for doctrines on the basis of which we could construct Hölderlin's philosophical system, and from this 'explain' the poetry—this being what one calls 'explaining.' We wish to spare ourselves such a manner of proceeding, not because we are of the opinion that philosophy has to be kept well away from Hölderlin's poetry, but because this widespread and customary way of proceeding has nothing to do with philosophy.

Yet if ever a poet demanded a *thoughtful* coming to terms with his poetry, it is Hölderlin, and this is not at all because as a poet he happened to be 'also a philosopher,' indeed one that we may without hesitation place alongside Schelling and Hegel. Rather, this is so because Hölderlin is one of our greatest—that is, one of our most futural—*thinkers,* because he is our greatest *poet.* A poetic turning toward his poetry is possible only as a *thoughtful* encounter with the *revelation of beyng* that is achieved in this poetry.

That said, the semblance and even the danger of talking and thinking the poetry to death will constantly accompany our work, all the more so, the less we know concerning *poetizing, thinking, and saying,* and the less we have experienced with regard to how and why these three powers belong most intimately to our original, historical Dasein. Our manner of proceeding in general thus stands entirely under the unique law of Hölderlin's work.

c) Concerning Our Particular Approach.
The Poetic Dasein of the Poet

We are beginning immediately with a poem and are thus neglecting to mention: Hölderlin was born on March 20, 1770, in Lauffen on the Neckar as the son of . . . and so forth. He published something like a novel, and in addition wrote this and that. From the nineteenth century to the present, his poetic work has been assessed in such and such a way. 'Life and work,' as they are called, and the history of their treatment are not something we wish to slight—quite to the contrary. In no other case are the historical Dasein of the poet, his need to create, and the destiny of his work so intimately *one* as they are with Hölderlin. Yet for this very reason we must not start by just giving a report that deals with his life, work, and history of his reception, so that we may then concentrate exclusively on 'just the poetry.' We shall encounter the Dasein of the poet in his own time and in each case from his own locale, and do so directly from out of the magnificent treasure of his letters, this Dasein without official position, without hearth and home, without success or renown—that is, without that entire sum of misconceptions that can accrue to a name; 'mentally ill,' as they say, at the age of thirty-five: *dementia praecox catatonica,* as medicine astutely diagnoses it. We shall also have to ponder the fact that the poet himself never published his real and greatest poetic works. We must come to terms with the fact that the Germans took a full hundred years to bring Hölderlin's work before us in a form that forces us to admit that we today are in no way equal to its greatness and futural power.

The purely material aspects of all this—life and works and the history of their treatment—that we have to take note of, learn, and work through, are readily accessible everywhere. However, the most industrious compiling and weighing up of circumstances, influences, precedents, and rules that contribute to the genesis of a poetic work are of no help to us unless we have first thoroughly comprehended the poetic work itself and the poetic Dasein of the poet within and for that work. And this is the point of our undertaking.

A word of Hölderlin's concerning the essence of poetry may serve to conclude these preliminary remarks. We cite from the letter that he wrote to his brother on New Year's day 1799, the last year of the eighteenth century that was then drawing to a close (III, 368ff.):

> So much has already been said about the influence of the fine arts on the education of the human being, but it has always sounded as though no one took it seriously, and this was natural, for no one gave any thought to what art, and in particular poetry [*Poësie*], is according to its nature. One simply viewed it in terms of its undemanding exterior, which admittedly cannot be separated from its essence, but is taken to constitute nothing less than the entire character of poetry; it was regarded as play, because it appears in the modest guise of play, and thus, consequentially enough, no other effect could arise from it than that of play, namely, distraction— almost the very opposite of the effect that it has when it is present in its

true nature. For then the human being gathers himself in its presence, and the poetry bestows a sense of repose—not some empty repose, but that living, vital repose in which all our forces are at work, and yet we do not take cognizance of them as active, simply on account of their intimate harmony. Poetry brings humans closer and brings them together, not like play, in which they are united only by each forgetting himself, so that the living peculiarity of no one comes to the fore.

Poetry [*Dichtung*] is not play, and our relationship to it is not one of playful relaxation that makes us forget ourselves, but rather the awakening and delineation of an individual's ownmost essence, through which he reaches back into the ground of his Dasein. If each individual proceeds from there, then a true gathering of individuals into an original community has already occurred in advance. The crude regimentation of the all too many within a so-called organization is only a makeshift expedient, but not the essence.

If we now attempt to approach that domain in which Hölderlin's poetry unfolds its power and indeed to expose ourselves to it, then we should know that in this endeavor neither swift intelligence, nor a blindly accumulated erudition, nor some contrived welling up of supposedly primal feelings, nor inflated rhetoric will help us, but only that *lucid seriousness* that is able to endure the momentousness of this task for a long time to come.

PART ONE
"GERMANIA"

We shall now read and listen to the poem "Germania." The authoritative edition from which I shall cite is the six-volume edition of Norbert von Hellingrath and his friends.[1] In von Hellingrath's edition, Hölderlin's entire work is distributed throughout the various volumes according to when the poems were composed. The letters are in each case ascribed to different periods and accordingly arranged throughout the various volumes. This is wholly appropriate to the character of Hölderlin's letters, which belong entirely to his work. Perhaps the German youth will one day come to remember the creator of their Hölderlin edition, Norbert von Hellingrath, who, at the age of twenty-eight, was killed in action at Verdun in 1916—or perhaps they will not.

The other critical edition by Franz Zinkernagel, which we must also necessarily employ in our actual work, collects all of Hölderlin's letters together in volume four.[2] Unfortunately we do not have the volume with the different versions.

---

1. Hölderlin, *Sämtliche Werke. Historisch-kritische Ausgabe*, begun by Norbert von Hellingrath, continued by Friedrich Seebass and Ludwig von Pigenot. Second edition. Berlin, 1923. The Roman numerals indicate the volume; page numbers are given in Arabic.

2. Hölderlin, *Sämtliche Werke und Briefe* in five volumes. *Kritisch-historische Ausgabe* by Franz Zinkernagel. Leipzig, 1914.

Germania[3]

I   Nicht sie, die Seeligen, die erschienen sind,
Die Götterbilder in dem alten Lande,
Sie darf ich ja nicht rufen mehr, wenn aber
Ihr heimatlichen Wasser! jezt mit euch
Des Herzens Licbc klagt, was will es anders
Das Heiligtrauernde? Denn voll Erwartung liegt
Das Land und als in heissen Tagen
Herabgesenkt, umschattet heut
Ihr Sehnenden! uns ahnungsvoll ein Himmel.
10   Voll ist er von Verheissungen und scheint
Mir drohend auch, doch will ich bei ihm bleiben,
Und rükwärts soll die Seele mir nicht fliehn
Zu euch, Vergangene! die zu lieb mir sind.
Denn euer schönes Angesicht zu sehn,
Als wärs, wie sonst, ich fürcht' es, tödtlich ists
Und kaum erlaubt, Gestorbene zu weken.

II   Entflohene Götter! auch ihr, ihr gegenwärtigen, damals
Wahrhaftiger, ihr hattet eure Zeiten!
Nichts läugnen will ich hier und nichts erbitten.
20   Denn wenn es aus ist, und der Tag erloschen,
Wohl trifts den Priester erst, doch liebend folgt
Der Tempel und das Bild ihm auch und seine Sitte
Zum dunkeln Land und keines mag noch scheinen.
Nur als von Grabesflammen, ziehet dann
Ein goldner Rauch, die Sage drob hinüber,
Und dämmert jezt uns Zweifelnden um das Haupt,
Und keiner weiss, wie ihm geschieht. Er fühlt
Die Schatten derer, so gewesen sind,
Die Alten, so die Erde neubesuchen.
30   Denn die da kommen sollen, drängen uns,
Und länger säumt von Göttermenschen
Die heilige Schaar nicht mehr im blauen Himmel.

III   Schon grünet ja, im Vorspiel rauherer Zeit
Für sie erzogen das Feld, bereitet ist die Gaabe
Zum Opfermahl und Thal und Ströme sind
Weitoffen um prophetische Berge,
Dass schauen mag bis in den Orient
Der Mann und ihn von dort der Wandlungen viele bewegen.
Vom Äther aber fällt

---

3. IV, 181ff.

40   Das treue Bild und Göttersprüche reegnen
Unzählbare von ihm, und es tönt im innersten Haine.
Und der Adler, der vom Indus kömmt,
Und über des Parnassos
Beschneite Gipfel fliegt, hoch über den Opferhügeln
Italias, und frohe Beute sucht
Dem Vater, nicht wie sonst, geübter im Fluge
Der Alte, jauchzend überschwingt er
Zulezt die Alpen und sieht die vielgearteten Länder.

IV Die Priesterin, die stillste Tochter Gottes,
50   Sie, die zu gern in tiefer Einfalt schweigt,
Sie suchet er, die offnen Auges schaute,
Als wüsste sie es nicht, jüngst da ein Sturm
Todtdrohend über ihrem Haupt ertönte;
Es ahnete das Kind ein Besseres,
Und endlich ward ein Staunen weit im Himmel
Weil Eines gross an Glauben, wie sie selbst,
Die seegnende, die Macht der Höhe sei;
Drum sandten sie den Boten, der, sie schnell erkennend,
Denkt lächelnd so: Dich, unzerbrechliche, muss
60   Ein ander Wort erprüfen und ruft es laut,
Der Jugendliche, nach Germania schauend:
"Du bist es, auserwählt
"Allliebend und ein schweres Glük
"Bist du zu tragen stark geworden.

V Seit damals, da im Walde verstekt und blühendem Mohn
Voll süssen Schlummers, trunkene, meiner du
Nicht achtetest, lang, ehe noch auch Geringere fühlten
Der Jungfrau Stolz, und staunten, wess du wärst und woher,
Doch du es selbst nicht wusstest. Ich miskannte dich nicht,
70   Und heimlich, da du träumtest, liess ich
Am Mittag scheidend dir ein Freundeszeichen,
Die Blume des Mundes zurük und du redetest einsam.
Doch Fülle der goldenen Worte sandtest du auch
Glükseelige! mit den Strömen und sie quillen unerschöpflich
In die Gegenden all. Denn fast, wie der heiligen,
Die Mutter ist von allem, und den Abgrund trägt
Die Verborgene sonst genannt von Menschen,
So ist von Lieben und Leiden
Und voll von Ahnungen dir
80   Und voll von Frieden der Busen.

VI O trinke Morgenlüfte,
    Biss dass du offen bist,
    Und nenne, was vor Augen dir ist,
    Nicht länger darf Geheimniss mehr
    Das Ungesprochene bleiben,
    Nachdem es lange verhüllt ist;
    Denn Sterblichen geziemet die Schaam,
    Und so zu reden die meiste Zeit
    Ist weise auch von Göttern.
90   Wo aber überflüssiger, denn lautere Quellen
    Das Gold und ernst geworden ist der Zorn an dem Himmel,
    Muss zwischen Tag und Nacht
    Einsmals ein Wahres erscheinen.
    Dreifach umschreibe du es,
    Doch ungesprochen auch, wie es da ist,
    Unschuldige, muss es bleiben.

VII O nenne Tochter du der heiligen Erd'!
    Einmal die Mutter. Es rauschen die Wasser am Fels
    Und Wetter im Wald und bei dem Nahmen derselben
100   Tönt auf aus alter Zeit Vergangengöttliches wieder.
    Wie anders ists! und rechthin glänzt und spricht
    Zukünftiges auch erfreulich aus den Fernen.
    Doch in der Mitte der Zeit
    Lebt ruhig mit geweihter
    Jungfräulicher Erde der Äther
    Und gerne, zur Erinnerung, sind
    Die unbedürftigen sie
    Gastfreundlich bei den unbedürftgen
    Bei deinen Feiertagen
110   Germania, wo du Priesterin bist
    Und wehrlos Rath giebst rings
    Den Königen und den Völkern.

Germania

I   Not those, the blessed ones who once appeared,
Divine images in the land of old,
Those, indeed, I may call no longer, yet if
You waters of the homeland! now with you
The heart's love has plaint, what else does it want,
The holy mourning one? For full of expectation lies
The land, and as in sultry days
Bowed down, a heaven casts today
You longing ones! its shadows full of intimation round about us.
10   Full of promises it is, and seems
Threatening to me also, yet I want to stay by it,
And backwards shall my soul not flee
To you, past ones! who are too dear to me.
For to see your beautiful countenance
As once it was, before, this I fear, deadly it is,
And scarcely allowed, to waken the dead.

II   Gods who have fled! You too, you present ones, once
More truthful, you had your times!
Nothing do I want to deny here, and ask nothing of you.
20   For when it is out, and the day extinguished,
It affects first the priest, yet lovingly follow
Him temple and image too and his custom
To the land of darkness and none is able still to shine.
Only, as from flames of the grave, there passes
Then overhead a wisp of golden smoke, the legend thereof,
And now it dawns around the heads of us who doubt,
And no one knows what is happening to him. Each feels
The shadows of those who once have been,
Those of old, who visit thus the Earth anew.
30   For those who are to come press upon us,
No longer does the holy host of humans divine
Tarry in the blue of the heavens.

III   Already nurtured for them, the field indeed grows verdant,
Prelude to a harsher time, the gift is readied
For the sacrificial meal and valley and rivers lie
Open wide around prophetic mountains,
So that into the Orient may look
The man and from there be moved by many transformations.
Yet from the Aether falls

40   The faithful image, and divine edicts rain down
Innumerable from it, and the innermost grove resounds.
And the eagle that comes from the Indus,
And over Parnassus'
Snowy peaks, flies high above the sacrificial hills
Of Italy, and seeks willing prey
For the Father, not as before, more practiced in flight
Ancient one, jubilant he soars over
The Alps at last and sees the many different lands.

IV   The priestess, quietest daughter of God,
50   She who too readily keeps silent in deep simplicity,
Her he seeks, who gazed with open eyes
As though unaware just now, when a storm
With deadly threat rang out above her head;
An intimation had the child of something better,
And eventually astonishment spread across the heavens
For there was One as great in faith, as they themselves,
The powers that bless from on high;
Wherefore they sent the messenger, who, quick to recognize her
Smilingly thinks to himself: You, unshatterable one,
60   Another word must test, and youthfully
He calls it loud, looking at Germania:
"You it is, the chosen one,
"All-loving and a grave good fortune
"Have you become strong to bear.

V   Since then, when hidden in the woods and flowering poppy
Full of sweet slumber, drunken, long you took
No heed of me, until lesser ones too sensed
Your virgin's pride and were astonished whose you were and
    whence you came,
Yet you knew it not yourself. I mistook you not,
70   And in secret, while you dreamt, I left for you
Departing at midday, a sign of friendship,
The flower of the mouth, and solitary was your speaking.
Yet a fullness of golden words too you bestowed,
Blissful one! with the rivers, and they streamed inexhaustibly
Into the regions all. For almost like the holy one,
Who is Mother of all, and carries the abyss,
Otherwise named the Concealed One by humans,
So is of loves and sufferings
And full of intimations too

80   And full of peace your breast.

VI   O drink morning breezes,
        Until you are open,
        And name what is before your eyes,
        No longer may the unspoken
        Remain a mystery,
        Though long it has been veiled;
        For shame is fitting for mortals,
        And thus to speak most of the time,
        Of gods is also wise.

90   Yet where more overflowing than the purest wellsprings
        The gold has become and anger in the heavens earnest,
        Between day and night
        Something true must once appear.
        Threefold you shall circumscribe it,
        Yet unspoken too, as it is found there,
        Innocent one, it must remain.

VII   O name you daughter of the holy Earth!
        Once the Mother. On the rock the waters rush
        And storms in the woods, and in her name too
100   From ancient times echoes the divinity of old once more.
        How different it is! And unmistakably gleam and speak
        From great distance also cheering things to come.
        But in the middle of time
        Peacefully with hallowed
        Virgin Earth lives Aether
        And gladly, to be remembered,
        The needless dwell
        Hospitably among the needless
        At your feast days
110   Germania, where you are priestess
        And defenselessly give counsel
        Around the kings and peoples.

Chapter One
Preparatory Reflection:
Poetry and Language

§ 2. Provisional Path of Approach to the Poem as a Piece of Text

a) The Overarching Resonance of the Telling as Origin for the Choice and Positioning of Words

The poem lies printed before us, a verbal construction that we can immediately read, repeat, and listen to. As this kind of linguistic construction it has a 'meaning.' The meaning is expressed on the one hand via the significance of the words whose content we can immediately grasp ("temple," "flames of the grave," "valley and rivers," "Alps"), and on the other via images ("the flower of the mouth" in line 72, for language), and via peculiar sequences of words, for example in strophe VI, lines 87ff.:

> Denn Sterblichen geziemet die Schaam,
> Und so zu reden die meiste Zeit
> Ist weise auch von Göttern.

> For shame is fitting for mortals,
> And thus to speak most of the time,
> Of gods is also wise.

This does not mean [as the German could conceivably be read (Tr.)] that it is appropriate for gods also to speak in such a way, if they wish to be wise. It means, rather, that to speak in such a way—namely *of the gods*—is something that is also indeed wise. Separating out words that belong together in this way here imparts a peculiar and significant compass to this hint concerning how to speak of the gods, and postponing the phrase "auch von Göttern" ["also of gods"] right until the end of the line sets it sharply into relief in such a way that nothing else follows it, for something different then begins: "Yet where more overflowing. . . ." In addition to the choice of words, positioning of words, and the sequencing of words, it is then above all the entire overarching resonance of the poetic telling that 'expresses' the so-called meaning. Yet this overarching resonance of the telling is not simply the result of the positioning of words and arranging of lines, but rather the reverse: The overarching resonance of the telling is the initial, creative resonance that first intimates the language; it is the origin not only for the arranging and positioning of the words, but also for the choice of words, an origin whose resonance constantly anticipates the use of words. This overarching resonance of the telling, however, is from the outset determined by the fundamental attunement of the poetry, which takes form within the inner outline of the whole. The fundamental attunement for its part grows out of the particular metaphysical locale of the poetry in question.

Yet all of this will have to become manifest to us directly and in its unity and purity with respect to the individual poems themselves. To start with, we shall seek a provisional, albeit tentative, path for approaching the effective domain of this particular poem.

b) 'Content and Form' of the Poem, 'Depiction in Images'

It has long been the custom with regard to a poem, as with artworks in general and in other domains too, to distinguish between 'content' and 'form.' The distinction is hackneyed, and can be used for anything and everything. It gives the appearance of being an absolute, supra-temporal determination, and yet it is entirely Greek, coming solely from Greek existence, and is therefore worthy of question, even if one were to say that something so ingrained and taken for granted can no longer be undone. Along the lines of this content–form distinction one can initially find an accommodating schema in analyzing the poem. The content is relatively simple and easy to identify: The old gods are dead, new ones are emerging. Germania has a special mission with regard to their arrival.

The form of the poem likewise presents no particular difficulties. It consists of seven sixteen-line strophes. The meter does not fit into any of the traditional poetic genres. Nor does the poem have any rhymes. A poem without meter and without rhymes is really no 'poem' at all; it is more prose than poetry. And this is how it appears, especially when we consider the altogether banal conjunctions, for example, "For full of expectation . . ." (line 6); or "For when it is out . . ." (line 20). "For"—a poet says "For" in a poem? And even 'it is out'! And yet— this commonplace, hackneyed, prosaic "For" sounds as though it were spoken for the first time, and this seeming prosaicness of the entire poem is more poetic than the slickest line-hopping and melodic rhyming of a song by Goethe or of any other singsong.

Furthermore, the poem "Germania" evidently gains greater power of poetic expression through the fact that its chief content—heralding the arrival of the new gods—is depicted in images: the messenger of the gods in the image of the eagle, Germania in the image of the dreamy child. It is indeed a cherished device for poets to symbolize what is actually real by means of the most sensuous possible images of what is, in fact, not real. This mode of depiction thus requires special consideration and 'investigation.'

One could, for instance, compare the image of the heralding of the gods here with the Annunciation to the Virgin Mary by the angel, and then further pursue the use of this motif by looking at how it is depicted in painting, for example, considering in turn how it is presented in different periods. One could also investigate where the figure of the eagle and other species of bird appear in the works of other poets, from Homer to Stefan George. Such 'research' projects are often a favorite occupation of academics, and are conducted along the lines of investigations such as that into the camel in Arabic literature (and this is not just made up). The explanation of poetic works is becoming ever greater in scope; and mostly nothing comes of it.

c) Hölderlin's 'Worldview'

It would surely be of greater importance to make some kind of statement assessing and evaluating the poem and this particular kind of poetry—that is, in this instance concerning the use of the aforementioned images. How does our poem measure up in that regard? Consider, for example, the image of Germania—a dreamy girl "hidden in the woods and flowering poppy" (line 65). This is more than a little 'romantic' when compared, say, to the Germania on the Niederwald monument: a fearsome woman with hair flying in the wind and a huge sword. By contrast, this Germania of Hölderlin is, as people say today, 'unheroic.' Yet we need not be surprised at this, for the use of this 'feminine' image manifestly fits in well with the 'worldview' of the poet. Hölderlin's 'worldview,' if the use of this fateful word in conjunction with Hölderlin's name is permitted for a moment, is expressed unmistakably in a manner 'internal' to the poem in its final lines. For there we read that Germania is to "defenselessly give counsel" to the peoples (line 111). Thus, Hölderlin is manifestly a 'pacifist' and stands for the defenselessness of Germania, and indeed for unilateral disarmament. That is very close to treason against one's country.

Yet this, after all, fits well the personality of the poet: He was unable to cope with life, nowhere managed to 'assert' himself, let himself be pushed from one house tutor position to another, and did not even manage to become a *Privatdozent* in philosophy, something he indeed tried to do in Jena.[1]

Thus this poem "Germania," together with its poet, seems altogether out of season for our tough times, provided that the interpretation we have given is true, and provided that we can truly see the 'character' of the poet if we measure him only according to his ability to muscle through. As evidence that this assessment is profoundly untrue, we cite in advance two passages from his correspondence. First, the end of the aforementioned letter to his brother on New Year's day (III, 371f.):

> I thank you a thousand times over for your encouraging remarks on my little poems, and for many another friendly and fortifying word in your letter. We must stick firmly together in all our need and in our spirit. Above all else we wish to adopt, with all love and with all seriousness, the great saying: *homo sum, nihil humani a me alienum puto;*[2] it is not meant to make us frivolous, but only to make us true to ourselves and perspicuous and tolerant toward the world, but in addition we do not wish to be hindered by any idle talk of affectation, exaggeration, ambition, exceptionalism, or such things; we wish only to struggle using all our strengths and to observe with full acuity and tenderness how we bring all that is human in us and in others into an ever freer and more intimate connection, whether depicted in images or in the real world, and if the realm of darkness should ever invade with *force,* then we shall throw our pens under the table and proceed in God's name to where the need is greatest, and to where we are most needed. Farewell!   Yours, Fritz.

The second passage is from a letter to his friend Neuffer half a year later, dated July 3, 1799 (III, 412f.):

> It cheers my heart when you devote yourself more and more to poetry. This epoch has cast such a heavy burden of impressions upon us that it is only, as I feel increasingly each day, through an extended period of activity that continues into old age, and through serious endeavors undertaken ever anew, that we may perhaps in the end be capable of producing that which nature in the first place gave us as our vocation, and which perhaps under other circumstances might have matured earlier, but hardly so completely. If we are called upon by duties that are truly sacred to us both, then we make a fine sacrifice to necessity too when we deny our love of the Muses, at least for a time.

Compare Fragment 17 (IV, 249, lines 18ff.):

> und Feuer und Rauchdampf blüht
> Auf dürrem Rasen,
> Doch ungemischet darunter
> Aus guter Brust, das Labsaal
> Der Schlacht, die Stimme quillet des Fürsten.

> and fire and smoke vapor blossoms
> On arid grass,
> Yet unmixed beneath it
> From a fine breast, the refreshment
> Of the battle, issues the voice of the prince.

Thus, the interpretation of the word "defenselessly" in our poem will not be so easy as the sound of the word suggests. In the end this procedure of ascertaining a 'worldview' from individual words and statements is altogether detrimental.

§ 3. Entering the Domain in Which Poetry Unfolds Its Power

We have recounted the main features of what is said in the poem and have described roughly how it is said. We have become acquainted with the poem, if only by way of a first read and a rough appraisal. And yet, becoming acquainted with a poem—even if this were to extend to the most minute details—does not yet mean *standing within the domain in which poetry unfolds its power.* Thus, we have to overcome the poem regarded as a piece of text that merely lies present before us. The poem must transform itself and become manifest as poetry.

It is indeed in keeping with a habitual, everyday attitude toward the poem that we pull it out during dull and empty hours, for instance, as a fleeting form of spiritual aid, only to then put it away again. Or that we take up poems as something lying present before us, dissecting and explaining them, while others occupy themselves with medieval papal documents, still others with the Civil Code, and others with guinea pigs and earthworms. Each time it is *we* who dispose over the poem as we will. But our task is the contrary: The poetry is to prevail over us, so that our Dasein becomes the living bearer of the power of this poetry.

Yet how is this to happen? How can a poem—I speak only of Hölderlin's poems—still become a power today, when altogether different 'realities' determine our Dasein? A poem: something flimsy, without resistance, evanescent, abstruse, and without substance—such a thing belongs nowhere anymore. For 'lyric' on handmade Japanese paper, bound in leather with gold trim can indeed be charming and pleasing, but this is not the space in which poetry belongs. Yet perhaps it is not at all the fault of the poem that we no longer experience any power in it, but has something to do with us, with the fact that we have forfeited our ability to experience, and with the fact that our Dasein is entangled in an everydayness that keeps it expelled from every domain in which art unfolds its power.

a) The Prevailing of Poetry in the Dasein of the Peoples

In the end, this is a situation that demands thorough examination. Especially if it should turn out to be true that the Dasein of the peoples in each case springs from poetry, and that poetry prevails even at their decline, if their decline is to be a great one and not a mere disintegration. Cf. Aphorism 9 (III, 246f.):

> For the most part poets have come to be formed at the beginning or at the end of a world period. With song the peoples arise out of the heavens of their childhood into active life, into the land of culture. With song they return from there into their original life. Art is the passage out of nature into culture, and from culture back to nature.

This goes together with the end of the first volume of *Hyperion* (II, 186):

> The first child of human, of divine beauty is art. In art, the divine human being rejuvenates and recovers himself. He wishes to feel himself, and therefore he places his beauty before him. In this way the human being gave himself his gods. For in the beginning the human being and his gods were One, when, unbeknown to itself, there was eternal beauty.—
>   I am speaking mysteries, but they are.—
>   The first child of divine beauty is art. Thus it was with the Athenians.
>   Beauty's second daughter is religion. Religion is love of beauty. The wise man loves her herself, infinite, all-encompassing; the people loves her children, the gods, who appear to the people in manifold forms. Thus it was also with the Athenians. And without such love of beauty, without such religion, every state is a bare skeleton without life or spirit, and all thinking and doing are a tree without a top, a column whose capital has been knocked off.

187f.:

> Good! someone interrupted me, that I can understand, but how it is that this poetic, religious people [the Athenians] should also be a philosophical people, this I cannot see.

Without poetry, I said, they would never even have been a philosophical people!

What, he replied, does philosophy, what does the cold sublimity of such knowledge have to do with poetry?

Poetry, I said, sure of my subject matter, is the beginning and end of such knowledge. Like Minerva from Jupiter's head, it springs from the poetry of an infinite, divine way of beyng. And thus what is irreconcilable in the enigmatic source of poetry in the end comes together in it once again.

And 191:

From mere intellect no philosophy can arise, for philosophy is more than just the limited cognition of what is present before us.

From mere reason no philosophy can arise, for philosophy is more than the blind challenge of a never-ending progression in unifying and differentiating a possible subject matter.

But if the divine εν διαφερον εαυτω lights up, the ideal of beauty that belongs to the striving of reason, then it does not challenge blindly, but knows why and wherefore it makes its claim.

If, like May Day in the artist's workshop, the sun of beauty shines into the work of the intellect, he does not go into raptures or abandon the necessity of his work, but fondly contemplates the feast day when he will walk in the rejuvenating light of spring.

If poetry is such a power, then the question of how a people stands in relation to it is simply the question: How do things stand with this people itself?

We wish to examine whether we yet stand in that domain in which poetry unfolds its power, and to do so not by having general discussions about art and culture, but by exposing ourselves to a particular poetry and its power—not just any poetry, but solely and precisely Hölderlin's poetry. It may be that we shall then one day have to be thrust out of our everydayness and thrust into the power of poetry, and that we shall never again return into that everydayness as we left it.

b) Working Our Way through the Poem as
a Struggle with Ourselves

Yet the only way in which we can attain the space of the poetry beyond the poem that lies present before us is the way in which the poet himself becomes master and servant of the poetry, namely, through a *struggle*. The struggle for the poetry in the poem is the struggle with ourselves, insofar as in the everydayness of Dasein we are expelled from the poetry, cast blind, lame, and deaf upon the shore, and neither see nor hear nor sense the surge of the waves in the sea. The struggle with ourselves, however, in no way means inspecting ourselves and dissecting our soul through some form of curiosity; nor does it mean some sort of remorseful 'moral' rebuke; this struggle with ourselves, rather, is a working our way through the poem. For the poem, after all, is not meant to disappear in the sense that we would think up a so-called spiritual content and meaning for the poem, bring it together into some 'abstract' truth, and in so doing cast aside the overarching resonance that oscillates in the word. To the contrary: The more powerfully the poetry comes to power, the more the telling of the word prevails in pressing upon us and tearing us away. And when it does so, the poem is no longer a thing lying present before us that can be read and listened to, as it appears initially whenever we regard language as a means of expression and reaching agreement— something that we have, as it were, in the same way that an automobile has its horn. It is not we who have language; rather, language has us, in a certain way.

Everyday things become worn out, blunted, used up, and empty through their being in use. Hölderlin's poems become more inexhaustible, greater, stranger from year to year—and can nowhere find definitive classification. They still lack their genuine historical and spiritual space. This space cannot come from without; rather, the poems themselves must create this space for themselves. If from here on we are not of a mind to hold out amid the storms of this poetry, then our attempt will indeed remain merely some kind of distraction for the curious.

We require no further extensive remarks to acknowledge that we shall not master Hölderlin's poetry. All of us together are, in our entire Dasein, too little prepared for such a task, and what is more, we lack all the weapons of thought that are needed for this struggle. What we can provide are barely even tentative directives, the kind of inconspicuous pointing that is meant to vanish again in turn, as soon as what the pointer is meant to indicate has been firmly grasped by our eyes and in our heart. What we bring to the poetry is at best like the scaffolding on the cathedral that is only there in order to be dismantled once again. We shall now attempt anew to approach the poetry of the poem. For this it is necessary for us first to clear up two textual questions.

c) Two Textual Questions

Those who were following the text in our first reading of the poem, if they did not have the von Hellingrath edition, must have noticed two deviations: (1) In strophe V, line 76, von Hellingrath reads:

Die Mutter ist von allem, und den Abgrund trägt

Who is Mother of all, and carries the abyss

The words "and carries the abyss" [*und den Abgrund trägt*] are missing in Zinkernagel and in your Reclam edition.[1] (2) In strophe VII, lines 101f., von Hellingrath reads:

Wie anders ists! und rechthin glänzt und spricht
Zukünftiges auch erfreulich aus den Fernen.

How different it is! And unmistakably gleam and speak
From great distance also cheering things to come.

We may make the general remark that the poem has been preserved for us in two handwritten fair copies; they are not drafts, unlike many of the poems from this period. Von Hellingrath designates these versions *a* and *b*. Version *b* breaks off at line 97; thus, it omits the entire last strophe (VII). When this strophe appears in print, it has been taken from the *a* version.

Regarding 1: It is this *a* version, which Zinkernagel and Vesper also use in reproducing the final strophe, that includes the words "and carries the abyss" in line 76. It is unclear why, although strophe VII is adopted from version *a*, line 76 is not also reproduced in its entirety. Nor is it clear why both strophe VII and the words "and carries the abyss" are missing from version *b*. And this quite apart from the fact that these words "and carries the abyss," which tell of the Earth, are so poetically appropriate and said in such a Hölderlinian manner that they ought not to be missing.

Regarding 2: Instead of *spricht* [speak], Zinkernagel and Vesper have the word *spielt* [play], a discrepancy in reading, but also of understanding in terms of the whole. I am unfamiliar with the handwritten manuscript of the poem, but I agree with the way in which von Hellingrath reads this. The word "play" seems to be suggested by the word *erfreulich* [cheering]. Yet if we merely take the latter in the straightforward meaning of pleasant, welcome, or notable, which fits with "play," then we are not understanding this in a Hölderlinian sense. Hölderlin does not mean the word *erfreulich* to be understood in the sense in which we say that trial runs of the new race car

1. Hölderlin, *Gedichte*, Gesamtausgabe, compiled by Will Vesper, Leipzig, 1921. Hölderlin, *Werke*, selected and with a biographical introduction by Will Vesper, Leipzig, 1928 (Helios-Klassiker edition).

that is supposed to reach 240 kilometers per hour produced quite 'encouraging' results. *Erfreulich* [cheering] here means heralding cheer or joy [*Freude*], not cheer in the sense of pleasure (as opposed to disagreeableness), but cheer in the eminent meaning of the Greek word χάρις—charm, enchantment, and therein unapproachable dignity. Yet this reading of *erfreulich* indicates only why we cannot read "play," and does not yet justify why we must read "speak." This can be shown only from our more extensive interpretation.

§ 4. Concerning the Essence of Poetry

a) The Commonplace Conception of Poetry as an Outward Manifestation of Lived Experiences

Our endeavors concern the poetry in the poem. Seen extrinsically, this entails a transition from one thing, the piece of text lying present before us that has a content and a form—both perhaps embellished—over to another, to the poetry. What is meant by 'poetry' here? We must, after all, know this in one way or another if we are not just to be thrust blindly from the poem into the poetry. For manifestly we are supposed to understand and comprehend the poetry, thus stand knowingly within it. We must therefore know of it, simply to be able to distinguish it properly from the poem. And if we are guided here by some idea or other of 'poetry,' then we must be familiar with it as such, especially if it is a commonplace conception that governs us all as though it were natural. In this respect, putting things in a deliberately crude way, we can say the following: We find poetry wherever there is poetizing. And poetizing—this is accomplished above all with the aid of the imagination. The poet imagines something, not just something arbitrary, but whatever he has 'experienced' either in the external world or within himself, a so-called lived experience [*Erlebnis*]. This is then thought out more fully and above all pictured and given the form of symbolic presentation—that is, poetized. Lived experience thus becomes condensed in poetry, and precipitates out in a form that can be extrinsically grasped: for example, in the form of the lyric poem. And one can describe these processes and lived experiences in the 'poetic soul' more profoundly—with the aid of modern 'depth psychology,' for instance. This will involve above all the comparison of various types of poet as representative of various genres of poetry, such as epic, lyric, and dramatic; depth psychology then becomes research into types, and these types can be further investigated in their diverse profiles in each case and in accordance with their belonging to a particular culture of a particular era.

How is poetry understood in all of this, in which lived experiences become condensed? It is represented as *an expression of lived experiences,* and the poem is then the precipitate of this expression of lived experience. These lived experiences can be regarded as the lived experiences of a single individual—in an 'individualistic' manner—or as the expression of a mass soul—'collectively'—or, with Spengler, as the expression of a cultural soul, or with Rosenberg as the expression of the soul of a particular race or as the expression of the soul of a people. All of these conceptions of poetry, which in part infuse one another, move within one and the same way of thinking. Whether we substitute the masses for the individual, or culture for the masses, or put race or the world in place of culture makes absolutely no difference with regard to the fundamental idea that guides these views. What remains decisive throughout is that poetry is conceived as the *outwardly manifest expression of soul, of lived experience.* And it is notable that all of these views can at any time claim to be correct and even be proven. Yet what is correct is not yet thereby true. This whole way of thinking in all of its forms is profoundly untrue and inessential. This becomes clear right away if, for instance, we consider a contemporary view of poetry that comes from this way of thinking and even bears a scientific and philosophical veneer. The writer Kolbenheyer states, "Poetry is a biologically necessary function of the people."[1] It does not take much intelligence to note that this is also true of digestion; it too is a biologically necessary function of a people, especially of a healthy people. When Spengler conceives of poetry as the expression of the soul of a particular culture, then this is true also of the manufacture of bicycles and automobiles. It is true of everything, which is to say, it does not hold true at all. By its very approach, this definition brings the concept of poetry into a realm where the slightest possibility of grasping its essence has been lost beyond hope. All of this is so wretchedly banal that we speak of it only reluctantly. Yet we have to point it out. For one thing, this way of thinking affects not only poetry, but all events and ways of being of human Dasein, which is why this guiding thread can easily be used to erect edifices concerned with the philosophy of culture and with worldviews. Secondly, however, this way of thinking is not the result of an accidental shallowness or inability to think on the part of certain individuals,

---

1. *"Lebenswert und Lebenswirkung der Dichtkunst in einem Volke,"* 1932. *"Unser Befreiungskampf und die deutsche Dichtkunst."* [*"The Value for Life and Effect on Life of Poetic Art in a People,"* 1932. *"Our Struggle for Liberation and German Poetic Art."*] Speech delivered to German universities in early 1932. In E. G. Kolbenheyer, *Vorträge, Aufsätze, Reden.* Darmstadt, 1966.

but has its essential grounds in the kind of being belonging to the human being of the nineteenth century and of modernity in general. If anything can and must be labeled with the widely abused term 'liberalistic,' it is this way of thinking. For it removes itself in principle and in advance from whatever it says and thinks, reduces it to a mere object of its opinions. In this way, poetry becomes one manifestation that can be directly encountered among others, a manifestation that, like every other, can then be defined in an equally indifferent way as an 'outward manifestation' of the soul churning behind it. We take manifestations as expressions. A dog's barking is also an expression. This way of thinking is intrinsically the accomplishment of a quite specific way of being belonging to the 'liberal' human being. It has remained prevalent in a host of forms and variations up to the present day, especially because it can be easily understood, concerns no one, and can be employed unproblematically in every context. Thus, this manner of representing things has altogether run riot—for example, among art historians and in the historiographical investigation of intellectual history. The fact that Nietzsche's work even today falls prey entirely to misinterpretation is in part essentially grounded in the dominance of this way of thinking, all the more because Nietzsche's own strength and art of critically dissecting cultural manifestations encouraged and apparently confirmed such thinking. It is almost as though we follow a natural tendency, therefore, when we repeatedly fall back into this way of thinking. And this is why our own undertaking must, if possible, be secured in advance from being misinterpreted along the lines of the said way of thinking.

Yet up to now we have only been making the following negative points, by way of rejection: (1) The poem is not a linguistic construction that simply lies present before us and is endowed with meaning and beauty. (2) Poetry is not the mental process of producing poems. (3) Poetry is not the linguistic 'expression' of lived experiences in the soul. A poem and poetry are presumably all these things too, and yet this view fundamentally misses their essence. But in what does the essence of poetry then consist? When are we finally going to say it in a positive manner? It cannot be said in a definition. It must first be experienced. Yet this experience also requires a directive.

b) The Provenance of the Word *Dichten,* to 'Poetize'

Dichten, to poetize—what does this word mean really? *Dichten* comes from the Old High German *tihtôn,* connected with the Latin *dictare,* which is an intensified form of *dicere,* meaning to say or tell [*sagen*]. *Dictare* is to say something once again, to recite it, 'dictate' it, to put something down in language, compose it, whether an essay, a report, a treatise, a written complaint or petition, a song, or something else.

All of these things are called *Dichten,* composing something in language. Only since the seventeenth century has the word *Dichten* been narrowed to mean the composition of linguistic forms that we call *poetisch* [poetic] and henceforth *Dichtungen* [poetry]. Initially, *Dichten* has no privileged relation to the 'poetic.' Thus, we cannot draw very much from this linguistic usage. Nor do we get any further if, for instance, we ask what 'poetic' means, so as to set off poetic *Dichten* against prosaic *Dichten* (composition). 'Poetic' [*poetisch*] comes from the Greek ποιεῖν, ποίησις—the making or producing of something. It lies in the same semantic field as *tihtôn,* only the meaning of the word is still more general. By this path we will not attain any knowledge of the essence of what is *dichterisch* or 'poetic.'

Nonetheless, we can avail ourselves of a clue that lies in the original meaning of *tihtôn* and *dicere.* This word belongs to the same root as the Greek δείκνυμι. It means to show, to make something visible, to make it manifest—not just in general, but by way of a specific pointing.

c) Poetizing as Telling in the Manner of
a Making Manifest That Points

Poetizing is a telling in the manner of a making manifest that points. This is not intended as a 'definition,' but only as an aid in helping us understand what Hölderlin says of poetizing and of the poet. Hölderlin tells us this often and in manifold ways, indeed constantly during the greatest period of his creative activity proper, a period to which our poem belongs: namely, 1799 and the years that follow. One might almost say: Poetry and the poet are the singular care of his poetizing. Hölderlin here is the *poet of the poet,* just as the thinker, who in his supreme creative accomplishment is most intimately related to the poet, wants to think and know—indeed *must* want to know—what thinking is and who the thinker is. Such poetizing about the poet and thinking about thinking can of course be a vacuous, unfruitful, and uncreative self-analysis, yet it can also be the most extreme opposite of this. And such is the case with Hölderlin. For now, we can initially only take note from the outside of what Hölderlin says concerning the poet. We may point, with utmost reservation and only as a stopgap, to a few passages whose selection is determined entirely by the interpretation of our poem "Germania." The first passage is taken from the poem "As when on feast day . . ." (IV, 153, lines 56ff.):

Doch uns gebührt es, unter Gottes Gewittern,
Ihr Dichter! mit entblösstem Haupte zu stehen,
Des Vaters Stral, ihn selbst, mit eigner Hand
Zu fassen und dem Volk ins Lied
Gehüllt die himmlische Gaabe zu reichen.

> Yet us it behooves, under God's thunderstorms,
> You poets! to stand with naked heads,
> To grasp the Father's ray, itself,
> With our own hands and shrouded in the song
> To pass on to the people the heavenly gift.

The poet harnesses the lightning flashes of the God, compelling them into the word, and places this lightning-charged word into the language of his people. The poet does not process the lived experiences of his psyche, but stands "under God's thunderstorms"—"with naked head," left without protection and delivered from himself. Dasein *is* nothing other than *exposure to the overwhelming power of beyng.* When Hölderlin speaks of the "poet's soul,"[2] this does not refer to some rummaging around in the lived experiences of one's own psyche, or to a nexus of lived experiences somewhere inside, but signifies the most extreme outside of a naked exposure to the thunderstorms. Regarding this, let us listen to a section from the letter to his friend Böhlendorff of December 4, 1801, shortly before his departure for Bordeaux from where, half a year later, he returned to his homeland as someone 'smitten' (V, 321):

> O friend! The world lies brighter there before me than hitherto, and more grave! it pleases me how things are going, it pleases me, just as in summer when "the ancient, holy father by his gentle hand blesses us with the lightning he shakes down from crimson clouds." For of all the things I can behold of God, this sign has become for me the chosen one. Before, I could rejoice over a new truth, a better view of that which lies over and around us, now I fear that things may go for me in the end as they did for the ancient Tantalus, who bit off more of the gods than he could chew. But I do what I can, and think, when I see, if I too must take my path the same way as the others, that it is godless and crazy to seek a path that would be safe from all danger of attack, and that for death, nature offers no remedy.

d) Poetizing as Receiving the Beckonings of the Gods and Passing Them on to the People

Thunderstorms and lightning are the language of the gods, and the poet is the one who has to endure this language without shirking, to take hold of it, and to place it into the Dasein of the people. Following the fundamental meaning of the root of the word, we determined poetizing as *a telling in the manner of a making manifest that points.* This corresponds to the way the language of the gods is characterized, as understood by Hölderlin in his knowing of an ancient piece of

---

2. "As when on feast day . . . ," IV, 152, line 44.

wisdom (cf. p. 114). Thus he says in the poem "Rousseau" (IV, 135, lines 39f.):

> . . . und Winke sind
> Von Alters her die Sprache der Götter.

> . . . and beckonings are
> From time immemorial the language of the gods.

Poetizing is a passing on of these beckonings to the people, or, from the perspective of a people, poetizing means placing the Dasein of the people into the realm of these beckonings, that is, a showing, a pointing in which the gods become manifest, not as something referred to or observable, but in their beckoning.

Even in the realm of the everyday, a beckoning is something other than a sign, and to beckon means something other than to point to something, or to merely draw attention to something. Whoever beckons does not just draw attention to himself—for instance, to the fact that he is standing at such and such a place and can be reached there. Rather, beckoning—for example, when departing—is the retaining of a proximity as the distance increases, and conversely, when arriving, is a making manifest the distance that still prevails in this felicitous proximity. The gods simply beckon, however, insofar as they *are.* In keeping with this essence of beckoning and its essential variants, we must understand beckoning as the language of the gods, and consequently understand poetizing as the beckoning shrouded in the word. There is nothing here of any 'expression of psychical lived experiences,' nor indeed of that other misinterpretation of poetry in which the object of poetry is just that which is poetized in whatever manner, whether by our imagination soaring over what is real, or by our reproducing what is real by working it over poetically. In both cases, poetry is understood as the non-real. Yet Hölderlin says in the last line of the poem "Remembrance" (IV, 63, line 59):

> Was bleibet aber, stiften die Dichter.

> Yet what remains, the poets found.

Poetizing is founding, a grounding that brings about that which remains. The poet is the one who grounds beyng. What we call the real in our everyday life is, in the end, what is unreal. In the beckoning of the gods being, as it were, built into the foundational walls of the language of a people by the poet, without the people perhaps having any intimation of this initially, beyng is founded in the historical Dasein of the people, a pointer and directedness are placed into this beyng and deposited there. Poetizing—the expression of psychical lived experiences? How far removed is all that! Poetizing—enduring the beckonings of the gods—the founding of beyng.

e) Everyday Appearance and the Being of Poetry

And yet—consider this poetizing and this Dasein of a poet if we measure it against the ready-made standards of the everyday with its demands and pretentions, its strife and quarrels, its harshness and impatience, its half measures and calculations, without all of which it could never be what it has to be. What is poetizing compared to this! Hölderlin knew, and names it "this most innocent of all occupations" in a letter to his mother. The letter dates, not from the time when he was a high school student, but from the period when he was beginning his greatest work. In this letter of January 1799, almost contemporaneous with the letter to his brother already cited, we read (III, 376f.):

> I am altogether in agreement with you, dearest mother!, that it will be good for me in future to try to make my own the least demanding office there can be for me, especially also because the perhaps unfortunate inclination toward poetry that, from my youth on, I always sought to counter by honest endeavors and by way of so-called more serious occupations is still in me, and judging from all the experiences I have undergone myself, will remain in me as long as I live. I do not wish to decide whether it is mere fancy or a true instinct of nature. But I do know this by now: that I have brought about profound conflict and discontent within myself by, among other things, pursuing with supreme attentiveness and effort occupations that seemed to be less suited to my nature, such as philosophy. And this was something well intentioned on my part, because I feared being called an idle poet. For a long time I knew not why the study of philosophy—which otherwise rewards with a sense of serenity the persistent hard work that it demands—made me only more unsettled and even passionate the more unreservedly I dedicated myself to it; and now I explain this to myself by the fact that I distanced myself from my own distinctive inclination to a greater degree than was necessary, and with this unnatural labor my heart sighed, longing for its own beloved occupation as the Swiss shepherds who join the military long for their valley and their flock. Do not say that I am just being carried away in a fit of enthusiasm! For why is it that I find peace and well-being, like a child, when I pursue this most innocent of all occupations undisturbed and with cherished leisure—an occupation that, admittedly, is honored only if it is masterly, and rightly so, something that mine is perhaps not by a long way. And this for the reason that, from the time I was a boy, I never dared to pursue it

to the degree that I pursued many other things, things I pursued perhaps too good-naturedly and conscientiously, on account of my circumstances and for the sake of the opinions of human beings. And yet every art demands an entire human life, and everything that the student learns, he must learn in relation to that art if he wishes to develop a disposition toward it and not just be stifled in the end.

Hölderlin's letters to his mother belong more than his other letters to his work, even though, or indeed because, he really is silent in them concerning his work and lovingly protects his mother in his reticence. Even in those places where he writes expressly concerning himself and his endeavors, he always speaks in a manner that is accessible and comprehensible to his mother. Indeed, Hölderlin unfolds the greatest intimacy precisely where he speaks to her from an immense distance toward his terrible calling. Where he follows his mother with an assent that is in each case genuine within its respective limits, he also indeed refuses himself to her in the end, gently yet firmly. The portion of the letter we have quoted documents this clearly in its beginning and its ending. Thus precisely these letters to his mother in their lucid intimacy bear witness to the immense need that attends his calling and to what is truly heroic in his Dasein, because they veil these things in a singular tenderness.

Poetry: "this most innocent of all occupations," seen from the perspective of the everyday. Poetry: a standing "under God's thunderstorms" that founds beyng, as experienced and comprehended in an originary manner by the Dasein of the poet. Poetry: It is both such appearance and such being. That everyday appearance belongs to poetry as the valley belongs to the mountain. Hölderlin's Dasein has held apart—and that means held together and sustained in supreme intimacy—this most extreme opposition of appearance and being in its greatest possible tension. Knowing this is the very first precondition for comprehending anything at all of what we call his apparent 'life story,' not to mention his so-called mental illness. Because such appearance and such being go together, there indeed appear to be very many poets, yet in truth there are but very few. There are both: many and few; what remains decisive is simply that we are able to distinguish them and know about the right measures for making a proper distinction—that we are sure of where the boundary line runs.

f) Poetry Not as Merit, but Exposure to Beyng

If poetry is not to be understood as the outward manifestation of a cultural soul or any other type of soul, then nor is it to be understood as a cultural achievement on the part of human beings. One can of course regard it in this way, just as sport and industry too are outward manifestations and achievements of this kind and can be described as such. If one grasps poetry in this way in the first instance and in this way alone, then one regards it as one of those human-made products whose production human beings have come to earn. Yet poetry for Hölderlin does not belong to the meritorious achievements and advances of culture, for he says:

Voll Verdienst, doch dichterisch wohnet
Der Mensch auf dieser Erde.

Full of merit, yet poetically
Humans dwell upon this Earth.

("In beautiful blue . . . ," VI, 25, lines 32f.)

All that the human being works and effects has its necessity and is "full of merit." Yet—in sharp opposition to this—none of this reaches *his dwelling upon this Earth,* his proper Dasein, for such beyng is "poetic" and has nothing to do with "merit" or cultural achievement or outward manifestations of soul. "Poetic" and poetical here mean that which sustains from the ground up the configuration of the being of the human being as a historical Dasein in the midst of beings as a whole. "Poetic" does not mean some kind of 'façon' or mode of providing additional embellishment for one's life, but is an exposure to beyng, and as such exposure is the fundamental occurrence of the historical Dasein of the human being. Human beings or a people can certainly be exiled from this poetic dwelling, but even then human beings still *are*; a people still *is*. This points to the fact that the historical being of humans is shot through with ambiguity, and indeed essentially so. The human being is and yet is not. It appears to be beyng and is not. And so too with poetry.

"Full of merit. . . ." In this context, we must admit and acknowledge the fact that the poem from which this quotation is taken does not come from the later period of the poet's creative activity, but from the time after he had already been treated in the Tübingen psychiatric clinic and deemed incurable, and had taken up residence in a small room provided by the carpenter Zimmer in Tübingen—from the time of his 'derangement.' Thus, the normal, run-of-the-mill human being may conclude that the poem does not count. Yet this is an erroneous conclusion here. We must express matters the other way around, and say that the poet's mental illness is a peculiar thing. Measles is measles and stomach cancer is stomach cancer, even though there are certainly various ways in which different people come to terms with it; but the illness as such is independent of this within certain essential limits. This is also true of certain kinds of so-called mental illness, although it is not true in every case. Here it can depend on who it is that is mentally ill. Such a case is the 'case' of Hölderlin. We shall now listen to the poem "In beautiful blue . . ." from the time of his 'derangement' (VI, 24ff.):

In lieblicher Bläue blühet mit dem
Metallenen Dache der Kirchthurm. Den
Umschwebet Geschrei von Schwalben, den
Umgiebt die rührendste Bläue. Die Sonne
Gehet hoch darüber und färbet das Blech,
Im Winde aber oben stille
Krähet die Fahne. Wenn einer
Unter der Gloke dann herabgeht, jene Treppen,
Ein stilles Leben ist es, weil,
10   Wenn abgesondert so sehr die Gestalt ist, die
Bildsamkeit herauskommt dann des Menschen.
Die Fenster, daraus die Gloken tönen, sind
Wie Thore an Schönheit. Nemlich, weil
Noch der Natur nach sind die Thore, haben diese
Die Ähnlichkeit von Bäumen des Walds. Reinheit
Aber ist auch Schönheit.
Innen aus Verschiedenem entsteht ein ernster Geist.
So sehr einfältig aber die Bilder, so sehr
Heilig sind die, dass man wirklich
20   Oft fürchtet, die zu beschreiben. Die Himmlischen aber,
Die immer gut sind, alles zumal, wie Reiche,
Haben diese Tugend und Freude. Der Mensch
Darf das nachahmen.
Darf, wenn lauter Mühe das Leben, ein Mensch
Aufschauen, und sagen: so
Will ich auch seyn? Ja. So lange die Freundlichkeit noch
Am Herzen, die Reine, dauert, misset
Nicht unglüklich der Mensch sich
Mit der Gottheit. Ist unbekannt Gott?
30   Ist er offenbar wie der Himmel? Dieses
Glaub' ich eher. Der Menschen Maas ist's.
Voll Verdienst, doch dichterisch wohnet
Der Mensch auf dieser Erde. Doch reiner
Ist nicht der Schatten der Nacht mit den Sternen,
Wenn ich so sagen könnte, als
Der Mensch, der heisset ein Bild der Gottheit.

Giebt es auf Erden ein Maas? Es giebt
Keines. Nemlich es hemmen den Donnergang nie die Welten
Des Schöpfers. Auch eine Blume ist schön, weil
40   Sie blühet unter der Sonne. Es findet
Das Aug' oft im Leben Wesen, die
Viel schöner noch zu nennen wären
Als die Blumen. O! ich weiss das wohl! Denn
Zu bluten an Gestalt und Herz und ganz
Nicht mehr zu seyn, gefällt das Gott?
Die Seele aber, wie ich glaube, muss
Rein bleiben, sonst reicht an das Mächtige
Mit Fittigen der Adler mit lobendem Gesange
Und der Stimme so vieler Vögel. Es ist
50   Die Wesenheit, die Gestalt ist's.
Du schönes Bächlein, du scheinst rührend,
Indem du rollest so klar, wie das
Auge der Gottheit, durch die Milchstrasse.
Ich kenne dich wohl, aber Thränen quillen
Aus dem Auge. Ein heiteres Leben seh' ich
In den Gestalten mich umblühen der Schöpfung, weil
Ich es nicht unbillig vergleiche den einsamen Tauben
Auf dem Kirchhof. Das Lachen aber
Scheint mich zu grämen der Menschen,
60   Nemlich ich hab' ein Herz.
Möcht' ich ein Komet sein? Ich glaube. Denn sie haben
Die Schnelligkeit der Vögel; sie blühen an Feuer
Und sind wie Kinder an Reinheit. Grösseres zu wünschen,
Kann nicht des Menschen Natur sich vermessen.
Der Tugend Heiterkeit verdient auch gelobt zu werden
Vom ernsten Geiste, der zwischen
Den drei Säulen wehet des Gartens.
Eine schöne Jungfrau muss das Haupt umkränzen
Mit Myrthenblumen, weil sie einfach ist
70   Ihrem Wesen nach und ihrem Gefühl.
Myrthen aber giebt es in Griechenland.

Wenn einer in den Spiegel siehet, ein Mann, und
Siehet darinn sein Bild, wie abgemahlt; es gleicht
Dem Manne, Augen hat des Menschen Bild, hingegen
Licht der Mond. Der König Oedipus hat ein
Auge zuviel vieleicht. Diese Leiden dieses
Mannes, sie scheinen unbeschreiblich,
Unaussprechlich, unausdrücklich. Wenn das Schauspiel

80   Ein solches darstellt, kommt's daher. Wie
Ist mir's aber, gedenk' ich deiner jezt?
Wie Bäche reisst das Ende von Etwas mich dahin,
Welches sich wie Asien ausdehnet. Natürlich
Dieses Leiden, das hat Oedipus. Natürlich ist's darum.
Hat auch Herkules gelitten?
Wohl. die Dioskuren in ihrer Freundschaft haben die
Nicht Leiden auch getragen? Nemlich
Wie Hercules mit Gott zu streiten, das ist Leiden. Und
Die Unsterblichkeit im Neide dieses Lebens,
Diese zu theilen, ist ein Leiden auch.
90   Doch das ist auch ein Leiden, wenn
Mit Sommerfleken ist bedekt ein Mensch,
Mit manchen Fleken ganz überdekt zu seyn! Das
Thut die schöne Sonne: nemlich
Die ziehet alles auf. Die Jünglinge führt die Bahn sie
Mit Reizen ihrer Stralen wie mit Rosen.
Die Leiden scheinen so, die Oedipus getragen, als wie
Ein armer Mann klagt, dass ihm etwas fehle.
Sohn Laios, armer Fremdling in Griechenland!
Leben ist Tod, und Tod ist auch ein Leben.

In beautiful blue with its
Metal roof the church tower blossoms. It
The swallows' cries swirl round, it
The most touching blue surrounds. The sun
Rises high above it and colors the tin,
Yet silently in the wind above
Crows the weathercock. If someone
Then descends beneath the bell, those stairs,
A still life it is, because,
10   When one's figure is so very detached, the
Plasticity of humans then emerges.
The windows from which the bells toll are
Like gateways in their beauty. Namely, because
The gateways are in keeping with nature, they bear
Likeness to trees in the woods. Purity
However is also beauty.
Within out of diversity a serious spirit arises.
Yet the images are so very simple, so very
Holy are they, that one really
20   Is often afraid to describe them. The heavenly, however,
Who are ever good, all at once, like the wealthy,

Have this virtue and joy. Humans
May imitate that.
May, when life is nothing but toil, a human
Look upward and say: thus
I too would be? Yes. So long as kindliness, in purity,
Still endures in the heart, humans
May measure themselves not unhappily
By divinity. Is God unknown?
30   Is he manifest like the heavens? This rather
I believe. The measure of humans it is.
Full of merit, yet poetically
Humans dwell upon this Earth. Yet the
Shadow of night with its stars is not purer,
If I could say such a thing, than
The human being: he is called an image of divinity.

Is there a measure on Earth? There is
None. For never do the worlds of the creator stem
The course of thunder. A flower too is beautiful, because
40   It blossoms under the sun. Often in life
The eye finds creatures that
Could be called much more beautiful
Than flowers. O! Well I know it! For
To have one's figure and heart bleed, and
No longer to be at all, does that please God?
Yet the soul, as I believe, must
Stay pure, else the eagle on pinions
Reach to the mighty with songs of praise
And the voice of so many birds. It is
50   The essence, form it is.
You beautiful stream, you seem touching
As you glide so clear, like the
Eye of divinity, through the Milky Way.
I know you indeed, but tears flow
From the eye. A cheerful life I see
Blossom round me in the forms of creation, for
I compare it not uncharitably to the solitary doves
In the churchyard. Yet the laughter
Of humans seems to grieve me,
60   For I have a heart.
Would I like to be a comet? I think so. For they have
The swiftness of birds; they blossom with fire
And are as children in purity. To wish for greater

Our human nature cannot presume.
Serenity of virtue merits also being praised
By the serious spirit that reigns
Between the three columns in the garden.
A beautiful virgin must wreathe her head
With myrtle blossoms, because she is simple
70 In her nature and in her feeling.
But myrtles are found in Greece.

When someone looks in the mirror, a man, and
Sees therein his image, as though it were painted; it resembles
The man, the human image has eyes, whereas
The moon has light. King Oedipus has perhaps
An eye too many. These sufferings of
This man, they seem indescribable,
Unspeakable, inexpressible. If the drama
Portrays such things, this is why. Yet how
80 Are things for me, if now I think of you?
Like streams the end of something tears me away,
That stretches out like Asia. Naturally
Oedipus has this suffering too. Naturally this is why.
Did Hercules too suffer?
No doubt. The Dioscuri in their friendship, did not
They too bear suffering? For
To quarrel with God like Hercules, that is suffering. And
The immortality amid the envy of this life,
To share in this is also a suffering.
90 Yet this too is a suffering, when
A human being is covered with freckles,
To be altogether covered with many a spot! This
Is what the beautiful sun does: namely,
It raises all things upward. It leads the young along their path
With the charms of its rays, like with roses.
The sufferings Oedipus endured seem thus, as when
A poor man laments that he lacks something.
Son of Laios, poor stranger in Greece!
Life is death, and death is also a life.

Cf. Hölderlin's "Remarks on Oedipus" (V, 180):

Because such human beings stand under violent conditions, their language, too, speaks in a more violent order, almost in the manner of Furies.

So far as a proper interpretation is concerned, this word replaces everything that has been written to this day in explanation of Sophocles' tragedy. We shall examine this statement in more detail later (p. 60f.).

g) Poetic and Thoughtful Telling

Yet if poetry and the poetic are thus identical with the fundamental occurrence of the historical Dasein of human beings—at once harmless and terrible—and if poetry is a *telling*—*language*, how is it then with language? We cannot yet take up this question here. But one thing is certain: If poetry is at once the most harmless thing and something terrible, and thus ambivalent and ambiguous, then poetic telling must also be such. The human being can take this harmlessness to be the only serious thing. Yet he can also misuse what is terrible as the mere play of psychic excesses. Poetic telling looks like a reciting that we can repeat. In the same direct way and indeed on the same level as we speak to our neighbor, we can also recite and listen to a poem together. And yet this telling is in the end something that is fundamentally quite different.

Matters stand in a corresponding—though not identical—way to the situation of *poetic* telling where the *thoughtful* telling of philosophy is concerned. In a real philosophical lecture, for example, the decisive issue is not really what is said directly, but what is kept silent in this saying. For this reason, one can indeed listen to and transcribe philosophical lectures without further ado, and yet in so doing constantly *mishear*—and this not in the incidental sense that one incorrectly apprehends individual words or concepts, but in the fundamental sense of an essential mishearing, in which one never notices what is really being spoken of, or to whom it is properly being spoken.

In the sciences, by contrast, and elsewhere too, the task is to directly grasp what is said. Admittedly, in order to simultaneously preserve in silence what is essential in one's saying, one cannot simply ramble on about something arbitrary in a confused manner. Rather, such telling demands of philosophy a rigor of thinking and of the concept that the sciences can never attain and indeed do not require. Thus, for example, the possibly philosophical statement may be made somewhere and on a certain occasion that what is decisive in philosophy and science—merely applied philosophy—consists in questioning, in persisting in the question. To this, 'one' retorts: Questioning? Surely not! The decisive thing is the answer. Every petit bourgeois understands that, and because he understands it, it must be right, and this can then all be called 'science in touch with the people.' If this kind of devastation of all proper thinking had no further consequences, then everything would be in order. For only someone who does not understand what is properly essential here can be surprised or even get worked up about such a misunderstanding and its unavoidability. Surprise or even a sense of outrage have no place here, just as little as when someone who sees a magnificent barnyard wished to rail against the fact that the barnyard also has a rather substantial manure pit beside it. What would a barnyard be without manure!

Saying and saying are not the same thing. To repeat a poem or even to be able to recite it by heart does not yet mean being able to follow poetically the telling of the poetry. We would thus do well to read again, and indeed frequently, the poem "Germania."

§ 5. The Question Concerning the 'We' in the Turbulence of the Dialogue

a) The 'I' in Refusal of the Gods of Old

Let us read the poem "Germania" again:

> Nicht sie, die Seeligen, die erschienen sind,
>
> Not those, the blessed ones who once appeared,

Who is speaking here? This is obviously a highly superfluous question, for who else should be speaking in the poem but its so-called author? Moreover, we then read straight after this:

> Sie darf ich ja nicht rufen mehr,
>
> Those, indeed, I may call no longer,
>
> (Line 3)

> . . . doch will ich bei ihm bleiben,
>
> . . . yet I want to stay by it,
>
> (Line 11)

> Nichts läugnen will ich hier und nichts erbitten.
>
> Nothing do I want to deny here, and ask nothing of you.
>
> (Line 19)

Who is this 'I'? Hölderlin? As author of the poem—yes, insofar as the author brings to language the entire poem as a linguistic construction. The poem as a whole is language and speaks. Certainly this is true of every poem, and yet there are differences here. The magnificent poem "Bread and Wine," from 1801, begins (IV, 119):

Rings um ruhet die Stadt; still wird die erleuchtete Gasse,

The town is peaceful round about; the lane, lit up, falls silent,

Here too the poem speaks, and in a certain sense Hölderlin speaks as author. Yet really no one is speaking there; rather: the town is peaceful round about, and the lit-up lane falls silent. Everything is peaceful and silent here. In our poem "Germania," however, the language of the poem expressly lets someone speak, and indeed in the first person. Yet not in such a way that the entire poem would be spoken in the first person by this 'I'; to the contrary: In line 19, the 'I' speaks for the last time. This 'I' has, in its telling, refused the gods of old, and only the legend of them now "dawns around the heads of us who doubt" (line 26).

b) The 'We,' the Man, and the Eagle.
The Speaking of Language

Und keiner weiss, wie ihm geschieht. Er fühlt
Die Schatten derer, so gewesen sind,

And no one knows what is happening to him. Each feels
The shadows of those who once have been,

(Lines 27f.)

The 'I' has become a 'we.' No one of us knows—each feels the shadow.

Denn die da kommen sollen, drängen uns,

For those who are to come press upon us,

(Line 30)

The poem, which began in the first person, now, no longer speaking in the first person, brings *us to language* as we await the dawning of the new gods that press upon us. Yet straightaway we find ourselves no longer in language; rather (lines 33ff.):

Schon grünet ja, im Vorspiel rauherer Zeit
Für sie erzogen das Feld, bereitet ist die Gaabe
Zum Opfermahl und Thal und Ströme sind
Weitoffen um prophetische Berge,
Dass schauen mag bis in den Orient
Der Mann . . .

Already nurtured for them, the field indeed grows verdant,
Prelude to a harsher time, the gift is readied
For the sacrificial meal and valley and rivers lie
Open wide around prophetic mountains,
So that into the Orient may look
The man . . .

"The man." Who is this man? He looks into the Orient, and from there is met by many transformations: Indus, Parnassus, Italy, the Alps. "The man" who looks and awaits has taken our place. The man sees the eagle and hears him call out loud (line 60) and say (lines 62ff.):

"Du bist es, auserwählt
"Allliebend und ein schweres Glük
"Bist du zu tragen stark geworden.

"You it is, the chosen one,
"All-loving and a grave good fortune
"Have you become strong to bear.

From here to the end of the poem the eagle speaks and the man listens. Of what does the eagle speak? Of language (lines 69ff.):

. . . Ich miskannte dich nicht,
Und heimlich, da du träumtest, liess ich
Am Mittag scheidend dir ein Freundeszeichen,
Die Blume des Mundes zurük und du redetest einsam.
Doch Fülle der goldenen Worte sandtest du auch
Glükseelige! mit den Strömen und sie quillen unerschöpflich
In die Gegenden all.

. . . I mistook you not,
And in secret, while you dreamt, I left for you
Departing at midday, a sign of friendship,
The flower of the mouth, and solitary was your speaking.
Yet a fullness of golden words too you bestowed,
Blissful one! with the rivers, and they streamed inexhaustibly
Into the regions all.

The eagle speaks of the solitary speaking of the girl and of the "fullness of golden words" that emanate in such solitary speech. Yet he speaks to her not only of the language that has been bestowed upon her and its solitary speech, but calls upon her to speak (lines 81ff.):

O trinke Morgenlüfte,
Biss dass du offen bist,
Und nenne, was vor Augen dir ist,
Nicht länger darf Geheimniss mehr
Das Ungesprochene bleiben,

O drink morning breezes,
Until you are open,
And name what is before your eyes,
No longer may the unspoken
Remain a mystery,

However, see lines 95f.: " . . . unspoken too . . . it [the true] must remain." Thus, she is to name and yet leave unspoken. Finally, the eagle
also says whom the girl is to name (lines 97f.):

O nenne Tochter du der heiligen Erd'!
Einmal die Mutter.

O name you daughter of the holy Earth!
Once the Mother.

and how she is to name the Mother. The poem is language. Yet who
properly speaks in the poem? The author, the 'I,' we, the man, the
eagle. They speak of language that is to name (speak) and yet in naming to leave unspoken.

If we have followed even vaguely the pointers just given, without
conceptually 'comprehending' the proper coherence of what has been
indicated, then it becomes clear how far we have now come from reporting the content of something said here. For this saying is manifold. That which is saying transforms itself into something said and
vice versa: The latter transforms itself into the former, a saying of the
saying. Everything turns around, so that "no one knows what is happening to him" (line 27). The poem is now already no longer a bland
text with some correspondingly flat 'meaning' attached to it; rather,
this configuring of language is in itself a *turbulence* that tears us away
somewhere. Not gradually; rather, we are torn away suddenly and
abruptly right at the beginning: "Not those . . . ," with this movement
coming to a mysterious rest in the final lines:

Und wehrlos Rath giebst rings
Den Königen und den Völkern.

And defenselessly give counsel
Around the kings and peoples.

Yet to where does this turbulence tear us? Into the speaking whose configuring of language is the poem. What kind of speaking is that? Who is speaking to whom, with whom, and about what? We are torn into a dialogue that brings language to language, and not as something arbitrary or incidental, but as the mandate given to the girl, to Germania: "O name you daughter . . ."; more properly speaking, the issue concerns naming and saying. Is this turbulence that tears us into the dialogue something other than the dialogue itself, or are they one and the same? Is this turbulence the poetizing we are seeking? In that case, the poetizing is not something we happen upon lying present before us. We shall not grasp the turbulence of the dialogue if we merely gape at it, rather than entering into its movement. But how are we to accomplish this? Our first task will be simply to begin to move, to abandon our peaceful position of spectator. This position must become unsettled so that our reading can no longer maintain the neutral position of uniformly reading off a text. Such a stance will already be unsettled if we now read along the lines of the hints provided and heed the beginnings of the various strophes.

c) The Beginnings of the Strophes

The beginning of each strophe is different, not just in terms of content, in the sense that there are different words in each case that mean something different, but insofar as the manner and status of the saying and the sayer are different.

I. "Not those . . . / Those, indeed, I may call no longer. . . ." Refusal in the first person.

II. "Gods who have fled!" First the refusal, now an appeal once more, and at the same time a retreat of the 'I' as it changes to 'we.'

III. "Already . . . indeed grows verdant . . ." We are told what we are seeing, but in this strophe there is a shift to the "man" as the one who is looking, who follows the eagle and listens to it.

IV. "The priestess, quietest daughter of God. . . ." He sees her look for the eagle. In this strophe there is, at the same time, a shift to the calling of the eagle.

V. "Since then, when hidden in the woods. . . ." The eagle's telling, and indeed telling of language and of the silent speech of the girl.

VI. "O drink morning breezes . . . / And name. . . ." This is the telling call to tell, but to tell in a manner that is to leave unspoken.

VII. "O name you daughter. . . ." The foretelling that points to what is to be said in an unsaid manner.

This hint concerning the beginnings of the strophes initially seems to give only an extrinsic guide that points us in the direction of the altered reading or listening, an indication of the manner in which each strophe in the turbulence of the poetizing turns at another point in the turbulence. More precisely: Since the turbulence does not exist independently from the outset, each strophe in this transformation, in this turning, first creates the turbulence and its various points, if one can speak at all of 'points' within a turbulence.

d) The Relation of Today's Human Being to the Greeks and Their Gods

Even now—and in a certain sense constantly and ineradicably—our initial mode of encounter with the poem as a piece of text lying present before us will continue to persist. On the other hand, however, we can now no longer altogether avoid the start of the poem and the way in which it tears us away. "Not those, the blessed ones. . . ." This "Not" tears us to a certain location from where, at the same time, we are supposed to accomplish a 'No,' a turning away. Yet why are we supposed not to be able to avoid this "Not those . . ."? Why are we supposed not to be able to refuse to accompany the telling of this "Not"? Not those, the gods of old. . . . Is it at all necessary for us to avoid in the first place? Surely this word speaks past us, no longer affects us, no longer applies to us. We have long since been done with the gods of old. Of what concern are, say, the Greeks still to us? The old, genuine humanism of the fifteenth and sixteenth centuries is in any case dead. The second wave, the neo-humanism of Winckelmann and Herder, of Goethe and Schiller, is merely an affair of cultural erudition, and barely that. What then followed in the second half of the century was already unmasked as groundless and vacuous by Nietzsche around the year 1870 in his lectures in Basel concerning the future of our educational establishments. What may still flicker up here and there as a third form of humanism is a predilection of individuals that carries no force and remains a flight from what is contemporary. Of what concern are the Greeks still to us, now that we have reached the point of henceforth no longer even learning their language, which is of no practical utility anyway!

This refusal of Hölderlin's therefore comes too late for us. It may have had some meaning for his era. Consider the revival of classical antiquity happening at that time. For Hölderlin in particular this refusal may have been of great consequence and import. Consider the 'enthusiasm for the Greeks' that carries and sustains the whole of *Hyperion*. Consider especially the harsh words about the Germans toward the end of *Hyperion* (II, 282ff.). Thus Hölderlin may now—barely a year and a half later—feel particularly pressed to make amends for that reprimand against the Germans. Back to the Germans and away from the Greeks! But that is his own personal affair. For us contemporaries, however, this "Not those, the blessed ones . . ." remains devoid of content. And whatever we are not burdened with, we do not need to shake off. This "Not those . . ." no longer speaks to us. Yet how, then, can we be torn away into the turbulence of the poetry of the poem starting from here? Indeed, does not the entire poem in the end remain without 'life' for us? And for Hölderlin only a sign of his restlessness, that lack of any constancy which, as is well known, is indeed characteristic of human beings who are nervous and high-strung?

These questions are manifestly not a matter of indifference for us, especially if what is demanded of us is to advance beyond the poem to its poetizing as what is essential.

e) The Question 'Who Are We?'

Yet if we admit so emphatically that this "Not those . . ." is no longer relevant for us, then this also begs the question: With what right do we make ourselves the measure of what the poem has to say? Answer: Because it is we who are meant to enter the domain in which the poetry unfolds its power. But do we know, then, *who we are?* If we do not know this, do we at least know where we can discover for ourselves a well-grounded answer to this question of who we are? If we do not even know that, do we then know the way in which we have to ask this question of who we are in order for it to lead us into the realm in which we may find an adequate answer? Yet if we do not even have a guideline and standard of measure for the asking of this question, why then do we wish to decide so readily that this "Not those . . ." is no longer relevant for us?

§ 6. Determining the 'We' from out of the Horizon of the Question of Time

a) The Calculable Time of the Individual and the Originary Time of the Peoples

Here it is more advisable to first listen to the poet, to what he says concerning us: ". . . no one [of us] knows what is happening to him" (line 27). Yet this 'us' and this 'we' of whom the poet speaks here are surely his contemporaries, the Germans of around 1801. Or do those of 1934 also belong to them? Or does Hölderlin mean the Germans of 1980? Or even those without a year? What reckoning of time is being used here, and which time is in the poetry? In the poem "To the

Germans," composed not long before "Germania," the poet says (IV, 133, lines 41ff.):

> Wohl ist enge begränzt unsere Lebenszeit,
>> Unserer Jahre Zahl sehen und zählen wir,
>>> Doch die Jahre der Völker,
>>>> Sah ein sterbliches Auge sie?

> Wenn die Seele dir auch über die eigne Zeit
>> Sich die sehnende schwingt, trauernd verweilest du
>>> Dann am kalten Gestade
>>>> Bei den Deinen und kennst sie nie.

> Our lifetime indeed is narrowly spanned,
>> We see and count the numbers of our years,
>>> Yet the years of the peoples,
>>>> Did ever a mortal eye see them?

> If your soul too beyond your own time
>> Transports you in its longing, mournfully you tarry
>>> Then on the cold shores
>>>> Alongside your own and never know them.

Cf. the start of the poem "Rousseau" (IV, 134):

> Zu eng begränzt ist unsere Tageszeit
>> Wir sind und sehn und staunen, schon Abend ists,
>>> Wir schlafen und vorüberziehn wie
>>>> Sterne die Jahre der Völker alle.

> The time of our day is too narrowly spanned
>> We are and look and are astonished, already it is evening,
>>> We sleep and like stars pass over
>>>> The years of all the peoples.

The time that pertains to the number of years of the brief existence of the individual can be surveyed. We can calculate this time and locate it numerically between the date of birth and date of death. But the time of the years of the peoples is concealed from us. If, however, someone is transported beyond his own time and its calculable 'today'—if someone is to be transported and freed like the poet—then he must alienate himself in turn from those to whom he belongs in his lifetime. He never knows his own and is himself a source of irritation for them. In search of the true time for his own time he removes himself from the time of the present day.

We do not know our proper historical time. The world hour of our people is concealed from us. We know not who we are when we ask concerning our being, our properly temporal being. Yet then it appears as rash conceit when we declare straightaway that we have long since been relieved of this denial of the 'gods of old.' Whether we of today affirm or no longer affirm humanism (assuming that we did cultivate the humanism of antiquity in some manner) is irrelevant with respect to the proper time of the world for the reason that this does not yet guarantee in the least that we are bound to the gods of old. Here the gods of old can quite happily remain objects of scholarly interest. Conversely, however, even if we do not have the Greeks in mind in a scholarly or erudite way, it is possible to be bound to the gods of old. A decision concerning such issues does not depend on a scientific observation regarding the extent to which antiquity lives on in the present day, or even on an assessment of the state of our contemporary high schools. And in that case we do not have the authority to refuse to accompany the telling of the poet's word merely on account of our know-it-all attitude and our small-minded cleverness. In that case, this disjointed and abrupt "Not those . . ." will indeed tear us into the turbulence of a dialogue in which the world time of the peoples and our world hour come to language. This "Not those . . ." with which our poem starts off is a temporal decision in the sense of the *originary time* of the peoples.

b) The Historical Time of the Peoples as the Time of the Creators

If, therefore, we wish to follow, if only by way of intimation, the telling of this "Not those . . ." and everything subsequent that is opened up with it, we must have some intimation of what the poet says concerning this time. Here at the beginning, however, we can provide only a few apparently scattered hints, and this in a makeshift fashion and with all the reservations that, following what was said earlier (in the Introduction), must attend such a procedure.

We heard already (p. 22ff.) that the historical Dasein of the peoples—its rise, its pinnacle, and its decline—springs from poetry, and from this a proper knowing in the sense of philosophy, and from both the effecting of the Dasein of a people as a people through the state: politics. This originary, historical time of the peoples is therefore the time of the poets, thinkers, and creators of the state—that is, of those who properly ground and found the historical Dasein of a people. They are those who properly create. Concerning this time, the poet says in the poem "To Mother Earth" (IV, 156, lines 63ff.):

> Und die Zeiten des Schaffenden sind
> Wie Gebirg, das hochaufwoogend
> Von Meer zu Meer
> Hinziehet über die Erde,

> And the times of the creator are
> Like a mountain range billowing high
> From sea to sea
> That draws across the Earth,

The times of the creators—a mountain range that billows high, the solitary peaks of the mountains extending into the Aether, which is to say, into the realm of the divine. These times of the creators tower out beyond the mere sequence of hurried days in the shallowness of the everyday, and yet are not a rigid, atemporal beyond, but rather times that billow up across the Earth, their own tide and their own law. In another great poem that has an intimate belonging to "Germania," namely, "Patmos" (three versions: IV, first 190, second, 199, third 227), the poet speaks explicitly of the "peaks of time" (lines 9ff.)[3]:

> Drum, da gehäuft sind rings [um Klarheit (3)]
> Die Gipfel der Zeit
> Und die Liebsten nahe wohnen [ermattend (2)] auf
> Getrenntesten Bergen . . .

> Therefore, since round about are heaped [for clarity]
> The peaks of time
> And the most loved dwell near [languishing] upon
> Mountains most separate . . .

"Therefore, since round about are heaped / The peaks of time. . . ." These peaks are quite near to one another, and so too are the creators who must dwell on them, where each one brings to fruition his vocation in each case and from there understands, from the ground up, the others on the other peaks. And yet, in this nearness they are precisely most separate by virtue of the abysses between the mountains where each one stands. Their nearness is the abyss, whereas on the shallow and level plane, by contrast, everything can drift far apart and be dispersed; things need not be near, and yet they readily and always com-

mingle, each with every other and many with each other. The time of
the creators and peoples is cleaved by an abyss; it is not the common
road on which everyone can race away and race past everyone else.
That time of the peaks, however—that billowing of the most separate
nearness of abyssal heights—can be intimated only by one who is like
the shepherd, who knows nothing other than the stony path and the
source, the alpine meadows and the clouds, the sun, and the storm.

c) A Textual Question: Different Versions of "Patmos"

Here we have occasion once again to point to the question of the text
and to examine the alterations among the different versions. People
usually call this 'philological technicalities.' There are such things, but
not in a work like Hölderlin's, and especially not if we move beyond
merely cataloguing the changes. Here the struggle for every word is a
pointer to understanding the poetry. Frequently, each newly formed
or newly inserted word raises the entire work to a new level in terms
of its inner cohesion, yet quite differently from a decisive stroke of the
sculptor's chisel. 'Aesthetic niceties'? Our pointing out such alterations has nothing to do with this either, nor does it have to do with
some empty curiosity that would seek to watch the poet in his workshop in order to learn how it is done.

Let us note the details of the alterations. The second version introduces the word "languishing." The creators are located on the peaks,
gifted with their vocation and with the resources of their creativity—
and yet are "languishing" on mountains most separate. They remain
behind in supreme solitude, not on account of mere inability belonging to a mediocre talent, but in the sense of falling short in the course
of accomplishing the supreme and sole vocation they must assume.
By introducing this opposition—up on the peaks near to one another
and yet languishing and without any help—the poet intensifies the
uniqueness of the creators and their times; and this intensified opposition is intensified once again in the third version by the insertion of
the words "for clarity." Despite supreme clarity and the purest vision,
there is a dwelling that languishes, a beyng that falls short. It is precisely the differences between the three versions that set into relief
the direction of the poetic telling and are therefore of inestimable significance for coming to terms with the poetry. We shall indeed have
to follow entire poems in this regard. Cf. also the beginning of "Patmos" (IV, 190, 199, 227):

Nah ist
Und schwer zu fassen der Gott.

Near is
And difficult to grasp the God.

(First and second versions)

Voll Güt' ist; keiner aber fasset
Allein Gott.

Full of goodness is he; yet no one alone
Grasps God.

(Third version)

d) Two Concepts of Eternity

This solitary, most intimate peaking of the times of the peoples and
of those creators is, however, for Hölderlin not a direct billowing over
into some timeless or supratemporal realm, an eternal realm in this
sense. Those who are up there on the remotest and supreme peaks of
time are indeed most harshly exposed to the lightning flashes of the
gods, but the God himself is "time." Hölderlin, in his "Remarks on Oedipus," speaks of the God who "is nothing other than time" (V, 181).

Ordinarily one tends to place the gods and the divine outside of time
and to address them as the eternal. Hölderlin too speaks of "eternity."[1]
However, the definition of eternity is not self-contained; rather, our
representation of what we call eternity and its concept are in each case
determined in accordance with our guiding representation of time.
There are two common concepts of eternity: (1) as *sempiternitas*—the
ongoing continuation of time, an unceasing 'and so on' with never a
final 'now'; and (2) as *aeternitas*—the *nunc stans,* the standing 'now,'
ever-enduring presence. Both concepts spring from ancient and/or
Christian thought and come together again in Hegel's philosophy,
where eternity is thought most richly and profoundly thereafter. Everything that subsequently follows is poor imitation.

These two concepts of eternity, however, also spring from a particular experience of time—namely, time as a *pure sequential passing of
'nows.'* In the first instance, time is a never-ending sequence of 'nows.'
In the second, time is an encompassing 'now' that remains standing
ahead of time. That concept of time, however, does not grasp the essence of time; nor does the concept of eternity that is altogether dependent upon it reach the essence of eternity, insofar as we are able
to think such a thing at all. Above all, these conceptions are inadequate for thoughtfully coming to terms with Hölderlin's poetic experience of time.

---

1. Fragment 4, "O Mother Earth!" IV, 239.

e) The Time That Is Essentially Long

For Hölderlin the gods are "nothing other than time," and 'the heavenly quickly passes by.'[2] Into this time of the gods tower the peaks of time as the times of the peoples. These times have their own measure.

> . . . Lang ist
> Die Zeit, es ereignet sich aber
> Das Wahre.

> . . . Long is
> The time, yet what is true
> Comes to pass.

("Mnemosyne," IV, 225, lines 17ff.)

Which time is long? It is "the time" of the everyday and the time on the peaks, yet each in a different way. Everyday time is "long" [*lang*] in boredom [*Langeweile*], where time holds us in limbo and in so doing leaves us empty, where we hurriedly and indiscriminately reach for whatever makes the long time pass or makes for diversion [*kurzweilig macht*].[4] The time of the peaks is long, because on the peaks reigns a persistent waiting for and awaiting *the event* [*Ereignis*], not boredom or diversion. There is no passing or even killing of time there, but a struggle for the duration and fullness of time that is preserved in awaiting. The time on the peaks is *essentially* long; for a making ready for the true that shall once come to pass [*sich ereignen*] does not happen overnight or to order, but consumes many human lives and even 'generations.' This 'long time' remains closed to all those who are overcome with boredom and have no intimation of their own boringness. This long time, however, "once" lets the true—the becoming manifest of beyng—come to pass. (Cf. "Germania," line 93: "Something true must once appear.")

f) The Creators' Knowing When It Is Not the Time for the True to Come to Pass

Who we are, we do not know, so long as we do not know our time. Our time, however, is that of the people between the peoples. Who knows this time? No one knows it in such a way that he could indicate it or 'date' it. Even those creators who dwell on the peaks of time do not know it. They know one thing only: namely, when it is *not* the time for the true to come to pass. Hölderlin says this at the beginning of the poem "The Titans" (IV, 208):

---

2. "Conciliator, you who never believed . . . ," IV, 163f., lines 49f.

Nicht ist es aber
Die Zeit. Noch sind sie
Unangebunden. Göttliches trift untheilnehmende nicht.

Yet it is not
The time. Still they are
Untethered. Divinity does not strike nonpartakers.

Thus the time is not yet. In that case, we must then defer that temporal decision that we grasped as the beginning of "Germania," for there, in the context of a refusal, there is supposed to be a decision between old and new gods. On the one hand, we have "Not those . . ." as a temporal decision, and then again "Yet it is not / The time," and this in a later poem! Thus the poet has again deferred that decision. In any case, he contradicts himself. This is indeed a contradiction if we set words and issues off against one another with our all-too-compliant common sense, and play off against one another the poet's various statements.

g) The Distinction between the Question *What* We Are and the Question *Who* We Are

Yet what does the beginning of "The Titans" say? This reference apparently tells us only when it is not time. Yet it tells us more: how long time is not, how long we can never experience who we are. Namely, so long as we are not 'partakers'—so long as we are "untethered." Accordingly, partaking and being tethered constitute a necessary condition for there coming to be time for us at all. Yet partaking in what? Tethered to what? This we are admittedly not told. The issue thus remains open and arbitrary, so that the important thing is simply that we partake at all—in existence [*Dasein*]—that we do not stand to one side of those tasks that press upon us, and that we intervene directly and seize upon what is nearest and undertake whatever is urgent. So it appears. For what someone undertakes, whatever he actually partakes in continually and not just from time to time, whatever everyone has and we ourselves in each case have as our occupation is, after all, how we determine what someone is and what we ourselves in each case are. This person makes shoes and thus *is* a shoemaker. That person is involved with instructing and educating and, in keeping with what he does, *is* a teacher. This one practices the art of weaponry and thus *is* a soldier. That one busies himself producing books that appear in the public catalogues of booksellers under the 'category' of 'philosophy,' and *is* therefore a philosopher. Whatever one in each case participates in continually, *what* he does, determines *what* he *is*.

Yet if we know *what* we are, do we then know *who* we are? No. It indeed remains unavoidable that we are such and such, and within certain limits this is not arbitrary or indifferent. Yet this does not decide about who we are, because what we busy ourselves with is unable to decide such a thing. Thus the 'partaking' of which the poet speaks cannot be meant in the sense of busying oneself with an occupation, or of being involved in whatever happens to be present at hand. The fact that we are not told what we are to partake in must be interpreted differently.

h) Partaking in the Poetry

The partaking is indeterminate, insofar as it does not concern this or that endeavor, and insofar as partaking is not something that happens to belong to our Dasein as one kind of comportment among others. The partaking to which the poet refers constitutes our Dasein as such a Dasein; it is that way of being of our Dasein that is concerned with beyng and nonbeing in general. In this partaking, the way in which we are what we do gets decided in advance and constantly. If we are not told what we are to partake in or to what we are to be tethered—if we are told only of partaking pure and simple, or of 'care'—then this precisely 'says' that such partaking is a necessary condition for the arising of *the* time when "divinity . . . strikes" us—when the lightning strikes.

Yet if it is the task allotted to the poetry to bring this lightning flash, shrouded in the word, into the Dasein of the people, then this word can address us only if we partake in the poetry—that is, in the dialogue. It indeed appeared as though we could, in complacent self-certainty, release ourselves from the task of accompanying the telling of that "Not those, the blessed ones . . . ," since it no longer applies to us. But now we see: Not only do we not know who we are, but we must in the end actually partake in the poetry in order to first create the necessary condition for it becoming the time in which we are then able to experience in the first place who we are. We do not understand the poetry if we measure it by the arbitrariness of our own superior knowledge and thereby seek to master it. We exclude ourselves from the poetic as the fundamental configuration of historical Dasein if we do not, through the poetry, first let the question of who we are become a *question* in our Dasein: one that we actually pose—that is, sustain—throughout our entire short lifetime.

§ 7. The Linguistic Character of Poetry

Thus we must increasingly relinquish our initial stance of reading poems in an arbitrary manner that we have simply happened upon without any preparation. The claim and power of poetry are opening themselves up in ever more disconcerting ways. However, our doubt and our resistance are equally increasing. For even if, in truth, the essence of poetry does reside in the fact that it exposes the historical Dasein of human beings to beings as a whole, it surely remains questionable to what extent a linguistic construction—a mere dialogue—is supposed to be able to accomplish such a thing in such an originary manner. Immediate realities can surely bowl us over in quite a different way. Real events tear us quite differently into existence [*Dasein*]; direct action brings quite different collisions with beings than this mere telling of a poetry. However lofty one may regard poetry as a calling, its purely discursive and linguistic character makes it impotent after all. Precisely because poetry is only language, and by essential necessity, it cannot effect any founding of beyng.

How do things stand concerning the linguistic character of poetry? How do things stand concerning language itself? How does language relate to the historical Dasein of human beings? Above all, how does Hölderlin himself experience and understand language? Only when we know this will our still-skeptical attitude toward the poetry become at least somewhat clearer, perhaps sufficiently clear to make a decision. Yet we also have to know how Hölderlin conceives of the relationship between language and the historical Dasein of human beings, because our poem in particular revealed itself to us in its poetic character as a peculiarly self-transforming telling of language. Here too some guiding indications must suffice initially. We shall point to five different contexts whose inner unity will soon become apparent of its own accord.

a) Language as the Most Dangerous of Goods

Yet in huts humans dwell, and wrap themselves in the garment of shame, for more intimate is more heedful too, and that they may preserve the spirit, as does the priestess the heavenly flame, such is their understanding. And for this reason free will and the higher power to command and to accomplish have been given to the godlike, that most dangerous of goods, language, has been given to humans, so that, creating, destroying, and perishing, and returning to the eternally living, to the mistress and Mother, that they may bear witness to what they are, their heritage, learnt from her, the most divine of her attributes, all-sustaining love.

(Fragment 13, IV, 246)[5]

Here language is conceived of as "that most dangerous of goods" that is proper to humans. We are not yet able to take the measure of what this is meant to say. Yet we can see straightaway the context in which language is here determined in such an alien way. The fragment speaks once more of human beings: namely, with respect to their fundamental position in the midst of beings. It speaks of their freedom, of the power of command and of accomplishment, of their creating and destroying, their perishing, and their return to the mistress and Mother—the Earth. The human being—not as one among the other things on the Earth that creep and fly, but as the meaning of the Earth, in the sense that with and through human Dasein each and every being first arises as such a being, closes itself off (comes under command), succeeds and fails, and returns again to the origin. Not the human being inanely idolized as some unrestrained creature that becomes the dupe of his so-called progress, certainly, but the human being as the *witness of beyng*, set into the midst of the most extreme conflicts and prevailing in his essence in the embrace of the simplest intimacy.

This fragment is laden with metaphysics that has not yet been thought through to its end, and this because the commencement of this metaphysics has not even been 'thought'—that is, thoughtfully placed into our historical Dasein.

Our undertaking is initially merely exploratory, and even this remains uncertain if we do not heed where this fragment occurs in the manuscripts. It is found in the Stuttgart foliobook, sheet 17b, whose content according to von Hellingrath seems to belong in essence to the years 1800 and 1801 (IV, 271). On this sheet we find the best-known poem of Hölderlin's later period, "Midpoint of Life" (IV, 60). On the same sheet we find a longer draft from which this poem was excerpted for an almanac publication in 1805. The draft proper, however, is concerned with the essence of the human being in the midst of beings, especially of nature (key words like "the rose," "the swans," and "the stag" are named), and of the poet's calling amid the historical Dasein of human beings. It is presumably no accident that immediately preceding it in the manuscript there stands the poem "As when on feast day . . ." (cf. p. 29). It is in this context that the word concerning language—that it is "that most dangerous of goods"—occurs. In language, the Dasein of human beings attains, or better, has from its very ground, its supreme danger. For in language, the human being ventures farthest: With language as such he first ventures forth into being. In language, there occurs the revelation of beings—not just a post facto expression of what is already unveiled, but the originary unveiling itself—yet for this very reason a veiling also, together with its preeminent derivative, *semblance*.

By virtue of language, the human being is the witness of beyng. He testifies on its behalf, stands up to it, and falls victim to it. Where there is no language, as in the case of animals and plants, there, despite all life, is no manifestness of beyng and, for this reason, there is no non-being either and none of the emptiness belonging to the Nothing. Plant and animal stand on this side of such things; here there reign only blind pursuit and opaque flight. Only where there is language does world prevail. Only where there is world—that is, where there is language—is there supreme danger: altogether *the* danger, which is the threatening of being as such by non-being. Language is dangerous not only because it brings the human being into a particular danger, but is *what is most dangerous*—the danger of dangers—because it first creates, and alone keeps open, the possibility of a threatening of beyng in general. Because the human being *is* in language, he creates this danger and brings the destruction that lurks within it. As what is most dangerous, language is what is most double-edged and most ambiguous. It places the human being into the zone of supreme achievement, yet at the same time holds him within the realm of abyssal decline [*Verfall*]. How we are to understand this will become clear from a second fragment on language.

b) The Decline of Language.
The Essence and Corrupted Essence of Language

But language—
In the thunderstorm speaks the God.
Now and then I tried language
it said there was wrath enough, and that held true for Apollo—

If you have love enough then always show rage out of love as well
Now and then I tried song, but they did not hear you.
For thus holy nature willed you sang you for her not singing in your youth
You spoke to the Godhead, but this you have all forgotten, that the
first-born are not mortals, that they belong to the gods. More common,
more everyday the fruit must first become, then it will become proper to
mortals.

(Fragment 3, IV, 237f.)

This text is less transparent. The word "but" points to the difficult, mysterious, and questionable aspect of language. "In the thunderstorm" names the relationship to the God and his language. What is essential for our context is the last section, specifically, the distinction between the "first-born" of language—that is, the creative, founding saying of the poet and the way in which what has been said becomes "more common," more everyday, as an inevitability in the realm of human Dasein. The supreme happiness of the first, creative telling is at the same time the deepest pain of loss, for first-born are sacrificed. The language that originarily grounds *beyng* stands within the fateful necessity of a decline, becoming leveled off into worn-out idle talk that nothing is able to escape, precisely because it gives rise to the semblance that in its manner of saying—if only it were a saying—beings would be reached and grasped. To say an essential word intrinsically entails also already delivering this word to the realm of misinterpretation, of misuse and deception—to the dangerousness of the most direct and contrary repercussions of its determination. Each—the purest and most concealed as well as the most commonplace and shallow— can become caught up in a clichéd way of talking.

The dangerousness of language is thus essentially double, and each of these dangers is fundamentally different: On the one hand, there is the danger of supreme proximity to the gods and thereby to being annihilated by their excessive character; at the same time, however, there is the danger of the most shallow turning away and of becoming entangled in worn-out idle talk and the semblance that goes with it. The manner in which these two conflicting dangers—the danger belonging to the essence of language, an essence difficult to endure, and that belonging to the playful corruption of its essence—intimately accompany one another heightens the dangerousness of language to the extreme. The dangerousness of language is *the most originary determination of its essence*. Its purest essence unfolds itself from the commencement in poetizing. Poetizing is the *originary language of a people* (cf. p. 198f.). Poetic saying, however, falls into decline and becomes genuine and then bad 'prose,' which eventually becomes idle talk. It is from this everyday use of words, this fallen version, therefore, that scientific reflection on language and the philosophy of language proceed, which then view 'poetry' as an exception to the rule. In this manner, everything gets turned upside down. Even when one conceives of language as a means of artistic creation, one remains fundamentally wedded to an instrumental view of language as expression. To conceive of language in this way is a well-established custom, because it seems plausible. Those aspects of language that appear to be most readily graspable, sound and letter, are a sign indicative of meaning, and meaning is a sign indicative of the matter. Thus one might regard it as an almost hopeless prospect ever to accomplish an essential transformation in the experience of the essence of language within the historical Dasein of a people. And yet this is what must occur if indeed a transformation of such Dasein back into the primordial realms of beyng is to be effected at all.

Certainly, the corrupted essence of language can never be eliminated. Yet it can be expressly acknowledged in its necessary domination. The corrupted essence of language can in this way be taken up as a danger and as resistance, as something that compels a constantly new assertion of the essence against the corrupted essence. To this realm of the necessary corruption of the essence of language, and of the semblance that is thereby fostered, there belongs also that state of affairs we encountered in our first attempt to grasp the poem. The poem allows itself to be reported, and indeed correctly, in the manner of paraphrasing its content. This possible reconfiguration into something we report can apply to all telling. For example, a prayer that calls upon the gods can be reported in statements: The man spoke to God, and his appeal has such and such content. Similarly, the kind of telling that is the asking of a question can be reproduced by reporting the content of the question. Such reporting carries with it the appearance of a reproducing, and yet this telling is the opposite of a genuine reproducing, repeating, or retelling in the manner of an appealing, for instance, or of an asking of the question. The unlimited possibility of transforming all originary saying into a kind of report of itself entails that language itself constantly endangers its own essence and thus remains inherently dangerous—indeed the more unconditionally so, the more essential the very telling is.

c) Language and the Human Being's Fundamental Orientations toward Beings as a Whole

Yet where the dangerousness of language is intimated or indeed comprehended as its essential ground, therein lies the insight that language and language are by no means the same. Rather, the fundamentally different 'conditions' of Dasein in each case demand their own language, because through this language they in each case first are as they are. This is indicated by Hölderlin in the "Remarks on Oedipus." Oedipus "has an / Eye too many perhaps" as we heard from that very late poem "In beautiful blue . . ." (VI, 26, lines 75f.). In the "Remarks on Oedipus," which he elaborated for his translation of Sophocles, Hölderlin conceives this in the following way: Oedipus "interprets the saying of the oracle too infinitely" (V, 177). In an astonishingly enraged curiosity, his desire to know rips through all barriers and demands to know more than he can bear or grasp. (Cf. the dialogue between Oedipus, Jocasta, and the messenger, V, 141, lines 928ff.) With regard to this, Hölderlin states (V, 180):

> Precisely this all-seeking, all-interpreting aspect is also the reason why his spirit ultimately succumbs to the raw and primitive language of his servants.

> Because such human beings stand under violent conditions, their language, too, speaks in a more violent order, almost in the manner of Furies.

These "violent conditions" do not refer to arbitrary circumstances in which a human being may become caught up, but to unique and unalterable fundamental orientations in which human beings stand toward beings as a whole and in which their destiny unfolds. Language, however, is not merely the expression thereof, their 'formulation' and communication to the public; rather, language sustains and guides the confrontation [*Auseinandersetzung*] with that which is violent and mighty. Language itself has this character of *being*, which it opens up and brings to humans. In language as such there occurs the confrontational setting apart [*Aus-einander-setzung*] of beyng and non-being: the confrontational encounter of forces and holding one's ground or succumbing in this struggle, but also stultification into the indifference of knowing it all and being capable of everything. How altogether remote all this is from the characterization of language according to its customary accomplishment of expression and its role as a means of exchange in coming to agreement! A fourth citation may serve to indicate this.

d) Language as the Human Being's Protection against the God

In the "Remarks on Antigone," Hölderlin sees language in a perspective that is almost the opposite of that view in which language grasps in the word the lightning flash of the gods: in language, the human being turns against the God and protects himself against the God, so as not to succumb to the God and thus not to destroy this fundamental relation toward beings. The full content of this point could be brought out only by going into the broader context. Here we wish merely to indicate the direction in which the human being in language exposes his Dasein, and the direction in which language carries his being (V, 255):

> It is a great resource of the secretly working soul that at the highest state of consciousness it evades consciousness, and that before the God that is present actually seizes it, it confronts this God with a bold, often even blasphemic word, thereby maintaining the sacred, living potential of the spirit.

e) Poetizing and Language as Configuring the Ground of Historical Dasein

From all that has been cited thus far, it must become clear that language is not something that the human being has among other faculties and tools. Rather, language is that which has the human being, that which configures and determines his Dasein as such in this way or that, and from the ground up.

The linguistic character of poetizing that we are inquiring after now shows itself quite differently to us. Language is not the mere external vocalization of inner poetic lived experiences, as though one were packaging them up to pass them along to other people. When in the last strophe of "As when on feast day . . . ," which we have already cited, Hölderlin speaks of the poets having to pass on to the people the lightning flashes of the gods "shrouded in the song" (IV, 153, lines 59f.), then this word concerning the shroud and shrouding has a quite different meaning. Poetizing is itself only that distinctive occurrence within the event of language in whose power the human being stands as historical. Poetizing configures the ground of historical Dasein: Language as such constitutes the originary essence of the historical being of humans. We cannot first determine the essence of the being of human beings, and then in addition or after the fact attribute language to them as a gift. Rather, the originary essence of their beyng is language itself. We can now better comprehend that it is no accident that, in asking the question of who we are, we find ourselves directed to first let ourselves into the dialogue of poetizing. Poetizing and language are not two separate things here; rather, both are the same configuration of the ground of historical being.

f) The Being of the Human Being as Dialogue.
Being Able to Hear and Speaking

How far Hölderlin penetrated poetically into this primal realm of poetic telling may now be attested to by a word that also brings together for us, out of an originary unity, everything that has been said thus far and by way of preparation concerning poetizing and language. (Cf. the Rome lecture of April 2, 1936, "Hölderlin and the Essence of Poetry."[1]) The poet says:

Viel hat erfahren der Mensch.
Der Himmlischen viele genannt,
Seit ein Gespräch wir sind
Und hören können voneinander.

Much have humans experienced.
Named many of the heavenly,
Since we are a dialogue
And can hear from one another.

---

1. *Erläuterungen zu Hölderlins Dichtung.* Fourth edition. Frankfurt, 1971. 33ff. Translated as *Elucidations of Hölderlin's Poetry* by Keith Hoeller. Amherst, New York: Humanity Books, 2000, 51ff.

This word comes from a fragment belonging to the elaboration of a major poem that remains without a title and begins: "Conciliator, you who never believed . . ." (IV, 162ff.). Von Hellingrath provides the text of this fragment in the Appendix to IV, 343.

We are a dialogue. What can this mean? It means that language constitutes and determines our being. This much we can say. Yet at the same time we enter the realm of the supreme dangerousness of language. For when we say we are a dialogue, this sounds like a straightforward answer to the question 'Who are we?' This statement comes close to sentences such as 'A straight line is the shortest distance between two points.' In the first case, we find 'how we are'; in the second, 'a straight line is. . . .' We have two definitions, concerning a straight line as such, and concerning ourselves as human beings, concerning the human being as such. Yet this makes everything fundamentally skewed and gives us to ponder. Not only have we torn the sentence altogether out of the poetic context to which the words belong; but in our intent to at once extract the main content of the line, we have been led astray into overlooking an essential word. The poet says: "Since we are a dialogue." "Since"—'since the time that. . . .' If we do wish to look for a so-called 'definition' of the human being here, then it is a historical one, relating to time, and—following what was said earlier (p. 47ff.)—evidently to the time of the peoples, which no one knows. It relates to that time which, as we heard, first comes to be only if we ourselves become 'partakers,' partaking in the dialogue, and only if we ourselves decide in favor of that which historically we can be. We understand the word of the poet only if, and only so long as, we ourselves enter into this decision and stand within it. With this proviso, we can now ask, and indeed must ask, what it means to say that we are a temporally determined, historically arising dialogue. Our task must be to anticipate our entire subsequent preoccupation with Hölderlin's poetizing if we wish to come to terms with and fathom in a purely thoughtful way the word of the poet concerning our beyng. At present, we can only indicate some points that may serve to guide our approaching questioning.

We are a dialogue. How do dialogue [*Gespräch*] and language [*Sprache*] relate to one another? In the dialogue, language occurs, and this occurrence is properly its beyng. We are an event of language, and this occurrence is temporal, yet not only in the superficial sense that it runs its course in time and can on each occasion be temporally measured with respect to its beginning, duration, and cessation. Rather, the event of language is the commencement and ground of the properly historical time of human beings. This dialogue does not arise at some point within a course of 'historical' events; rather, ever since such dialogue has been occurring, there first *is* and has been time and history at all. This dialogue that is a commencing, however, is poetizing, and "poetically dwell / Human beings upon this Earth."[2] Their Dasein as historical has its steadfast ground in the dialogue of poetizing.

Yet what we are saying here still leaves many things obscure. We are a "dialogue." Yet we do not speak incessantly. Nor does our Dasein expend itself in talking. Dialogue—this is always something transitory, something we enter into temporarily, as we are accustomed to do. We are surely other things besides. At most, we are caught up *within* the process of the dialogue, but are surely not *the dialogue itself.* Or are we a dialogue in the sense in which one says that this or that incident—say, the burning of the university building—is the talk of the day or of the town? We are a dialogue in the sense that there is talk about us? Yet precisely such things need not touch our beyng.

Thus the saying must indeed be understood literally. Our beyng occurs as dialogue, in the happening of the gods' addressing us, placing us under their claim, *bringing us to language* with respect to whether and how we are, how we respond, by committing our beyng to them or by way of a telling refusal. Our beyng therefore occurs as dialogue insofar as we, speaking as thus addressed, bring beings as such beings to language, open up beings in what and how they are, yet at the same time also cover over and dissemble them. Only where language occurs do being and non-being open up. We ourselves are this opening up and veiling.

Yet we are a dialogue also insofar as the gods do not address us, insofar as their beckonings remain absent, whether because they are abandoning us and leaving us to ourselves, or because they are sparing us. That we are a dialogue means at the same time and equiprimordially: we are a *keeping silent.* But it also means that our beyng occurs in discourse concerning beings and non-beings, so that we become enslaved to talking away about things without thinking. We are then a kind of idle talk, for the latter is the corrupted essence that necessarily belongs to the essence of the dialogue. In other words, we must fathom the entire dangerousness of language in order to experience what the event of language, the dialogue, is *as the dialogue that we are.* We are a dialogue in commencing and thus in ending history, as the supremely violent word, as poetizing, as keeping silent, and—as idle talk.

---

2. "In beautiful blue . . . ," VI, 25, lines 32f.

The fragment just cited thus brings together everything that we have to ponder concerning language, if we are not to mistake its essence and regard it merely as a means of coming to agreement. Yet one difficulty still persists. For this very fragment appears to say the opposite of what we wished to show: namely, that language is not only and not in the first instance something that serves to enable mutual agreement and communication. How did the lines read?

Seit ein Gespräch wir sind
Und hören können voneinander.

Since we are a dialogue
And can hear from one another.

This clearly says that language enables us reciprocally to inform one another about our lived experiences. In this fragment it is therefore indeed being referred to only as a means of expression and of coming to agreement, and everything that we just now read into this line 'we are a dialogue' becomes untenable. Yet let us look more carefully and seriously. In the first place, the line does not read: 'since . . . and therefore we . . . '—with the aid of such means—can come to agreement. It says, rather: since we are and have been a dialogue, since that time we can hear from one another. Saying and being able to hear are at least equiprimordial. And being able to hear is not at all the consequence of speaking with one another, but rather the reverse: It is the condition thereof. Being able to hear is not something subsequently added to being able to talk, just as little as the latter is merely added to the former. The two are essentially unified, as are being able to talk and keeping silent. Only whoever can keep silent can also talk. Someone who is mute by birth can indeed never say anything, but for this reason he can never keep silent either. Keeping silent, as a not-saying, is not always negative: It can be very positive and highly telling; indeed, it can even say what is properly the case. (Whoever keeps silent in the face of the continual use of cheap or commonplace remarks is saying something, even if this is understood only by those who understand such silence.) Ever since we have been a dialogue, since then also—but not simply as a consequence of this—we can hear from one another. Yet even if we wish to interpret these lines in such a way as to conceive of being able to hear from one another as a consequence of the dialogue, reading the "And" as a consequential 'and,' precisely then we must conceive of dialogue in the originary sense that we have indicated and not as a coming to agreement. To what extent?

g) Being Exposed to Beings, the Individual and the Community

Since we have been a dialogue, we have been exposed to beings open-ing themselves up, and only since then has it been possible for the be-ing of beings as such to encounter and determine us at all. Yet this, the fact that beings are manifest in advance for each of us in their be-ing, is the precondition for someone being able to hear something—that is, something about beings, from another, whether these beings are those that we are not (nature) or that we ourselves are (history). Being able to hear does not first bring about the relation of one to another—that is, community—but rather presupposes it. This origi-nary community does not first arise through the taking up of recip-rocal relations—only society arises in this way. Rather, community *is* through *each individual's* being bound in advance to something that binds and determines every individual in exceeding them. Something must be manifest that is neither the individual taken alone nor com-munity as such. The comradeship of soldiers on the front is based nei-ther on the fact that people had to join together because other human beings, from whom one was removed, were absent; nor did it have its basis in people first agreeing to a shared enthusiasm. Rather, its most profound and sole basis lies in the fact that the nearness of death as a sacrifice placed everyone in advance into the same nothingness, so that the latter became the source of an unconditional belonging to one another. Precisely death—which each individual human being must die for him- or herself, and which individuates each individual upon themselves to the most extreme degree—precisely death and the readiness for its sacrifice first of all creates in advance the space of that community out of which comradeship emerges. Then comrade-ship springs from anxiety? No and yes. No, if like a petit bourgeois one understands anxiety as merely a helpless quaking in a panic-stricken state of cowardliness. Yes, if anxiety is conceived as the metaphysi-cal proximity to what is unconditional, a proximity bestowed only to a supreme steadfastness and readiness. If we fail to compel into our Dasein powers that bind and individuate just as unconditionally as death as free sacrifice, that is, powers that attack at the roots of the Dasein of each individual, and that stand just as profoundly and en-tirely within a genuine knowing, then no 'comradeship' will emerge; at most, we shall attain an altered form of society.

What does this have to do with our question? Everything. Being able to hear from one another is possible only if each individual is ex-posed in advance to the nearness and distance of the essence of things. This, however, occurs through language, not as a means of coming to agreement, but as the originary founding of being. Only when we return to ourselves from out of the essential power of things experienced in advance do we come to one another and come to *be* with and for one another—of ourselves, and in the strict sense of this phrase 'of ourselves.'

If indeed it is the dialogue, then, that enables us to hear from one another, the dialogue is to be conceived not as communication, but as the fundamental event of our being exposed to beings. The possibility of a misinterpretation of this fragment is thereby eliminated.

h) Summary

With regard to its importance for what is to follow, we shall give a brief summary of what has been said about poetizing and language. We are inquiring concerning the linguistic character of poetizing. Because poetizing is merely something said, and not something actually produced or real, as a mere telling it seems to remain without any effective power. What is the situation regarding the effective power of language and consequently of poetizing, their power of being? How does Hölderlin understand language? We have interrogated five decisive contexts with regard to language.

1. Language is the most dangerous of goods for the human being, for it first exposes humans to the realm of being and thereby of nonbeing, and thereby to the realm of the possible threatening or loss of being.

2. Language is dangerous in a second sense, because by its very essence it bears decline within it, whether into a mere reciting or reporting of what has been said, or the decline that falls into idle talk.

3. Language thus sustains and determines in its very ground the Dasein of human beings, grounding (and not merely expressing) the respective way in which the human being stands and holds his ground amid essential conditions. In violent conditions, language has the manner of the Furies (Oedipus).

4. Language is not only the veiled passing on of the beckonings of the gods, but can become that whereby the human being, within decisive fundamental orientations, turns against consciousness, blasphemically against the gods, so as precisely thereby to preserve a relation to them (Antigone).

5. Language is therefore not something that the human being has, but the reverse: that which has the human being. What the human being is—we are a dialogue. We are since we have been a dialogue, addressed and brought to language.

Poetizing founds beyng. Poetizing is the primordial language of a people. Within such language, there occurs a being exposed to beings as they thereby open themselves up. As the accomplishment of such exposure, the human being is historical. The human being 'has' a history only because and to the extent that he is historical. Language is the ground of the possibility of history, but language is not something like an invention that is first made within the course of the historical creation of culture.

i) The Absence of Language in the Animal and in 'Nature'

The originary origin of language as the essential ground of human Dasein, however, remains a mystery. Especially when we ponder the fact that even where there is 'life' (plant, animal), language does not also occur without further ado, even if it seems as though it were merely a matter of eliminating some persistent inhibition in order for the animal to speak. And yet! The leap from living animal to the human being who tells is just as great as, or still greater than, that from the lifeless stone to the living.

Why does the animal not speak? Because it does not need to speak. Why does it not need to speak? Because it does not have to speak. It does not have to, because it is not compelled to. It is not compelled to do so, because it is closed off with respect to beyng as such. Neither being nor non-being, nor the nothing nor emptiness are accessible to it. Why is being closed off from the animal? Because it is not within language. So, the animal does not speak because it is not within language. This sounds like a statement that says the same thing twice, and thus says nothing. And yet it does say something: namely, that the animal's not speaking is not due to some particular cause or inhibition, but is synonymous with the essential otherness of its beyng. In keeping with this otherness, the animal is captivated by whatever presses upon it from its environment and its own kind, and remains caught up within this captivation. This does not preclude the animal living in its own ways of dealing with things and fulfilling its vital urge within this captivated entanglement.

Yet this apparent nearness and at the same time essential distance of the animal to the human first becomes a genuine question when we give thought to the real absence of language that we find in nature as a whole, where, on the other hand, nothing can 'speak' more insistently to us than the prevailing of nature in its greater and in its smallest aspects.

That is to say, we will not succeed simply by placing nature with its absence of language and human beings who speak alongside one another as different kinds of things. We shall first approach our questioning here if we ponder fundamentally how poetizing as the fundamental event of the historical Dasein of human beings relates—if we may put things this way at all—to *nature,* prior to all natural science. The whole of natural science—indispensable though it is within certain present-day limits (for instance, for the manufacture of rubber and of alternating current)—for all its exactness leaves us fundamentally in the lurch here regarding what is essential, because it de-'natures' nature.

j) Poetizing and Language in Their Originary Belonging to the History of the Human Being

Along two separate paths we have now come to see that poetizing configures the ground of historical Dasein. Language as dialogue is the fundamental event of historical Dasein. As an originary dialogue, poetizing is the origin of language, the human being's most dangerous of goods, with which he ventures forth into being as such, stands firm there or falls, puffing himself up and becoming stultified in his decline into idle talk.

This may suffice for the purposes of making visible the essential unity of poetizing and language and their originary belonging to the history of the human being. For now, all this has been undertaken only to serve as an appropriate preparation for our concern with the poetizing of the poem "Germania," of this dialogue in which, in the context of a decision concerning the world time of our people, language itself comes to language.

Our concern with the poetizing, however, underwent a recoil right at the outset, one that placed in question our accompanying the telling of the whole poetizing in its possibility and necessity. It has now become manifest that our hesitation arose from our ignorance concerning the kind of "time" that is at stake, an ignorance concerning the essence of the dialogue and of language, and an ignorance concerning the necessity of asking the question of who we are. Our hesitation and even our stepping back from accompanying the telling was therefore not a decision at all, not a knowing resolve. Yet, on the other hand, an inclination provoked by something or other to go along with others in reading the poem is not a decision either, for—to the extent that it is necessary to say such a thing at all—it is not a matter of persuading you or certain individuals to willingly read along here, in this lecture, for instance. Rather, what has to be decided is an engagement in asking the question of who we are; whether we are a dialogue or just some idle talk; whether we let ourselves enter into the originary historicality of our historical Dasein or merely hang around on the periphery; whether we have a truthful knowing of our beyng and, as a consequence and in the first instance, of beyng as such, or merely stagger around in various ways of talking; and whether we truly know what we do not know and cannot know, so as to become strong ourselves by genuinely running up against these barriers and setting resistance against resistance. This is the decision through which our accompanying the telling of every poem of Hölderlin's poetizing—our entering into its dialogue—must repeatedly pass.

Chapter Two
The Fundamental Attunement of Poetizing
and the Historicality of Dasein

§ 8. *Unfolding the Fundamental Attunement*

a) The Provenance of Poetic Telling from out
of the Fundamental Attunement

All that has been said thus far fails to eliminate the suspicion that perhaps a certain non-genuineness remains in play when we accompany the saying of the "Not those . . . ," the refusal of the gods of old. Come what may, we must transpose ourselves into the position of the poet and proceed as if. . . . We still fail to experience anything coming from ourselves or directly affecting us that compels us to this refusal. Yet—is it indeed a refusal? IV, 181f.:

> I Nicht sie, die Seeligen, die erschienen sind,
>   Die Götterbilder in dem alten Lande,
>   Sie darf ich ja nicht rufen mehr, wenn aber
>   Ihr heimatlichen Wasser! jezt mit euch
>   Des Herzens Liebe klagt, was will es anders
>   Das Heiligtrauernde? Denn voll Erwartung liegt
>   Das Land und als in heissen Tagen
>   Herabgesenkt, umschattet heut
>   Ihr Sehnenden! uns ahnungsvoll ein Himmel.
> 10   Voll ist er von Verheissungen und scheint
>   Mir drohend auch, doch will ich bei ihm bleiben,
>   Und rükwärts soll die Seele mir nicht fliehn
>   Zu euch, Vergangene! die zu lieb mir sind.
>   Denn euer schönes Angesicht zu sehn,
>   Als wärs, wie sonst, ich fürcht' es, tödtlich ists
>   Und kaum erlaubt, Gestorbene zu weken.

II Entflohene Götter! auch ihr, ihr gegenwärtigen, damals
   Wahrhaftiger, ihr hattet eure Zeiten!
   Nichts läugnen will ich hier und nichts erbitten.
20 Denn wenn es aus ist, und der Tag erloschen,
   Wohl trifts den Priester erst, doch liebend folgt
   Der Tempel und das Bild ihm auch und seine Sitte
   Zum dunkeln Land und keines mag noch scheinen.
   Nur als von Grabesflammen, ziehet dann
   Ein goldner Rauch, die Sage drob hinüber,
   Und dämmert jezt uns Zweifelnden um das Haupt,
   Und keiner weiss, wie ihm geschieht. Er fühlt
   Die Schatten derer, so gewesen sind,
   Die Alten, so die Erde neubesuchen.
30 Denn die da kommen sollen, drängen uns,
   Und länger säumt von Göttermenschen
   Die heilige Schaar nicht mehr im blauen Himmel.

 I Not those, the blessed ones who once appeared,
   Divine images in the land of old,
   Those, indeed, I may call no longer, yet if
   You waters of the homeland! now with you
   The heart's love has plaint, what else does it want,
   The holy mourning one? For full of expectation lies
   The land, and as in sultry days
   Bowed down, a heaven casts today
   You longing ones! its shadows full of intimation round about us.
10 Full of promises it is, and seems
   Threatening to me also, yet I want to stay by it,
   And backwards shall my soul not flee
   To you, past ones! who are too dear to me.
   For to see your beautiful countenance
   As once it was, before, this I fear, deadly it is,
   And scarcely allowed, to waken the dead.

II Gods who have fled! You too, you present ones, once
   More truthful, you had your times!
   Nothing do I want to deny here, and ask nothing of you.
20 For when it is out, and the day extinguished,
   It affects first the priest, yet lovingly follow
   Him temple and image too and his custom
   To the land of darkness and none is able still to shine.
   Only, as from flames of the grave, there passes
   Then overhead a wisp of golden smoke, the legend thereof,

And now it dawns around the heads of us who doubt,
And no one knows what is happening to him. Each feels
The shadows of those who once have been,
Those of old, who visit thus the Earth anew.
30   For those who are to come press upon us,
No longer does the holy host of humans divine
Tarry in the blue of the heavens.

Were we correct in asserting that the beginning of the poem tears us away to a locale starting from which we are supposed to say a 'No'? Or were we completely mistaken, misreading this beginning because we were still grasping too precipitously after some ascertainable content? Instead of comprehending that the locale and the 'there' from which the poet speaks can be experienced only in terms of the whole orientation in which the poetic telling occurs? This is indeed the case. Despite our considerable preparation in many respects, we have yet to ponder the fact that the voice [*Stimme*] of the telling must be attuned [*gestimmt*], that the poet speaks from out of an attunement [*Stimmung*], an attunement that determines and attunes [*be-stimmt*] the ground and soil and that permeates [*durchstimmt*] the space upon which and within which the poetic telling founds a way of being. This attunement we name the fundamental attunement of the poetizing. By fundamental attunement, we do not mean some vague emotional state that merely attends the telling. Rather, the fundamental attunement opens up the world that in the poetic telling receives the stamp of beyng. Before we ponder specifically the essence of a fundamental attunement, so as to comprehend thereby something of the essence of human, historical Dasein, we wish to set into relief the fundamental attunement of the poetizing that bears the title "Germania." With regard to this task, we shall read only up to a particular point: namely, line 38.

The words "Not those . . ." in their abrupt severity awaken the appearance of a rejection, a no longer wanting to know. Yet the beginning of the second strophe, in which the 'I' continues to speak, calls out: "Gods who have fled!" This surely tells us that the gods themselves have gone—'the day is extinguished,' the people were no longer able to keep them and had to become blind in the night—'it is out.' What is the point of a refusal here? That presence of the gods is past. However, when we establish this—say as a historical fact—this tells us nothing whatsoever of the history that is at stake here, just as little as when we give assurances that there still is a Christendom today. When we speak this way, we do so only as those who have no ties, forgetting that a godless time is not nothing, but an uprising of the

Earth that can neither be alleviated, nor even recognized, whether by the mere continued existence of various denominations, or by an organizational change in the governance of the church on the part of the state.

The gods of a people cannot be acquired so readily. The flight of the gods must first become an experience, and this experience must first thrust our Dasein into a fundamental attunement in which a historical people in its entirety endures the need of its godlessness and of its fragmentation. It is this fundamental attunement that the poet founds within the historical Dasein of our people. Whether this occurred in the year 1801 or has yet to be apprehended and taken hold of in the year 1934 is unimportant, for numbers of years are indifferent with respect to the time of such decision.

b) Renouncing Calling the Gods of Old as Sustaining a Conflict. The Fundamental Attunement of Mourning and Its Three Aspects

The "Not those . . ." is no refusal, but introduces the words "Those, indeed, I may call no longer" (line 3). The "indeed" [ja] intensifies and lends finality to the 'not being permitted.' The abrupt "Not" at the beginning by no means refers to the severity of a rejection, but to the gravity of a necessary renunciation. With what is the renunciation concerned? With the "Divine images in the land of old" (line 2)? No. It concerns the calling of these gods. Someone who has nothing, who can have nothing, and wants to have nothing is also unable to renounce; he cannot even experience the necessity of a renunciation. Yet if the poet speaks from such a necessity, then he indeed wants something. He wants to call—that is, he does not merely wish to do so. Rather, wanting to call means standing firm within this calling. What kind of a calling is this? It is not a calling summoning those who are close and familiar to him, nor is it a calling through which the caller draws attention to himself, but rather that calling in which we await that which is called as such, and through the calling first place that which is awaited at a distance from us, as something yet distant, so as thereby to simultaneously be deprived of its nearness. This calling is the sustaining of a conflict between the opening up of a readiness and the absence of fulfillment. The enduring of such a conflict is *pain, a suffering*, and the calling is therefore *plaintive* (lines 3ff.):

> . . . wenn aber
> Ihr heimatlichen Wasser! jezt mit euch
> Des Herzens Liebe klagt,

. . . yet if
You waters of the homeland! now with you
The heart's love has plaint,

This pain of calling, this plaintiveness, springs from and oscillates within a *fundamental attunement of mourning.*

With regard to this and every fundamental attunement, however, it must be said from the outset that what is at issue here is not some weak resignation that submerges itself in so-called feelings, a kind of sentimentality that merely 'broods over' the state of one's own soul. In particular, this mourning is not some impotent collapse into oneself. Fundamental attunements—to use a customary distinction here—do not concern the soul, but the spirit. Pain and suffering in general *are* only by virtue of our enduring a conflict. Animals too can indeed endure pain and suffering, but their suffering and being in pain is not sorrow, just as stomach pains are not in themselves sorrow, nor the kind of pain that mourning is. Nor are these merely a 'higher' kind of feelings, but rather something essentially different.

Renouncing the calling of the gods of old is the decisiveness of a willingness to be deprived: "Nothing do I want to deny here, and ask nothing of you" (line 19). This decisiveness springs from the intimate superiority of the fundamental attunement of mourning. For this attunement makes all the many insignificant things a matter of indifference and maintains itself within the untouchability of one thing alone. And yet it is not some kind of wounded or disgruntled withdrawal; an empty, despairing rejection; or even obstinacy. Rather, this originary mourning is the *lucid superiority of the simple goodness of a grave pain—a fundamental attunement.* It opens up beings as a whole differently, and in an essential manner. Here we must pay heed to the following: Attunement, as attunement, lets the manifestness of beings occur.

Yet we must clarify still further the poetic configuration of the fundamental attunement. "The heart's love has plaint" (line 5). According to ancient wisdom, love is a willing: namely, willing that the beloved, in his or her being, be such as they are, stand firm in their essence. A willing—the heart's love—"what else does it want / The holy mourning one?" (lines 5f.). The mourning is a holy one, not some arbitrary sadness about some individual thing; rather, the entire fundamental attunement is holy.

To attunement there belongs, on the one hand, that which attunes (cf. below, on the 'inner ground' of attunement, p. 78ff.), then that which is attuned in the attunement, and finally the reciprocal interrelatedness of that which is attuned and that which attunes. Here we must pay heed to the fact that attunement does not start from a subject and an object that lie independently present at hand, such that an attunement would impose itself between the two and go back and forth between subject and object. Rather, the attunement and its arising or receding is what is originary, first drawing the object into the attunement in its own particular way in each instance, and making the subject that which is attuned. Considered more profoundly, however, the subject–object relationship that is commonly represented is here altogether inadequate for comprehending the essence of attunement. That relationship was conceived with respect to the representational relation between subject and object, so that the attunement, conceived as a feeling, is then merely something added on—a coloring.

c) The Fundamental Attunement and the Holy.
A Threefold Sheer Disinterestedness

The entire fundamental attunement as such is holy in the three respects mentioned. Yet what does "holy" mean? Hölderlin often employs this naming, and always does so in an essential manner in terms of the reach of the particular fundamental attunement of his poetizing. To cite just a few instances:

> Und trunken von Küssen
> Tunkt ihr das Haupt
> Ins heilignüchterne Wasser.

> And drunken with kisses
> You dip your heads
> Into the holy-sobering water.

("Midpoint of Life," IV, 60, lines 5ff.)

> Denn so wollte die heilge Natur . . .

> For thus holy nature willed it . . .

(Fragment 3, IV, 238)

> Süss ists zu irren
> In heiliger Wildniss,

> Sweet it is to wander
> In holy wilderness,

(Fragment 18, Tinian, IV, 250)

O nenne Tochter du der heiligen Erd'!

O name you daughter of the holy Earth!
("Germania," line 97)

Und was ich sah, das Heilige sei mein Wort.

And what I saw, may the holy be my word.
("As when on feast day . . . ," IV, 151, line 20)

Und es wurzelt vielesbereitend heilige Wildniss.

And there is rooted much-readying holy wilderness.
("The Titans," IV, 208, line 22)

Hölderlin names the holy something 'disinterested' [*uneigennützig*]. 'Disinterest' here refers not merely to a relinquishing of self-interest for the benefit of the common interest, but rather to that disinterest-edness that removes all self-interest even from the common interest— that is, removes from it its tendency toward self-limitation. It refers to a disinterestedness that no longer stands at all within the realm of utility—and nor, therefore, within that of what is useless either, since the latter is still evaluated with reference to interest. In what sense can Hölderlin understand the holy as that which is disinter-ested? Hölderlin clarifies his own understanding of the holy precisely with reference to what we are naming a 'fundamental attunement,' which in the language of Hölderlin's time is called 'sentiment' [*Emp-findung*], and which even at that time was subject to manifold interpre-tations, yet in its metaphysical essence was neither fully experienced, nor for that matter comprehended or grounded. The fact that this has not been accomplished to the present day is no accident, but has its grounds in the unbroken hegemony of the thinking of modernity— not so much in the form in which it was originally coined, but as the commonplace way of thinking and distilled mode of experience that characterize our contemporary everydayness.

We find this elucidation of the holy in a passage from the exceed-ingly difficult essay that bears the title "On the Operations of the Po-etic Spirit" (III, 277ff.). The essay remains incomprehensible without a genuine understanding of the innermost core and of the funda-mental questions of the philosophy of Kant and above all of German Idealism. Yet an understanding of this philosophy remains but one precondition among others. One cannot simply 'trace Hölderlin back' to that philosophy—in accordance with the usual method—and say, for instance, that he transforms the metaphysics of Schelling or Hegel into poetry. When dealing with these greats, it is always a mistake to try to figure out the details of who said what first and influenced the other; for only one who is himself great and open can truly be influenced. For this reason, genuine influence is extremely rare, whereas ordinary understanding is of course of the opinion that everything is influenced by everything. And this is indeed correct where everything remains merely small and mediocre and excluded from that which is great. It requires a supreme mustering of thoughtful energy and the longest endurance of a dialectical and metaphysical comprehension in order to follow the thinker-poet in his essay. Historically it belongs to the period of his first stay in Homburg following his flight from Frankfurt: the years 1798 to 1800. Toward the end of the essay, we find a concluding passage that tells us about the holy as the disinterested (III, 300ff.):

> Thus in an overly subjective state, just as in an overly objective one, the human being seeks in vain to attain his vocation, which consists in this: that he comes to recognize himself as a unity contained within divine, harmonious opposites, just as, conversely, he comes to recognize the divine, united, harmonious opposites as a unity contained within him. *For this is possible only in beautiful, holy, divine sentiment,* in a sentiment that is beautiful because it is neither merely pleasant and happy, nor merely sublime and powerful, nor merely unified and peaceful, but that is all at once, and can be such only in a sentiment, one that is holy because it is neither disinterestedly given over to its object, nor merely disinterestedly resting on its own inner ground, nor merely disinterestedly hovering between its inner ground and its object, but is all at once, and can be such only in a sentiment, one that is divine because it is neither mere consciousness, mere reflection (subjective or objective) with the loss of inner and outer life, nor mere striving (subjective or objective) with the loss of inner and outer harmony, nor mere harmony, as with intellectual intuition and its mythic image of a subject-object, with the loss of consciousness and of unity, but because it is all this at once, and can be such only in a sentiment, one that is transcendental and can be such only because in its unifying and in the reciprocal interaction of the said qualities it is neither overly pleasant and sensuous, nor overly energetic and wild, nor overly collected [*innig*] and enthusiastic, neither too disinterestedly given over to its object, i.e., in excessive self-forgetfulness, nor too disinterestedly resting on its inner ground, i.e., in an overly authoritarian manner, nor too disinterestedly hovering between its inner ground and its object, i.e., in an overly indecisive and empty and indeterminate manner, neither overly reflected,

overly conscious of itself, excessively discerning and for this very reason not conscious of its inner or outer ground, nor overly animated, too much caught up in its inner and outer grounds, and for this very reason not conscious of the harmony of inner and outer, nor overly harmonious, and for this very reason insufficiently conscious of itself and of its inner and outer grounds, for this very reason too indeterminate and less receptive to, and less capable of enduring, the genuine Infinite, which is determined by it as a *determinate*, actual infinity, as lying outside.

The holy is a complete disinterestedness—that is, one that is not one-sided. Disinterestedness can become one-sided with respect to those sides belonging to its essential structure. There are three 'sides':

1. The inner ground of disinterestedness. This ground belongs to disinterestedness as a kind of resting within itself, a manner of genuine self-steadfastness.

2. Its relationship to the objects as such. It is open to its objects and given over to them, and in this process retracts its own self-interest.

3. The relating as a relating between the inner ground and the object, their between, whereby the inner ground is secured and at the same time the object is promoted, raised up into its own good and its own essence and set free.

Disinterestedness is one-sided in relation to side 1 if it congeals into authoritarianism; one-sided in relation to side 2 if, becoming entirely absorbed in its object, it loses itself; and one-sided in relation to side 3 if it merely hovers between its inner ground and its object and remains empty, neither becoming set on itself, desiring nothing for itself, nor losing itself in the object, failing to take the object into its care.

Where all three of these sides, by contrast, are equiprimordially alive in the free superiority of a devotion fulfilled within a certain attunement, there occurs there pure disinterestedness, the holy.

d) A Holy Mourning 'with' the Homeland
as the Power of the Earth

Mourning, within which the necessary renunciation of the calling of the gods of old resonates, is holy in this manner. Not that mourning ossifies and turns to stone in a despair that pushes everything away; rather, the gods of old remain too dear to it. Mourning does not lose itself in merely abandoning itself, without abode, to those who have fled; it asks for nothing and does not seek to force anything. Mourning does not float off into a vacuum, because, as will become apparent, it precisely founds a new relationship to the divine.

The fundamental attunement is a *holy mourning*. This adjective 'holy' raises the attunement beyond all contingency, but also beyond all indeterminacy. Mourning is neither an isolated pining over some loss or other; yet nor is it that floating, hazy, and yet burdensome sadness about everything and nothing—what we call melancholy—which can in turn be shallow or profound depending on its fundamental differences in depth and extent. Yet even this character of the holy does not exhaust the essence of the fundamental attunement that prevails here. We experience this if we avoid taking the plaint that resonates in mourning as an isolated calling and see it instead as it understands itself: as having plaint 'with the waters of the homeland'. Plaint, and mourning especially, are a plaint and mourning 'with' the homeland. What does this mean? Perhaps that the poet is reading the feelings in his soul into the processes of nature, the flowing of the water, the rustling of the forest, and so on, and is thus symbolizing his nonsensuous, inner lived experiences through something external that can be grasped sensuously? Given all that has been said thus far, we shall hardly be inclined to come to terms with the poetizing in such a facile manner, or to inquire in this direction at all. The 'I' that is doing the telling here has plaint with the homeland because this 'I' self, as standing within itself, experiences itself precisely as belonging to the homeland. Homeland—not as a mere birth place, nor as a mere landscape familiar to us, but *as the power of the Earth* upon which the human being "dwells poetically,"[1] in each case in accordance with his historical Dasein. This homeland does not at all first require attunements to be transferred into it, because it is precisely that which attunes, and it attunes all the more directly and steadfastly when human beings stand fundamentally open to beings within a fundamental attunement. The way in which mourning stands within itself is a standing open to the prevailing of that which thoroughly attunes and embraces the human being. The land lies full of expectation beneath the stormy heaven that bows down, casting its shadows around nature as a whole in the homeland. In such homeland, the human being first experiences himself as belonging to the Earth, which he does not make empathetically subservient to his attunements. Rather, the reverse is the case: From out of the Earth, it first becomes possible for him to experience the nothingness of his individuated I-ness, which sets out by setting itself over and against everything, only to place it at its mercy as an object and empathize with it in its lived experiences.

e) The Transposition of the Human Being Together with Beings into Attunement

Because we have long been misled and regard the human being from the outset as a corporeal thing fitted out with a soul and its processes,

---

1. "In beautiful blue . . . ," IV, 25, line 32.

and because in addition we take the soul to be an 'I' in the first instance, we locate 'moods' within this 'I-subject.' Since cognition and willing as subjective processes at least always relate to and have to do with objects, yet moods, for the most part, also lack this relation to objects—they are naturally something purely 'subjective.' Since these moods or attunements are located within the 'I,' they must arise there too; that is, they must be caused in turn by other corporeal and psychological conditions. 'Moods' come to be located in the subject, and this subject in turn transfers them into the objects with the aid of so-called empathy. Attunements are then something like gloves: sometimes worn, sometimes set aside somewhere.

In contrast to this view, we have to say: Attunements are not placed into the subject or into objects; rather we, together with beings, are *trans-posed* into attunements. Attunements are powerful forces that permeate and envelop us; they come over us and things together with one fell swoop. That sounds fantastical. Yet far more fantastical—that is, far more remote from all true reality—is that representation of the human being as a corporeal thing endowed with a soul, a representation that is so commonplace and that leaves us so completely at a loss if our task is indeed to intimate the essence of attunement in the right way, that is, as it concerns the Dasein of the human being. It would be equally erroneous to place attunements in the subject as only 'subjective appearances'—as appearances arising in the interiority of the subject, like air bubbles in a glass of water—or to seek to explain them in terms of the effects of things acting upon our nerves. Rather the Dasein of the human being is transposed into attunements equiprimordially together with beings as such. The words "with you" (line 4) tell of this equiprimordiality. The holy mourning (plaint) with what belongs to the homeland is no accident and no poetical embellishment. Here, rather, something fundamental and essential is said poetically concerning beyng pure and simple.

f) The Fundamental Attunement as a Mourning with the Rivers of the Earth of the Homeland

Yet why "waters of the homeland" precisely (line 4)? Conventional poets sing of forest and meadow, brook and shrub, mountain and sky. Why precisely "waters" here? And which waters are meant? To the more immediate homeland of the poet belong the Neckar and the upper Danube. Cf. Fragment 27 (IV, 258f.):

Ihr sichergebaueten Alpen!
Die

Und ihr sanftblikenden Berge,
Wo über buschigem Abhang

Der Schwarzwald sausst,
Und Wohlgerüche die Loke
Der Tannen herabgiesst,
Und der Nekar

       und die Donau!
Im Sommer liebend Fieber
Umherwehet der Garten
Und Linden des Dorfs, und wo
Die Pappelweide blühet
Und der Seidenbaum
Auf heiliger Waide,

You solidly built Alps!
That

And their mountains' serene gaze,
Where over the bushy slope
The Black Forest rustles
And sweet fragrance flows down
From the curls of the fir trees,
And the Neckar

       and the Danube!
In summer the garden
Wafts lovingly fever all around
And lindens of the village, and where
The black poplar blossoms
And the silk tree
On sacred pasture,

Here we find a telling of the homeland, yet with mountains and the Alps also named, as well as the Black Forest, a garden, and the linden trees of the village. Why in "Germania" do we find precisely the "waters"? Why are they too addressed as "You longing ones" (lines 8f.)?

   . . . umschattet heut
Ihr Sehnenden! uns ahnungsvoll ein Himmel

   . . . a heaven casts today
You longing ones! its shadows full of intimation round about us.

The poet speaks of himself and of the "waters of the homeland" in the plural "us." Compare also lines 35f.:

... und Thal und Ströme sind
Weitoffen um prophetische Berge,

... and valley and rivers lie
Open wide around prophetic mountains,

And if we look at Hölderlin's late poetizing in the proximity of "Germania," we encounter major poems with the titles "At the Source of the Danube" (IV, 158ff.), "The Rhine" (IV, 172ff.), "The Ister" ("Ἴστρος, the Greek name for the Danube: IV, 220ff.), "Peaceful the Branches of the Neckar" (Fragment 12, IV, 246), and "The Fettered River" (IV, 56). Cf. "The Main" (III, 54f.) and "The Neckar" (III, 59f.).

These river poems are not only contemporaneous with "Germania" from a superficial perspective, but are intrinsically connected to it. Our preparatory interpretation of "Germania" is indeed meant to afford us a midpoint from which to comprehend the poetic dimension of these river poems.

In addition, we possess translations and remarks from Hölderlin's late period concerning fragments of Pindar. One of these fragments bears Hölderlin's title, "That Which Animates." In his comments on it, we find a discussion of what the poet means by a river and river spirit (V, 272f.):

That Which Animates.

The power of honey-sweet wine, after
The Centaurs had learned of it,
Vanquishing men, suddenly
Their hands pushed away the white milk and the table too, spontaneously
And drinking from the silver horns
They became enchanted.

The concept of the Centaurs is presumably that of the spirit of a river, insofar as the latter cuts paths and limits, with violence, upon the originarily pathless, upward-flourishing Earth.

Their image is therefore in the place of nature, where the shore is rich in rocks and grottos, *especially in places where the river originally had to abandon the chain of mountains and tear out its path at an angle.*

Centaurs are therefore also originally teachers of natural science, because nature can best be discerned from that perspective.

In such regions the river originally had to wander around before it tore out a path for itself. Thus there came to be formed—as around ponds—damp meadows and caves in the Earth for mammals, and the Centaur was meanwhile a wild shepherd, akin to the Odyssean Cyclops; the waters longed for and sought out their direction. Yet the more the drier of its two banks formed more firmly and gained direction by its firmly rooted trees and thickets and its vines, the more too the river, receiving its movement from the shape of its bank, had to take on direction until, driven on by its origin, it broke through at a spot where the mountains that contained it were most fragile.

The Centaurs *thus learned the power of honey-sweet wine.* They took on movement and direction from the securely formed bank, rich in trees, and *with their hands threw away the white milk and the table.* The wave that had formed suppressed the peace of the pond, and the mode of life of the banks too became altered; the storms and the assured princes of the forest that swept over the woods incited the leisurely life of the moorland; the stagnant water was repelled by the steep bank *until it grew arms* and thus acting alone, with its own direction, *drinking from silver horns,* it made a path for itself and gained a determinate orientation.

The songs of Ossian in particular are veritable Centaurs' songs, sung with the river spirit, and as though from the Greek Chiron, who also taught Achilles to play the lyre.

The river violently creates paths and limits on the originally path-less Earth. (Since the flight of the gods, the Earth has been pathless.) This perspective already illuminates to what extent mourning and plaint are a mourning precisely with the rivers of the Earth of the homeland: because, through the arrival of the new gods, the entire historical, Earthly Dasein of the Germans is to be pointed on a new path and created a new determinacy and orientation. The river spirit is not an opposition of water to land; rather, the waters in their ac-companying plaint have a longing for the paths of a land that has be-come pathless. They tear the entire land toward an encounter with the awaited gods.

g) The Opening Power of the Fundamental Attunement. Preserving the Divinity of the Old Gods While Mournfully Renouncing Them

From here, a further essential characteristic of the prevailing funda-mental attunement becomes clearer. This mourning is not the wander-ing around, with neither hope nor goal, of some attunement without root. Rather, such being attuned takes root in the land and places the land into an awaiting under the threatening heavens. To such self-composed readiness, with which the land awaits an approaching thunderstorm, there belongs the superior composure of a mournful plaint; whence the words (line 11):

. . . doch will ich bei ihm bleiben,

. . . yet I want to stay by it,

by these heavens, that is, to endure amid the threatening of the land, which lies "full of expectation" (line 6). Mourning is not a hanging on to the past, but a standing firm within oneself and withstanding the 'there' [da] and here. The poet knows all too originarily that a mere clinging to others is not love, is not a will that the beloved be. It is because these gods are too dear to him that he lets them be dead, for their flight does not destroy their having been, but rather creates and maintains it. The will to reawaken them, a violently deceptive reaching beyond the limit of death, would only tear them into a non-genuine, non-godlike proximity and bring about, rather than a new life, their death.

For the calculative intellect, renunciation means a relinquishing and a loss. True renunciation—that is, a renouncing that is sustained and brought about by a genuinely expansive fundamental attunement—is creative and productive. In releasing what was previously possessed, it receives, and not as some kind of subsequent reward; rather, a mournful enduring of the necessity of renunciation and of letting go is in itself a receiving.

Only if we fathom the entire expanse of this holy mourning, steadfast within itself and rejecting everything contrived, can we encounter and understand the decisive word of the whole first strophe, and thereby of the entire poem. This word has the linguistic form of a question and reads (line 5):

. . . was will es anders

. . . what else does it want

—it, the holy mourning heart. In our customary way of characterizing forms of speech, we can here find a so-called rhetorical question: a way of saying which, despite its interrogative form, is not a question, but an answering and assuring, a saying of assuredness and decidedness. The holy mourning is resolved to renounce the gods of old, but what does the mourning heart want other than this: in relinquishing the gods to preserve untouched their divinity, and thus to maintain itself precisely in this preserving renunciation of the distant gods in the nearness of their divinity. No longer being allowed to call upon the gods of old, this will to acquiesce in their renunciation, what else is it?—it is nothing else than the sole possible, resolute readiness for awaiting the divine; for the gods as such can be relinquished in such renunciation only if they are retained in their divinity—and the more intimately they are thus retained. Where the most beloved has left, love remains behind, for otherwise the former could not have left at all.

That the gods have fled does not mean that divinity too has vanished from the Dasein of human beings. Here it means that such divinity precisely prevails, yet as something no longer fulfilled, as becoming dark and overcast, yet still powerful. If someone wished to escape from the realm of divinity—granted that such a thing could be possible at all—for such a one there could not even be dead gods. Whoever says in all seriousness 'God is dead,' and like Nietzsche devotes his life to this predicament, is no atheist. Such is the opinion only of those who relate to and treat their God in the same way as a pocketknife. When the pocketknife is lost, it is indeed gone. But to lose God means something else, and not only because God and a pocketknife are intrinsically different things. Thus atheism is altogether a strange state of affairs; for many who sit in the cage of a traditional religious belief that has so far failed to astound them, because they are either too cozy or too smart for that, are more atheistic than the great skeptics. The necessity of renouncing the gods of old, the enduring of this renunciation, is the *preserving* of their divinity.

If the attuning, opening power of the fundamental attunement lies herein, and the fundamental attunement sustains and bestows an attuned determinacy on the course of the poetic telling, then this essential word (line 5) must engender the progression to the second strophe. But first let us read the first strophe once again, this time with a more lucid knowledge (IV, 181):

I Nicht sie, die Seeligen, die erschienen sind,
   Die Götterbilder in dem alten Lande,
   Sie darf ich ja nicht rufen mehr, wenn aber
   Ihr heimatlichen Wasser! jezt mit euch
   Des Herzens Liebe klagt, was will es anders
   Das Heiligtrauernde? Denn voll Erwartung liegt
   Das Land und als in heissen Tagen
   Herabgesenkt, umschattet heut
   Ihr Sehnenden! uns ahnungsvoll ein Himmel.
10   Voll ist er von Verheissungen und scheint
   Mir drohend auch, doch will ich bei ihm bleiben,
   Und rükwärts soll die Seele mir nicht fliehn
   Zu euch, Vergangene! die zu lieb mir sind.
   Denn euer schönes Angesicht zu sehn,

Als wärs, wie sonst, ich fürcht' es, tödtlich ists
Und kaum erlaubt, Gestorbene zu weken.

I Not those, the blessed ones who once appeared,
Divine images in the land of old,
Those, indeed, I may call no longer, yet if
You waters of the homeland! now with you
The heart's love has plaint, what else does it want,
The holy mourning one? For full of expectation lies
The land, and as in sultry days
Bowed down, a heaven casts today
You longing ones! its shadows full of intimation round about us.
10   Full of promises it is, and seems
Threatening to me also, yet I want to stay by it,
And backwards shall my soul not flee
To you, past ones! who are too dear to me.
For to see your beautiful countenance
As once it was, before, this I fear, deadly it is,
And scarcely allowed, to waken the dead.

We no longer read anything of a refusal. We also have the intimation that what is at stake is not at all the superficial historical comparison between a previous state of the ancient world and way of relating to it and some subsequent, contemporary state—that it is not some question or other of humanism—but that what prevails here is the time of peoples, and what stands in question is a world destiny of the Earth of the homeland.

Yet not only does nothing of a refusal happen in the first strophe. The "Not" with which it begins is fundamentally not at all a denial that stands alone, nor the kind that pertains to renunciation, but finds its full and authentic significance in the phrase "what else does it want" (line 5), speaking of the holy mourning heart. Earlier (p. 74) we already pointed to the opening of the second strophe, and emphasized that the gods themselves have fled, after all, and that there is therefore no need to refuse them. Yet this does not yet lead us to the proper content of the second strophe and its inner connection to the first. Rather, we must hold together in their unity line 5 (first strophe) and line 19 (second strophe): "what else does it want" and "Nothing do I want to deny here, and ask nothing of you." This word is supreme resolve—namely, in taking over our abandonment by the gods of old. The fundamental attunement of holy mourning thus becomes intensified here into its innermost superiority. Mourning becomes a knowing of the fact that truly taking seriously the gods that have fled, as having fled, is in itself precisely a remaining with the gods, with their divinity as a divinity that is no longer fulfilled. No longer wanting anything or asking anything of the gods does not mean decline into some crude form of godlessness or empty despair; it is not a listless and contrived coming to terms with their death. Rather, this wanting is the wanting of line 5 ("what else does it want"): displacement into and maintaining oneself purely within the space of a possible new encounter with the gods.

h) The Essentially Lawful Sequence of Decline Belonging to a Historical Dasein within the Need of the Absence of the Gods

The fact that this no longer wanting anything in one respect at the same time and essentially remains and becomes supreme willing in another respect, is told by the second strophe. For this reason, the second strophe brings a further essential unfolding of the fundamental attunement of the poetizing. In both strophes we find a will: the will that what is willed be as it is. Such willing is the essence of that love of which we are told (line 5): it has plaint. At the supreme peak of abandonment that is knowingly taken over, there occurs the sudden, innermost turnaround of this abandonment into a knowing awaiting. Such awaiting displays itself as knowing awaiting in our being told expressly of the occurrence of the flight of the gods, of being abandoned, and of desolation (lines 20ff.):

> Denn wenn es aus ist, und der Tag erloschen,
> Wohl trifts den Priester erst, doch liebend folgt
> Der Tempel und das Bild ihm auch und seine Sitte
> Zum dunkeln Land und keines mag noch scheinen.

> For when it is out, and the day extinguished,
> It affects first the priest, yet lovingly follow
> Him temple and image too and his custom
> To the land of darkness and none is able still to shine.

First it affects the priest—namely, the flight of the gods; temple and image and custom follow after. Lovingly, being of the same will, and staying close to him, they too fall into abandonment, desolation, and impotence. The poet tells of this in the poem "To Mother Earth" (IV, 156, lines 47ff.):

> Die Tempelsäulen stehn
> Verlassen in Tagen der Noth,
> Wohl tönet des Nordsturms Echo

50   – – – tief in den Hallen,
        Und der Reegen machet sie rein
        Und Moos wächst und es kehren die Schwalben,
        In Tagen des Frühlings, nahmlos aber ist
        In ihnen der Gott, und die Schaale des Danks
        Und Opfergefäss und alle Heiligtümer
        Begraben dem Feind in verschwiegener Erde.

        The pillars of the temple stand
        Abandoned in days of need,
        The north storm's echo rings indeed
50   – – – deep within the chambers,
        And the rain makes them pure
        And moss grows and the swallows return,
        In days of spring, yet nameless is
        The God within them, and the cup of thanks
        And vessel of sacrifice and all holy shrines
        Abandoned to the foe in Earth's silent seclusion.

When the poet in the poem "Germania" speaks of temple, image, and custom following the priest, this does not refer to a one-time historical process, but means the essentially lawful sequence of stages of decline of a historical Dasein as such within the need of the absence of the gods. The poet here tells—that is, he tells it in *founding*—how beyng happens, formerly and in the future. For this reason, we must elucidate this essential lawfulness for ourselves.

Custom and tradition are found only where temple and image, as the historical Dasein of the gods, tower over and are binding for our everyday activity and living. Image and temple, however, are found only where those great individuals exist who, in knowing and creating, directly endure and bring to resolution in the created work the presence and absence of the gods. Such works are not there in order to further or enrich a so-called 'culture.' Culture and the furthering of culture, culture clubs, and even cultural programs exist and make sense only where historical Dasein stands under the domination of what is today called 'liberalism.' The Greeks had no time for 'culture'; such exists in late antiquity. Only insignificant times—eras when our entire Dasein declines into something contrived—foster the true, the good, and the beautiful and then have corresponding ministries in their state. Yet even where temple and image and custom continue to be present and to exist for decades, or even for centuries—and, in so doing, keep alive an effective morality for individuals and for groups—still everything is fundamentally already untethered. Creative forces run riot as the achievements of individuals and acquire their value as contributions to the furthering of culture and progress. Why, really, and to what end, no one knows.

The possibility of a monumental unsettling of the historical Dasein of the people has faded. Temple, image, and custom are not in a position to assume the historical mission of a people as a whole from the ground up and to compel it into a new mandate. The temples, besides edifying individuals and providing for the salvation of individual souls, are limited to the securing of the authoritative powers and spheres of influence of the churches. The churches likewise participate in the gradual decline into culture, in a noncreative way, moreover, and in such a way that they continually and skillfully assimilate themselves to whatever is in each case contemporary. Thus today, for instance, we get to read things concerning church dogmatics that appear almost as though they were written by Nietzsche, which is certainly a rather perverse state of affairs.

Conversely, however, there is also no creation of any decisive relationship of the people to the ground and abyss of its historical Dasein if there is only a fostering of custom, which taken by itself can be edifying, but which becomes a misunderstanding when the opinion arises that the preservation of national tradition [Volkstum] comes about through the increased hiring of professors of indigenous knowledge [Volkskunde] and primal history. All of this remains merely an altered form of the pursuit of culture and can never be what it is meant to be, so long as the gods have fled. Image and temple can never come about through market competition, if the God is dead. There can be no priests if the lightning flashes of the gods fail to strike, and they will never strike unless the Earth of the homeland and its entire people as this people come to stand in the realm of the thunderstorms. Yet the people will never enter this realm of the thunderstorms until, as a whole in its historical Dasein as such, it brings to essential experience and to a long endurance the innermost need of the death of the gods.

i) The Enduring of Abandonment by Those Who Doubt

Just as, at the beginning of the flight of the gods, it strikes first the priest—this does not, of course, mean the pastors—so too a priest or priestess must once again be struck if there is to be a new arrival of the gods: a priest or priestess who, in a concealed and unrecognized manner, awaits the messenger of the gods, so that temple, image, and custom can lovingly follow them. Unless this happens, the peoples will lurch toward their end without prospect of salvation, in spite of the airplane and radio and conquest of the stratosphere. For things to proceed otherwise, the godlessness of our entire historical Dasein must first be experienced; that is, our Dasein must be open to such experience, and, if it is closed, it must be opened up, and indeed by those who truly endure such fleeing of the gods. They are *those who doubt,* around whose heads there dawns the legend of what has been, and they are those of whom no one knows what is happening to him, whereas the self-assured and able-bodied know-it-alls always know what is happening to them, since they promptly see to it that nothing whatsoever can happen to them.

The doubt of those who doubt is sustained by a genuine will to know, and stands firm in the face of a true not-knowing. In true doubt there comes to pass [*ereignet sich*] the collision of knowing and not-knowing, and there is temporalized that originary need that transposes our Dasein into fundamental attunements. Here, accordingly, doubt does not mean a merely corrosive denial, driven on from one reservation to another, nor the blind assertion, weary of all questioning, that after all, we can know nothing. In doubting, the most profound abandonment is endured. And precisely in such abandonment, the individual comes to vanish as an individual with his special and personal needs. The more originarily our Dasein is experienced and told of as worthy of question, the more genuinely this is a telling that stands for everyone. Now, where even the individual in his particular relation to particular gods has been abandoned, where only the preservation of the divinity of the gods that have fled remains—there the 'I' recedes and the telling is a word of the 'we.'

The poet tells of this monumental doubt, which encompasses the entire historical Dasein of the people and transports us toward the mystery, in the poem "To the Germans" (IV, 132f.):

> Spottet nimmer des Kinds, wenn noch das alberne
> Auf dem Rosse von Holz herrlich und viel sich dünkt,
> O ihr Guten! auch wir sind
> Thatenarm und gedankenvoll!

> Aber kommt, wie der Strahl aus dem Gewölke kommt,
> Aus Gedanken vieleicht, geistig und reif die That?
> Folgt die Frucht, wie des Haines
> Dunklem Blatt, der stillen Schrift?

> Und das Schweigen im Volk, ist es die Feier schon
> 10   Vor dem Feste? die Furcht, welche den Gott ansagt?
> O, dann nimmt mich, ihr Lieben!
> Dass ich büsse die Lästerung.

> Schon zu lange, zu lang irr' ich, dem Laien gleich,
> In des bildenden Geists werdender Werkstatt hier,
> Nur was blühet, erkenn ich,
> Was er sinnet, erkenn ich nicht.

Und zu ahnen ist süss, aber ein Leiden auch,
Und schon Jahre genug leb' ich in sterblicher
Unverständiger Liebe
20   Zweifelnd, immer bewegt um ihn,

Der das stetige Werk immer aus liebender
Seele näher dem Sterblichen und lächelnd da,
Wo ich zage, des Lebens
Reine Tiefen zu Reife bringt.

Schöpferischer, o wann, Genius unsers Volks,
Wann erscheinest du ganz, Seele des Vaterlands,
Dass ich tiefer mich beuge,
Dass die leiseste Saite selbst

Mir verstumme vor dir, dass ich beschämt ᴗ –
30   Eine Blume der Nacht, himmlischer Tag, vor dir
Enden möge mit Freuden,
Wenn sie alle, mit denen ich

Vormals trauerte, wenn unsere Städte nun
Hell und offen und wach, reineren Feuers voll
Und die Berge des deutschen
Landes Berge der Musen sind,

Wie die herrlichen einst, Pindos und Helikon
Und Parnassos, und rings unter des Vaterlands
Goldenem Himmel die freie,
40   Klare, geistige Freude glänzt.

Wohl ist enge begränzt unsere Lebenszeit,
Unserer Jahre Zahl sehen und zählen wir,
Doch die Jahre der Völker,
Sah ein sterbliches Auge sie?

Wenn die Seele dir auch über die eigne Zeit
Sich die sehnende schwingt, trauernd verweilst du
Dann am kalten Gestade
Bei den Deinen und kennst sie nie.

Never mock the child, when foolish yet
Magnificent upon his wooden horse he thinks much of himself,
O, you good ones! we too are
Poor in deed and rich in thought!

Yet does perhaps the deed, spirited and mature, emerge from
thoughts,

As the ray of light emerges from the clouds?
Does the fruit ensue from silent script,
As it does from the grove's dark leaf?

And the silence among the people, is it already the celebration
10   Before the festival? the fear that announces the God?
O, take me then, you beloved ones!
That I may atone for the blasphemy.

Too long, too long already I wander, like the layman,
Here in shaping spirit's emergent workshop,
I recognize only that which blossoms,
What spirit has in mind, I know not.

And to intimate is sweet, but a suffering too,
And for enough years I have lived already in mortal
Uncomprehending love
20   Doubting, always there moves around him,\

Who brings the steady work, ever from a loving
Soul, nearer to the mortal and smiling there,
Where I waver,
Brings life's pure depth to fruition.

Creative one, O when, genius of our people,
When will you fully appear, soul of the fatherland,
That I may bow more deeply,
That the gentlest chord itself

Will fall silent for me before you, that I ashamed ◡ –
30   A flower of the night, heavenly day, before you
Might end with joys,
When all those with whom I

Previously mourned, if our towns now
Bright and open and awake, full of pure fire
And the mountains of the German
Land are mountains of the Muses

Like the once magnificent, Pindos and Helicon
And Parnassus, and round about beneath the fatherland's
Golden heavens the free,
40   Clear, spiritual joy gleams

Our lifetime indeed is narrowly spanned,
We see and count the numbers of our years,

> Yet the years of the peoples,
>   Did ever a mortal eye see them?
>
> If your soul too beyond your own time
>   Transports you in its longing, mournfully you tarry
> Then on the cold shores
>   Alongside your own and never know them.

Through everything that we have discussed thus far, the place of this poem within Hölderlin's later poetizing as a whole has already become clear, and its connection with "Germania" visible. Both poems are the same poetizing, and only together do they testify to the inexhaustible that remains to be said here.

j) The Completion of the Prevailing Fundamental Attunement into Its Full Essence: The Distress of Holy Mourning as Readiness

We return to "Germania." The sudden, inner turnaround from abandonment into awaiting announces itself in the ending of the second strophe through a reversal of temporality: Those who thus have been press upon us, come toward us as already pressing. Strictly speaking, however, the talk of a sudden turnaround from abandonment into expectation is misleading. For the fundamental attunement of abandonment is so little able to vanish and be replaced by an awaiting that, precisely in abandonment, there resonates an awaiting—an awaiting that thus lets the abandonment become distress.

As distress, however—that is, insofar as it stands firm before the pressure of those who press upon us—the distress of holy mourning becomes a *readiness*. In this way, the fundamental attunement prevailing in this poetizing is first completed into its full essence. Yet insofar as the fundamental attunement prevails throughout and in its attuning permeates the whole of beings, the Earth of the homeland too enters into this attunement. The superiority of holy mourning is sustained by such readiness that withstands the distress, which is why we are also told of this readiness last, as concluding the unfolding of the fundamental attunement, at the beginning of the third strophe (lines 33ff.):

> Schon grünet ja, im Vorspiel rauherer Zeit
> Für sie erzogen das Feld, bereitet ist die Gaabe
> Zum Opfermahl und Thal und Ströme sind
> Weitoffen um prophetische Berge,
>
> Already nurtured for them, the field indeed grows verdant,
> Prelude to a harsher time, the gift is readied

For the sacrificial meal and valley and rivers lie
Open wide around prophetic mountains,

Once again we find this "indeed" or "yes" [*ja*], as at the beginning: "Those, indeed, I may call no longer." In each case the "indeed," the "yes," is an unconditional decidedness: at the beginning, in the will to renounce; now, in being ready; each the echo of the other, and both united in telling of the unconditional nature of the attunement, which is why we name this a *fundamental* attunement. As such, it attunes human being and Earth equiprimordially, indeed—contrary to our received opinion—the Earth even before, for the Earth is ready so "that . . . may look . . . / The man" (lines 37f.). The latter does not empathetically and subsequently import an initially and properly 'subjective' attunement into the landscape, but the reverse: The readied Earth is the condition for the man's being able to look and wanting to look. In the word "may," there resonates the double meaning of being able and willing.

§ 9. Historical Time and Fundamental Attunement

a) The Experience of the Earth of the Homeland in the Lucidity of a Questioning Knowing Concerning the Historical Mission of a People

The poet tells of the field's growing verdant, of the valley, and of the flowing of the rivers that are open wide around prophetic mountains. This is a strange geography: a description of the Earth that we barely understand at first, assuming that we are concerned with a description at all here. Here the Earth is experienced in advance in the lucidity of a questioning knowing concerning the historical mission of a people. The Earth of the homeland here is not a mere space delimited by external borders, a realm of nature, or a locality constituting a possible arena for this or that event to be played out there. The Earth, as this Earth of the homeland, is nurtured for the gods. Through such nurturing it first becomes homeland, yet as such it can once again fall into decline and sink to the level of a mere place of residence, which accordingly goes hand in hand with the advent of godlessness. The coming to be of homeland does not happen through mere settlement, either, unless it is accompanied by a nurturing of the Earth for the gods, in which the Earth is held open for an encounter with the prevailing of the gods in the course of the changing seasons of the year and their festivals. This occurs in 'prelude' to a harsher time, so that the Earth then first comes fully and properly into play, i.e., history and historical time. History is the monumental play that the gods play with the peoples and with a people; for the great times and eras of world time are a play, according to the word of an ancient Greek philosopher, Heraclitus, whom they call the obscure one, and whose most profound thoughts were thought anew precisely by Hölderlin. See Fragment 52:

αἰὼν παῖς ἐστι παίζων, πεσσεύων. παιδὸς ἡ βασιληίη.

"The time of the world—a child it is, playing, moving the board pieces to and fro, of [such] a child is sovereignty [over being]." In such play of the gods stands the Earth.

b) Provenance of the Pivotal Times of the Peoples from out of the Abyss

In the Earth's becoming homeland, it opens itself to the power of the gods. The two are the same and include within them a third element: that in the storm of the divine, the Earth itself comes to be torn open in its grounds and abysses. The latter can certainly become covered over, and do so together with the decline of the homeland. The Earth then becomes a mere site of use and exploitation. By contrast, when the Earth manifests herself in the disinterestedness of authentic Dasein, she is holy—holy Earth. The holy one,

> Die Mutter ist von allem, und den Abgrund trägt

> Who is Mother of all, and carries the abyss

("Germania," line 76)

In this abyss, the firmness and individuatedness of all ground retreats and everything yet finds its way to a constantly dawning new becoming. For the human being, who 'dwells poetically upon this Earth,' he and he alone *belongs* to the abyss that the Earth carries. This Earthly dimension of the Earth is unattainable even for the heavenly.

> . . . Nicht vermögen
> Die Himmlischen alles. Nemlich es reichen
> Die Sterblichen eh' in den Abgrund. Also wendet es sich
> Mit diesen.

> . . . The heavenly
> Are not capable of all. Mortals rather
> Reach into the abyss. Thus things turn
> With them.

("Mnemosyne," IV, 225, lines 14ff.)

The great, pivotal times of the peoples always emerge from the abyss, and, in each case, in accordance with the extent to which a people reaches into it—which is to say, into its Earth—and possesses home-land. For this reason, pivotal times of a people are not experienced, let alone comprehended, on the shallow plain of the platitudes of the day's gossip and its ever-skewed considerations, or all the contingencies to which it clings, blind with respect to origin and advent of the necessary. The necessary cannot be arrived at by calculations balancing cause and effect, but is a grounding only within the abyss.

> . . . Und gewaltig dämmerts
> Im ungebundenen Abgrund
> Im allesmerkenden auf.

> . . . And mightily it dawns
> Within the unbound abyss
> Within the all-divining.

("The Titans," IV, 210, lines 72ff.)

Whoever knows only the day, and indeed the everyday, recognizes nothing and knows nothing, just as he also does not know the night,

> . . . wenn alles gemischt
> Ist ordnungslos und wiederkehrt
> Uralte Verwirrung.

> . . . when all is mixed
> Disorderdly and there returns
> Primordial confusion.

("The Rhine," closing lines, IV, 180)

When the poet tells of the Earth and names meadows of the home-land and valley and rivers, this is all far removed from every kind of poetic depiction of nature, whether the latter is sweet and dreamy or rapturous and sublime, or whether it is faithfully preserving and pro-claiming mysteries.

The fundamental attunement of a holy mourning in readied dis-tress, out of which it is no longer an 'I' who speaks, but a 'we,' is thus a truthful preserving of the heavenly that have fled and thereby an awaiting of the newly threatening heavens, precisely because it is 'Earthly.' 'Earthly' does not mean created by a creator-god, but rather an uncreated abyss within which all emergent happening quivers and remains held.

c) Primordial Movedness of Fundamental Attunement.
Having-Been and Past

Already the fact that we cannot and may not directly name the fundamental attunement with a single word points to the fact that the attunement in itself—as both attuning and attuned—is reciprocal and thus a properly primordial movedness. This movedness we wish now to clarify in concluding our interpretation of lines 1 to 38.

The gods of old, as those that have fled, are precisely there in no longer being permitted to call upon them; they are there not as present, but rather, in the renunciative Dasein, they are there as having been, i.e., as still being. In being absent, they come to presence precisely in the absence of that which has been. That which has been, and its having-been, is something fundamentally different in principle from that which is past and its being past. It is true that we do not name either one unequivocally in our language, in part because in our customary referring to time and temporal moments we indeed fail to experience any distinctions. That which has been is for us the past, and vice-versa. However essential language can be in its telling, our immediate word usage is just as often contingent and arbitrary. That is, the use of language is not a matter of official or pedantic 'terminology,' and it would run counter to the meaning of language to try to regulate all word usage in a terminological way. If, however, we decide to go with a particular designation in order to name the difference in meaning between having-been and past, we do so out of the necessity of establishing an essential difference within the essence of time. Whether one is named having-been and the other past, or vice-versa, is arbitrary within certain limits and a matter of one's feel for language. What we want to name that which 'has been,' the poet indeed names that which is 'past' (lines 12f.):

> Und rükwärts soll die Seele mir nicht fliehn
> Zu euch, Vergangene!

> And backwards shall my soul not flee
> To you, past ones!

Yet he understands passing here in a specific sense, as we shall document (p. 110f.).

What is past is unalterably closed off, unable to be brought back; it lies firmly in the past, which, as our language fittingly says, is a space of time—a storeroom, as it were—in which everything that has expired or passed away collects. Even if it were possible for something that is past to recur once more in all its details and circumstances, it would never be the same; that point of time—the previous 'now' from which what was passing receded back into the past, taking it itself along with it—is irretrievably gone. What is past lies before the gate to the present and can never again enter back through this gate. That which has been, however, is that which still presences, which we ourselves in a certain way are, insofar as, bringing it before us, preserving it and carrying it forward, or even pushing it away or wanting to forget it, we let it stand forth into our Dasein. The shadows of those who once have been visit us anew, come toward us, are of the future [zu-künftig]. Conversely, however, in withstanding the distress, in the pressure of those who press upon us, we do not experience something altogether other, but divinity and that for which, in the prelude to a harsher time, the Earth already made herself ready before this.

d) Temporalizing of Originary Time as the Fundamental Occurrence of the Fundamental Attunement

Within this prevailing forward of that which has been into the future—which, directed backward, opens up that which earlier already readied itself as such—there prevails the approach of a coming [das Zu-kommen] and a still-presencing (future and having-been) in one: originary time. The temporalizing of this time is the fundamental occurrence of that attunement in which the poetizing is grounded. This originary time transports our Dasein into future and having-been, or better: makes our being enraptured as such, provided that our being is authentic. Inauthentically, it is always—in contrast to such rapture—merely sitting tight on an ever-changing present-day. I have provided an account of the essential constitution of this originary temporality and its essential possibilities in the treatise Being and Time.[1]

The poet on a number of occasions names this time the "time that tears,"[2] because it is within itself the oscillation that tears us away into the future and casts us back into having-been. Within the rhythm of this being torn back and forth into an ever-new preservation of what has been and an ever-new awaiting of that which is to come, there is temporalized the time of a people. By virtue of this time, a people enters into the standing open of valley and flowing rivers for that which is told from the mountains concerning what is to come,

---

1. Tübingen, 1977 (14th edition). Gesamtausgabe Bd. 2. Frankfurt, 1977. §§65ff. Translated as Being and Time by John Macquarrie and Edward Robinson. New York: Harper & Row, 1962.

2. Fragments on the motif of the "Titans," IV, 217, line 67; "Remarks on Antigone," V, 254; and elsewhere.

from those peaks of time upon which the creators dwell. In such time, as it quivers within the fundamental attunement—to say it more truly, as it quivers as the said fundamental attunement—in the Dasein of the people 'there comes to be' time; there comes about that right time, which is no inopportune time—the latter, as with everything forcibly contrived and produced in a merely calculative manner, remaining something hated by the gods.

> Denn es hasset
> Der sinnende Gott
> Unzeitiges Wachstum.

> For the God that muses
> Hates
> Untimely maturation.
>   (Fragments on the motif of the "Titans," concluding lines, IV, 218)

The beginning of this poem reads (IV, 215):

> Wenn aber die Himmlischen haben
> Gebaut, still ist es
> Auf Erden, und wohlgestalt stehn
> Die betroffenen Berge. Gezeichnet
> Sind ihre Stirnen.

> Yet when the heavenly have
> Built, it is quiet
> On Earth, and finely formed stand
> The mountains in question. Their brows
> Are marked.

e) The Decision in Favor of the Authentic Time of Poetizing as a Decision to Enter into the Fundamental Attunement

Such authentic time, however, is difficult to recognize, and knowledge of it can readily be destroyed by the daily events that are all too familiar and by the eternally yesterday. No amount of accumulated historical knowledge is of any help here. Exchanging hitherto known and referenced historical materials for different ones also remains useless, if the historicality of Dasein fails to become sovereign over our mere everydayness. For we can never have our authentic time—our true history—so long as we are not historical. And we are not historical so long as we remain incapable of experiencing the power of temporality from the ground up, and in such a way that we stand in the very midst of its tearing us away, which also means, so long as we remain wedded to an image of eternity that is merely constant presence and, as such, is comfortable to think; whereas eternity becomes ancient and has been: "ancient eternity becomes ever more concealed" (Fragment 4, "O Mother Earth!" IV, 239).

> So ist schnellvergänglich alles Himmlische.

> Thus everything heavenly passes quickly.
> > ("Conciliator, you who . . . ," Appendix, IV, 341, line 5)

To pass does not here mean to perish, but rather to pass by, not to remain, not to remain there constantly present, i.e., thought in terms of the issue, to presence as something that has been, to come to presence in a coming that presses upon us.

Because we are here concerned with something other than things that are present at hand or not present at hand—things whose appearing can be directly ascertained—our experience of such eternities and times is also of a different character, one that must appear incongruous to our everyday way of experiencing time. In the ensuing lines of the poem just cited, we are told that something is indeed first recognized as what it is when it has passed, in memory (ibid., lines 5ff.):

> So ist schnellvergänglich alles Himmlische. Aber umsonst nicht.
> Und des Maases allzeit kundig rührt mit schonender Hand
> Die Wohnungen der Menschen
> Ein Gott an, einen Augenblick nur
> Und sie wissen es nicht, doch lange
> Gedenken sie dess und fragen, wer es gewesen.
> Wenn aber eine Zeit vorbei ist, kennen sie es.

> Thus everything heavenly passes quickly. Yet not in vain.
> And ever knowing the measure, with protective hand, a God
> Touches the dwellings of humans,
> Just for a moment,
> And they know it not, yet long
> They ponder it, and ask who it was.
> But when a time has passed, they know it.

The passing character of that which is eternal is not in vain. Rather, passing by is precisely the kind of presence belonging to the gods: the fleeting character of a scarcely graspable beckoning that, in the flash of its passing over, can indicate all bliss and all terror. The God has his own measures; just for a moment [*Augenblick*] he lingers, scarcely touching the dwellings of humans, and the latter do not properly know what it is—nor indeed can they know it, so long as they cling to the kind of knowing by which they know things and circumstances and themselves all at once. Yet the passing over was after all not nothing, and "long / They ponder it, and ask who it was" (lines 9f.).

Pondering long and retaining in memory are the manner in which the proximity of the gods is, so to speak, unfolded—not, of course, a mere musing that clings to something after the fact, but an actual inquiring after. "But when a time has passed, they know it" (line 11). When inquiringly they have endured the long time in its having-been, then true knowledge comes to them. Then what has been—that which still presences—comes toward them. The mission that is intimated opens up their mandate, and the latter grounds the former anew.

We said earlier (p. 69) that in the words "Not those . . ." at the beginning of the poem there lies a temporal decision. Only now do we correctly understand what is meant: not the mere choice between an old and a new, between what was then and what is today. Rather, what is to be decided is this: whether we decide in favor of the authentic time of poetizing with its having-been, future, and present, or whether we continue to cling to the everyday experience of time that regards everything in a merely 'historiographical-chronological' way. If we regard that which is temporal only in the way in which we habitually take it—namely, by reckoning with it—then we are governed by the *corrupted essence of time*. This corrupted essence of time, precisely those aspects of it with which we are commonly familiar in a more or less knowing way, is not nothing, but is a power in its own right, and one that belongs to the essence of time. The decision is whether we merely remain wedded to the corrupted essence of time, without even recognizing it as such, or whether we experience the essence of time and are willing to place its corrupted essence into confrontation with it. For the essence of time can no more be experienced by itself alone, let alone possessed, than can its corrupted essence ever be denied.

To decide in favor of the authentic time of poetizing means, however, to enter into the fundamental attunement of a holy mourning in readied distress. This cannot be unconditionally brought about in a violent or contrived manner. Thus our task is to bring ourselves before the decision as to whether, in where we are setting out from, we experience from the ground up the fact that, and the way in which, we want to partake in creating the presuppositions for such experience, or whether we work against this, if only through an indifference or being at a loss. An authentic decision for or against our entering into the fundamental attunement of the poetizing presupposes that we are strong enough to experience a need, a need from which distress and readiness first arise. There is indeed already plenty of deprivation, neediness, and lack. And yet, despite all the hardship and adversity in this, it fails to reach into that realm in which an overall threat to our spiritual and historical Dasein makes itself felt. Only in such a dimension can it be decided whether we still want to call—whether this calling is in advance originary in such a way that we then no longer move within personal lived experiences or views or within such individual groups or denominations, but rather are compelled by the historical Dasein of the people, by its innermost and most far-reaching need.

The poet's telling is founding. Our poetizing founds and grounds a locale of Dasein in which we do not yet stand, yet to where the poetic telling seeks to impel us—a locale to which we bring ourselves whenever we respond to and understand in a fitting way this founding, grounding telling, that which is now being said—that is, whenever we want to arrive at the ground that is being laid in this grounding that founds. For manifestly lines 39ff. first bring to language the proper content of the telling.

§ 10. The Locale of Dasein Founded in "Germania" within the Horizon of the Heraclitean Thought

a) The Poetic Telling of the Fundamental Attunement from a Standing within and Sustaining of Essential Conflicts

α) The Nexus of Occurrence of the Images and the Attuning Power of the Fundamental Attunement

It seems that we should now pursue the further occurrences in the poem—the arrival of the eagle and its word to the girl—while merely re-experiencing the fundamental attunement, perhaps only imaginatively, and in this way come to 'understand' the core content of the poem in terms of the fundamental attunement. To our intellectual reckoning, this proves to be the next step. Yet this would once again be an avoidance of the poetizing.

The eagle (its flight and its tidings) and the girl and her silent receiving of the mission—both are images that present imagistically an entire nexus of occurrence. These images demand, in the first place, a proper interpretation. Yet before we can attempt such an interpretation, we must be clear as to why images are used here at all, and why precisely these ones in their intuitable, straightforward, and immediately familiar content. Manifestly, there are no difficulties in answering this second question. For the more familiar and unforced the intuitable character of an image, the more compelling and penetrating its imagistic force. And especially if—as is the case here in the poem "Germania"—what is at stake is the telling of ultimate, fundamental orientations of Dasein and of its relations of being, the fundamental relationship of a people to its gods, then no choice remains but to have recourse to images that are as vivid as possible. For otherwise the poetic discourse would run the risk of forgoing all intuitable content, in the manner of a metaphysical treatise. Poetizing would go astray into an abstract discussion of concepts. And this ought also to have adequately clarified and answered the first question as to why the nexus of occurrence is presented imagistically here at all.

What we just presented is commonplace knowledge to everyone who has even a remote intimation of the essence of poetic telling. The language of poets is always a language of images. And yet, this is not sufficient for understanding Hölderlin's poetizing. Indeed, what was just said, plausible though it may be, is likely to lead our interpretation astray before we have even begun.

It cannot escape notice that we are now attempting to grasp the further content of the poetizing, which first authentically brings what is essential, without relating it to the fundamental attunement—as though the fundamental attunement were to be enunciated and dealt with in a first part of the poetizing (lines 1–38), so as then to make room for another theme that is presented in the image of the eagle and the girl. If, however, the fundamental attunement of the poetizing truly is as we discovered it to be, then it must, after all, attune and determine the telling of the entire poetizing. Indeed, its attuning power must first unfold itself precisely in the ensuing part of the poetizing. It appears that now the man comes into play, who, in holy distress, is supposed to stand firm in the face of the pressure of those who, in their coming, press upon him. Yet there is no mention whatsoever of this "man" in what follows. Furthermore, the transition from line 38 to line 39 remains obscure initially. It is questionable as to whether what is said from line 39 on may be grasped at all as something that the man now sees. For that to be the case there would have to be a colon at the end of line 38, following ". . . from there be moved by many transformations" and indicating that from line 39 on, these transformations, or one of the many transformations, are being presented. One can equally well, or with even greater legitimacy, see here the commencement of something quite different: "Yet from the Aether falls. . . ." For the "yet" [aber] surely brings a contrast and introduces something new. Admittedly, the "yet" in Hölderlin's poetizing is distinctly polysemous, and nonetheless generally essential and difficult in its content.

In the end, we will do more justice to this new beginning (lines 39ff.) and to the "yet" if we understand the whole as meaning that the man, in awaiting, looks and looks. In the meantime, however, something else is happening: that very thing that is told of in the image of the eagle and the girl. This happens, so to speak, behind the man's back, as he is still looking back and persisting within the fundamental attunement, an attunement that, as we know, also reaches forward as readied distress.

Yet then it is entirely incomprehensible as to how the occurrence that is narrated in the said nexus of images is meant to be connected with the fundamental attunement. For the girl in her entire beyng and stance cannot be made into the bearer of the fundamental attunement; nor is the arrival of the eagle at all an arrival of the new gods, to which the fundamental attunement, as an awaiting, remains related. The eagle is, after all, only the messenger of the gods.

It is advisable for us not to diminish this absence of any immediately clear connection between fundamental attunement and the essential imagistic content of the poetizing. On the other hand, we must surely expect that if the fundamental attunement of the poetizing will retain its attuning power anywhere, it will be in the essential part of the poem, thus itself remaining poetically intact and not dissipating. Where do we find a way out here? A way that will let us comprehend this poetizing in the poet's sense?

β) Fundamental Attunement and "Intimacy."
The Preserving Veiling of the Fundamental Attunement
through the Nexus of Images of the Poetizing

We must free ourselves from the commonplace view of what images and the intuitable content of poetizing are supposed to accomplish, even though this view is often entirely correct. According to such a view, these images are meant to clarify as much as possible, to make familiar and bring close to us the true states of affairs that the poet wishes to name poetically and to found. In the poetizing we are considering here, however, and in all poetizing of this kind, making things sensuously intuitable has precisely the opposite task. Because what is at stake here is the poetic founding, not of some arbitrary feeling, but of a fundamental attunement in which the historical Dasein of a people and its decision is meant to find its locale, the fundamental attunement must for this reason be maintained, preserved, and sheltered in its untouchable greatness. The task of the image is not to clarify, but to veil; not to make familiar, but to make unfamiliar; not to bring closer, but to place into a distance—and this all the more, the more originary the fundamental attunement is and the further it extends and compels the destiny of a people and its relationship to the gods together into one. The fundamental attunement is originary above all because it does not extrinsically juxtapose the most extreme contraries—namely, decisive renunciation and unconditional awaiting—but rather lets them spring forth out of a unique and primordial essence of temporality.

The originarily unitary nexus of the farthest-reaching conflicts is what Hölderlin, especially in his later period, names with his own word "intimacy" [*Innigkeit*] (cf. p. 225ff.). We encounter this word repeatedly, in the most varied contexts, and in a number of variations and constructions. It is one of Hölderlin's key words. Its content cannot, of course, be captured in some scholarly definition. We wish only to ward off one misunderstanding at the outset: "Intimacy" does not mean the mere 'interiority' of sensation, in the sense of the closing off within oneself of a 'lived experience.' Nor does it mean an intensified degree of 'warmth of feeling.' Intimacy is also not a word that belongs in the context of the 'beautiful soul' and that way of conceiving the world. For Hölderlin, the word carries nothing of the flavor of some dreamy, inactive sentimentality. Quite to the contrary. It means, first, supreme force of existence [*Dasein*]. Second, this force evinces itself in withstanding the most extreme conflicts of beyng from the ground up. In short, it is an attuned, knowing standing within that sustains the essential conflicts of that which, in being opposed, possesses an original unity—the "harmoniously opposed" with which we are already familiar from the essay on the operations of the poetic spirit (III, 300). In his New Year's letter to his brother, which we have already mentioned several times, Hölderlin says of the Greeks (III, 366):

> that among the ancients, where each belonged with his senses and his soul to the world that surrounded him, there is much greater intimacy to be found in individual characters and relationships than, for example, among us Germans . . .

Openness for beings—letting oneself enter into them and withstanding their divisiveness—does not exclude intimacy, but precisely first grants the authentic possibility for its power, a power that unifies in its very grounds. In his magnificent poetizing of Greek existence [*Dasein*] in the "Archipelago," Hölderlin names the Greeks "the intimate people" [*das innige Volk*] (IV, 91, lines 86ff.):

Denn des Genius Feind, der vielgebietende Perse,
Jahrlang zählt' er sie schon der Waffen Menge, der Knechte,
Spottend des griechischen Lands und seiner wenigen Inseln,
Und sie deuchten dem Herrscher ein Spiel, und noch, wie ein Traum, war
Ihm das innige Volk, vom Göttergeiste gerüstet.

For the foe of genius, the far-governing Persian,
For years now has been counting his multitude of weapons and soldiers,
Mocking the Greek land and its few islands,
And they seemed like a game to the ruler, and even like a dream was
To him the intimate people, armed with the spirit of the gods.

"Intimacy," however, has a decisive significance in Hölderlin's essay entitled "Ground for Empedocles" (III, 316ff.), where Hölderlin deals not only with his own poetry of the same name, but with tragic poetry as such, and that means with tragic beyng. To be considered together with this is the short essay "Becoming in Dissolution" (III, 309ff.). In the "Ground for Empedocles" we read (III, 317):

It is the deepest intimacy that expresses itself in the tragic dramatic poem.

Hölderlin also knows a "modest," a "bold," and an "excessive" intimacy (ibid.). And in this context there belongs a word that concerns us and tells us about the poetic conception of "intimate" sensations—that is, fundamental attunements (III, 319ff.):

for the most intimate sensation is exposed to transitoriness precisely to [the] extent that it does not deny the true, actual, and sensuous relations (and for this reason it is also a law of lyric if whatever is intimate can there be maintained as in itself less dead, thus more readily to deny the physical and intellectual nexus).

Here it is clearly said that the nexus of beings whose being is to be founded in the poetizing—here, the fundamental relationship of a historical people to the gods—the fundamental attunement in the original unity of its conflict, must be denied, precisely so as to preserve the "most intimate sensation," the fundamental attunement, from transitoriness, from being prematurely eroded and flattened. The fundamental attunement is for this reason not something that may be made directly 'popular.' In the nexus of images in the poetizing we are considering, therefore, we are not to be on the lookout for their greatest possible clarifying force. To the contrary: We must attempt to appropriate this nexus of images in its power of veiling.

Here a new perspective opens up into the essence of the truth that is proper to such a poetizing, and accordingly into the essence of the originarily founding, poetic language. If indeed we consider such language in terms of its capacity for expression, then it is here precisely not supposed to express anything, but to leave the unsayable unsaid, and to do so in and through its saying.

If the essence of truth is to be sought in the manifestness of beings, then concealment and veiling prove to be a particular way that is proper to manifestness. The mystery is not a barrier that lies on the other side of truth, but is itself the highest figure of truth; for in order to let the mystery truly be what it is—concealing preservation of authentic beyng—the mystery must be manifest as such. A mystery that is not known in its power of veiling is no mystery. The higher our knowing concerning the veiling and the more genuine the saying of it as such, the more untouched its concealing power remains. Poetic saying of the mystery is *denial*.

b) The Locale of Dasein Founded in "Germania"

α) The "Fatherland" as the Historical Beyng of a People

Our interpretation of the poem is thus faced with altogether unique tasks: on the one hand, the task of grasping in itself, in terms of its own intuitable content, the nexus of occurrence indicated by the images; on the other hand, the task of grasping this whole as denial and displacement of what is authentically to be said. At the same time, there lies herein the question of whether—faced with a poetic saying of this kind—interpretation does not in principle reach a limit here, and what kind of limit this is.

In any case, we stand at an important place in the course of our concern with Hölderlin's poetizing. We stand before the closed door to that of which this poetizing authentically and ultimately tells, that which the poet names the 'most forbidden fruit' that 'each shall taste last': "the fatherland." For the poet, this does not mean some dubious greatness of an even more dubious patriotism full of noise. He means the 'land of the fathers'; he means us, this people of this Earth as a historical people, in its historical being. Such beyng, however, is founded poetically, articulated and placed into knowing in thinking; it is rooted in the actions of those of the Earth who are responsible for the establishing of the state, and in historical space. This historical beyng of the people—the fatherland—is sealed in a mystery, and indeed essentially and forever. Yet for this reason too we shall by ourselves never come before the closed door that leads to it; by ourselves,

we simply run around somewhere and everywhere. Our interpretation of the poem "Germania" thus far was to provide us with the
sign pointing the way to this door. Why we began the lecture course
with precisely this poem may now have become clearer. It should
also have become clear, however, that we must now leave this poem
standing, untouched, as it were, until we gain a richer and more intimate comprehension of the poetic saying of the poet, in which the
poet struggles to attain the locale to which the fundamental attunement of the poem "Germania" tears us, and which its authentic content precisely denies. Only at the end of our endeavors may we venture to accompany the telling of the poetizing of "Germania" that we
have interrogated thus far.

We have indeed on a number of occasions already drawn on 'excerpts' [*Stellen*] from the circle of poetic works in which "Germania"
stands, but only 'excerpts'. From the course that our interpretation of
the poem "Germania" has taken hitherto—a course that for some was
perhaps already too tedious and laborious—we ought to have learned
how inadequate an extrinsic appeal to 'excerpts' remains, especially
when we have not sufficiently comprehended the fundamental orientation of the poetic telling. In view of the fact that we are now drawing the circle of poems to be interpreted more broadly, and seeking to
grasp the poetizing in a more comprehensive way, it is necessary, at
the transition point where we now stand, to undertake a fundamental reflection on Hölderlin's poetizing and on the poet.

What is most concealed with respect to our everyday dealings with
beings, and most forbidden with respect to our ever contingent and
roaming curiosity, is the "fatherland." Certainly, this is not something
remote lying somewhere behind things or hovering above them. *The
"fatherland" is beyng itself,* which from the ground up bears and configures the history of a people as an existing [*daseienden*] people: the his-
toricity of its history. The fatherland is not some abstract, supratemporal idea in itself; rather, the poet sees the fatherland as historical in
an original sense. The proof that this is the case lies in the fact that
the poet's fundamental metaphysical reflection on that being and remaining that the poets found, thus standing firm in the face of dissolution, from the very outset refers to the "fatherland." The "fatherland"
does not, in this context, play the extrinsic role of a case that suggests
itself in order to cast light upon dissolution and becoming in dissolution by way of an example. Rather, the beyng of the fatherland—
that is, of the historical Dasein of a people—is experienced as the authentic and singular beyng from which the fundamental orientation
toward beings as a whole arises and attains its configuration.

β) The Decline of the Fatherland as the Emergence
of a New Unity of Nature and Humans

The fatherland in decline, nature and humans, insofar as they stand in a particular relation of reciprocity, a *particular* world that has become ideal, and constitute the nexus of things, and dissolve themselves to this extent: so that out of them and out of the generations that remain and out of the forces of nature that remain, which are the other real principle, a new world, but also a new and particular relation of reciprocity may form, just as that decline proceeded from a pure yet particular world.

(Becoming in Dissolution, III, 309)

What is decisive in reflecting upon the decline is not the process of decline, but the emergence of a new unity, starting from which what existed hitherto is comprehended as dissolving itself. The decline is therefore a historically distinctive moment, one that can extend over a century, because here the unexhausted—the inexhaustible that belongs to the new commencement, the *possible*—can bring itself to power, granted that those human beings are there who are capable of experiencing in advance this inexhaustibility of the possible as such: of founding it, of knowing it, and of bringing it about.

> *This decline or transition of the fatherland* (in this sense) feels itself within the parts of the existing world in such a way that in precisely [that] moment and to that degree in which what exists dissolves itself, the newly entering, the youthful, the possible feels itself also. For how could dissolution be felt without unification, so that if what exists is meant to be felt and is felt in its dissolution, then *in this process* the *unexhausted* and *inexhaustible* character of the *relations* and *forces,* as well as that dissolution, must be felt more through this unification than vice versa; for from nothing comes nothing, and if we take this in terms of degree, it would mean as much as that that which proceeds toward negation, and insofar as it disappears from actuality and is not yet something possible, could not act. But the *possible,* which enters into *actuality,* as *actuality dissolves itself*—this acts, and it brings about both the feeling of dissolution and the recollection of what has been dissolved.

(ibid., 310)

We take from these passages the essence of that originary beyng in which the poet comprehends the flight of the gods of old and the emergence of the new gods. These passages attest to how passionately the poet is concerned to think together the passing away as arising, going as a coming, to thoughtfully become master of this conflict—that is, to endure it and think it through.

c) On Hölderlin's Understanding of Being.
The Power of the Heraclitean Thought

α) Hölderlin and Heraclitus

In all of this, that understanding of beyng that gained power at the commencement of Western philosophy—and in the meantime has, in genuine and non-genuine variations, dominated German thought and knowing, particularly since Meister Eckhart—lies near and is once again powerful. It is the conception of being that we find in a thinker with whom Hölderlin knew himself to have an affinity: Heraclitus. We possess only fragments of his philosophy. With reference to what has been said thus far, yet also with a view to what is to follow, we shall cite several sayings of Heraclitus. We must here forgo any interpretation. See Fragment 51:

οὐ ξυνιᾶσιν ὅκως διαφερόμενον ἑωυτῶι ὁμολογέει. παλίντροπος ἁρμονίη ὅκωσπερ τόξου καὶ λύρης.

"They fail to understand [namely, those who simply proceed with their existence (*Dasein*) in an everyday manner] that, and in what way, whatever is by itself at variance is nevertheless in agreement with itself; counter-striving harmony it is, as with the bow and the lyre" [where the ends that stretch apart are tensed together, a tension which, however, first makes possible precisely the release of the arrow and the resonance of the strings, that is: beyng]. And then an example, in Fragment 48:

τῶι οὖν τόξωι ὄνομα βίος, ἔργον δὲ θάνατος.

"The name of the bow is life [βίος], its work, however, death" [the most extreme opposites of beyng together in one].

Yet—as is already clear from the first fragment cited—this comprehension of beyng is closed to everyday understanding: namely, the insight that whatever is most intensely counter-striving is fundamentally the harmony of whatever belongs together. When everyday understanding sees harmony, it is merely superficial agreement that exists temporarily and remains without force. Whence Fragment 54:

ἁρμονίη ἀφανὴς φανερῆς κρείττων.

The harmony that does not show itself to the habitual way of seeing—that is, which remains merely a divergence of opposites for such seeing—this concealed harmony is more powerful than that which is visibly manifest, more powerful because it is the power proper to beyng as such. The poet thinks and poetizes in the direction of this ἁρμονίη ἀφανής when he says the words *Innigkeit* and *innig—das innige Volk*.[1] Yet it must be noted: This ἁρμονία—harmony—is not some indifferent accord, that is, one without tension; it is not at all an agreement that comes about by leveling out and setting aside oppositions, but the converse: Opening up the conflicting parties proper opens up the harmony. It places the conflicting powers into their limits in each case. This placing of limits is not a restrictive limitation, but rather a de-limiting, the emergent setting out and fulfillment of the essence. If all beings thus stand in harmony, then precisely strife and battle must determine everything fundamentally. From this, we can first comprehend Heraclitus through one of his two sayings with which people are generally familiar, but in a corrupt and distorted form: "Battle is the father of all things." The saying, however, properly and in its entirety reads thus (Fragment 53):

Πόλεμος πάντων μὲν πατήρ ἐστι, πάντων δὲ βασιλεύς, καὶ τοὺς μὲν θεοὺς ἔδειξε τοὺς δὲ ἀνθρώπους, τοὺς μὲν δούλους ἐποίησε τοὺς δὲ ἐλευθέρους.

"Battle is for all beings indeed the creator, yet for all beings also the ruler, and it indeed makes some manifest as gods, others as humans, bringing some to light as slaves, yet others as masters." The saying is so profound in content that we cannot even remotely analyze it here. Just two things may be pointed out. Battle is the power that creates beings, yet not in such a way that, once things have come to be by way of it, battle then withdraws from them. Rather, battle also and precisely preserves and governs beings in their essential subsistence. Battle is indeed creator, yet also ruler. Wherever battle ceases as a power of preservation, standstill begins: a leveling out, mediocrity, harmlessness, atrophy, and decline. Such battle, however—and this is the other thing that must briefly be pointed out—is here not arbitrary discord or dissension or mere unrest, but the strife of profound conflict between the essential powers of being, such that in the battle the gods first come to appear as gods, humans as humans, over against one another and thereby in their intimate harmony. There are no gods and humans in themselves, or masters and slaves in themselves who then, because they are such, enter into strife or harmony. Rather, the converse is the case: It is battle that first creates the possibility of decision with regard to life and death. By proving themselves in one way or another, beings in each case first become what and how they

---

1. "The Archipelago," IV, 91, line 90.

are, and this 'are'—being—prevails in its essence only as such proving. Another saying, Fragment 80, belongs together with the one just cited:

εἰδέναι δὲ χρὴ τὸν πόλεμον ἐόντα ξυνόν, καὶ δίκην ἔριν, καὶ γινόμενα πάντα κατ᾽ ἔριν καὶ χρεών.

"Yet there is need to know: battle is constantly there participating [in all beings], and therefore 'right' is nothing other than strife, and all beings that come into being are by way of strife and necessity." δίκη ἔρις—right *is* strife. According to common understanding, right is something inscribed independently somewhere, and with its aid and through its application strife is precisely decided and eliminated. No! Originarily and in keeping with its essence, right first emerges as such in strife; in strife it forms itself, proves itself, and becomes true. It is strife that establishes the sides, and one side is what it is only through the other, in reciprocal self-recognition. For this reason we never grasp a being if we consider only one side, yet neither do we grasp it if we merely add on the other side as well: Rather, we grasp it when we comprehend both sides in their belonging together and know the grounds for such comprehension. Heraclitus expresses this in another saying, Fragment 67:

ὁ θεὸς ἡμέρη εὐφρόνη, χειμὼν θέρος, πόλεμος εἰρήνη, κόρος λιμός, ἀλλοιοῦται δὲ ὅκωσπερ πῦρ, ὁπόταν συμμιγῇ θυώμασιν, ὀνομάζεται καθ᾽ ἡδονὴν ἑκάστου.

"The God is day and night, winter and summer, war and peace, satiety and hunger; he changes however like fire; every time the latter is mixed with incense it is named [which means: it is] according to the scent [of the incense] at that time."

Only on the basis of what has been said does that word of Heraclitus —which, like the saying concerning battle as father of all things, is mostly repeated thoughtlessly—gain its proper content: πάντα ῥεῖ: "everything flows." This does not mean that everything is continually in a process of change and without subsistence, but rather that you cannot take up position on any one side alone, but will be carried, through strife as conflict, to the opposite side. And only in the back and forth of the movement that is battle do beings have their being. Flowing does not here mean simply the stubborn, constant dissolution and annihilation of things, but the converse: The flowing pertaining to conflict, i.e., conflictual harmony, creates precisely subsistence and steadfastness, beyng. (The opposition between Heraclitus and Parmenides does not lie where it is commonly sought.)

If, however, beings can thus never be grasped one-sidedly, then the naming of beings and the saying of beyng finds itself in a peculiar difficulty, above all wherever being as a whole and in its essence is to be said and made manifest. For a word indeed names a being in such or such a way, for example, in Fragment 67: God—war. The word makes the being manifest. Yet at the same time it also conceals, if we stick to this naming taken on its own. For the God is equally 'peace.' For this reason, the authentic, essential saying of beings is of a properly primordial kind: It is originarily that kind of saying that is proper to the gods. See Fragment 93:

ὁ ἄναξ, οὗ τὸ μαντεῖόν ἐστι τὸ ἐν Δελφοῖς, οὔτε λέγει οὔτε κρύπτει ἀλλὰ σημαίνει.

"The lord, whose oracle is at Delphi [the God Apollo], neither says, nor does he conceal, but rather *beckons*." Originary saying neither merely makes beings directly manifest, nor does it simply conceal them altogether. Rather, this saying is both together in one, and as this one is a beckoning—in which what is said points to the unsaid, and what is unsaid to what is said and to be said—the elements that stand in conflict to the harmony that they are, the harmony to the conflict within which alone harmony oscillates.

'Beckonings are the language of the gods,'[2] we heard earlier from Hölderlin (p 31). This echo of Heraclitus is not accidental. In his poetizing that founds being, Hölderlin's entire thinking and understanding of beyng was subject to the power of Heraclitus, and remained so from his student years in Tübingen to the years of his greatest creativity and well beyond. The wisdom of Heraclitus was condensed in an almost formulaic manner into the words of Fragment 50: ἓν πάντα εἶναι—One is all. But "One" does not mean uniformity, empty sameness, and "all" does not mean the countless multitude of arbitrary things: rather, ἕν, "One" = harmony, is all—that which arises in each case essentially constitutes beings as a whole as diverse and in conflict with one another.

The power of Heraclitean thought over the poet's existence [*Dasein*] is attested to by the fact that well into the period in which the gods with their lightning flashes had spared him already and placed him under the protection of what we, with our fragile and short-sighted standards, call 'mental illness,' the poet still had to struggle with that saying, ἓν πάντα.

From the summer of 1807 until his death in the summer of 1843 Hölderlin lived in Tübingen with the carpenter Zimmer. In the 1820s

---

2. "Rousseau," IV, 135, lines 39f.

he became friends with the young student Wilhelm Waiblinger, who already visited him in his final year as a high school student, and saw all the manuscripts and drafts of the poet. (Cf. the diary entry of July 3, 1822, VI, 403f.) In 1830 in Rome, Waiblinger wrote an essay entitled "Friedrich Hölderlin's Life, Poetry, and Madness" (VI, 409–442). It indeed contains quite a bit of false information concerning superficial details of the poet's life prior to his illness, details that could not have been known without the study of sources. What is valuable, however, is the depiction of what he himself experienced in his familiarity with the poet over the course of several years. We cite one passage that shows how Heraclitus was still somehow present for the poet (VI, 427):

> What he is able to occupy himself with for days at a time is his *Hyperion*. When I visited him, I heard him a hundred times outside issuing declamations in a loud voice. His pathos is great, and *Hyperion* almost always lies there open; he often read to me from it. (Cf. II, 188f.)

β) Hölderlin and Hegel

It is no accident that Hegel who, in the sole philosophical system to be found in Western philosophy, thought the thoughts of Heraclitus in terms of their ground and to their end, was a contemporary and student companion of Hölderlin. Hölderlin and Hegel grew up in a common spiritual world and together struggled to shape it anew. One of them went the path of the poet, the other, that of the thinker. Instead of explaining Hölderlin on the basis of Hegel's system, as is customary, and of also recording influences of the poet on the thinker, we must learn to experience the great conflict between the two precisely in their most lofty heights and their solitary peaks in each case, in order thus to first comprehend something of their true harmony. We cannot and shall not speak of Hegel within the context and charge of this lecture course, however. Nevertheless, some hints are necessary in order to clarify Hölderlin's own relationship to Heraclitus proceeding from Hegel, and above all to bring more sharply into relief the sense of Hölderlin's foundational word, "intimacy."

The two Swabians Hölderlin and Hegel had been close friends especially since 1790, which marked the beginning of their study of theology together. The third Swabian in the group was Schelling, who was some five years younger than the other two. From the autumn of 1790, the three seminarians even lived together in the same dormitory in Tübingen, the *Augustinerstube*. In that era, and even in the last century too, it was the custom to record companionship of the heart by entries in a friendship book addressed to one another. We still possess such a friendship book entry of Hölderlin's for Hegel (VI, 232):

Goethe
Desire and Love are
the pinions of great deeds.
Tüb.
v. 12 Febr.   Written for remembrance
1791   your friend
S(ymbolum). Εν και παν   M. Hölderlin.

Hölderlin and Hegel passed their theological exam in the same year, 1793. In the autumn of that same year Hölderlin went to Waltershausen as a house tutor in the residence of Charlotte von Kalb. Hegel went as a house tutor to Bern in Switzerland. Yet they were to spend decisive years in immediate proximity to one another once more, years that were indeed the most decisive for each. From the end of the year 1795, Hölderlin had been a house tutor in Frankfurt am Main. At the beginning of 1797 Hegel too took up a house tutor position in Frankfurt that was arranged for him by Hölderlin. During this Frankfurt period, Hölderlin found the path to his great poetizing, while Hegel found his proper way into philosophy. For both, confrontation with the Greek world stood at the center of their poetizing and thinking during this period. When Hegel in 1801 began to give his lectures in Jena as a *Privatdozent* in philosophy, he had become someone other than he was before his Frankfurt period, and had become so by virtue of a creative confrontation with Greek philosophy in the proximity of the poet. In the year 1801, Hegel began his proper path of a difficult and great labor of thought. For Hölderlin, the same year is already the year of his greatest creative work. Hegel's path, after a few detours, led to a prominent career and public acclaim. In 1801, Hölderlin wrote a word in which he knowingly saw himself to be in an altogether opposite predicament (cf. p. 120f.).

Hegel comprehends philosophy as infinite thinking. Finite thinking only ever thinks one side, thinks one-sidedly, finitely. That thinking that thinks one side and the opposing side reciprocally—that is, that thinks their conflict in its unity—is infinite. What is one-sided, finite, is dead. But this one-sided aspect is not to be rejected as a negative nothing, nor blindly passed over; rather, the one side is, as this one, to be held over against the other and to be endured in its opposition. This is why Hegel, on page 26 of the Preface to the *Phenomenology of Spirit*, his first major work, and at the same time his greatest work, which appeared in 1807, writes the following:[3]

---

3. Fourth edition, 34. Hegel, *Werke*, Jubiläumsausgabe. Edited by H. Glockner. Volume 2. Stuttgart, 1964.

Death, if that is what we wish to call that non-actuality, is what is most terrifying, and to hold fast to what is dead requires the greatest strength. Beauty, lacking strength, hates the understanding for asking of her something she is unable to do. But the life of Spirit is not the life that shrinks from death and preserves itself untouched by devastation, but rather the life that endures death and maintains itself within it. Spirit wins its truth only when, within absolute dismemberment, it finds itself. It is this power, not as something positive that closes its eyes to the negative, as when we say of something that it is nothing or is false, and then, having done with it, turn away and move on to something else; on the contrary, Spirit is this power only by looking the negative in the face and tarrying with it. This tarrying is the magical force that converts the negative into beyng.[6]

This Preface has appeared as a separate publication in the well-known Insel series.[4] The Preface was completed the evening before the battle in Jena and Auerstedt. That same day, Hegel saw Napoleon ride through the city.

Hegel here provides a magnificently structured view of the fundamental orientations assumed by the spiritual powers of his era (around 1806), not as an observer, but as one who is conscious of himself being on the verge of launching a major strike. This Preface concludes a work that is governed by the clear knowledge that philosophy is labor. See pages 53f.:[5]

In the case of all other sciences, arts, skills, and crafts, everyone is convinced that a complex and laborious process of learning and practice is necessary for competence. Yet when it comes to philosophy, there seems to be a currently prevailing prejudice to the effect that, although not everyone who has eyes and fingers, and is given leather and tools, is at once in a position to make shoes, everyone nevertheless immediately understands how to philosophize, and how to pass judgment on philosophy, since he possesses the criterion for doing so in his natural reason—as if he did not likewise possess the measure for a shoe in his own foot. It seems that philosophical competence consists precisely in a lack of knowledge and study, as though philosophy left off where they began. Philosophy is frequently taken to be a formal kind of knowledge, devoid of content, and the insight is sadly lacking that, whatever truth there may be in the content of any discipline or science, it can only deserve the name if such truth has been engendered by philosophy. Let the other sciences try to argue as

4. Leipzig, 1920. Frankfurt, 1964.
5. Fourth edition, 61f.

much as they like without philosophy—without it they can have in them neither life, Spirit, nor truth.[7]

As absolute thinking, Hegel's thought seeks to bring opposites into a universal fluidity and thus to resolution. Hegel's infinite thinking, however, is not some thought-up formula, but has arisen from, and is sustained by, a fundamental experience of Western existence [*Dasein*] and of the essence of its Spirit. To this essence belongs the pain of being torn into extreme oppositions. The knowledge of existence being dismembered in this way is what Hegel calls the "unhappy consciousness."[6] It is the proper spur of Spirit, which drives its happening in the most diverse configurations and stages of world history, and thus drives Spirit to itself, to its essence. Spirit knows itself in philosophy as absolute knowing itself. And in this knowing, it is at the same time truly actualized.

For Hegel, however, the actuality of Spirit in history is the state, and the state can only be what it has to be if it is permeated and sustained by the infinite force of infinite Spirit—that is, if it actualizes universally in a living unity the most extreme opposition between the free independence of the individual and the free power of the community. In his *Philosophy of Right,* §185,[7] Hegel says that former states were not yet able to be founded upon the developed principle of Spirit. The grounds for their decline lie in the fact that the truly infinite force was lacking: the force that is to be found only in that unity that lets the opposition within reason unfold into its entire strength, and that has conquered it, thus fulfilling itself within it and holding the opposition together within itself.

Hegelian thinking is inspired by a new, creative retrieval and enactment of the original thought of Heraclitus. In this retrieval, the entire history of World Spirit that has, in the meantime, run its course is conceptually integrated into the 'flux' of this thinking and differentiated in terms of its essential stages.

Hölderlin too, however, was subject to the power of the Heraclitean thought. A later thinker, Nietzsche, would also come under its power. Indirectly, the commencement of German philosophy with Meister Eckhart fundamentally stood under this power. The name Heraclitus is not the title for a philosophy of the Greeks that has long since run its course. Just as little is it the formula for the thinking of some universal world humanity in itself. Presumably, it is the name of a primordial power of Western-Germanic, historical Dasein, and indeed in its first confrontation with the Asiatic.

6. Hegel, *Werke.* Volume 2, 166ff. (II, 158ff.). Stuttgart 1964, 4th edition.
7. Hegel, *Werke.* Volume 7, 265f. (VIII, 249f.). Stuttgart 1964, 4th edition.

d) Founding of the Need Pertaining to a New Commencement
of Our Historical Dasein within the Metaphysical Need
of the Western World

We are not to think that we could escape from this power, that we could be released from a new confrontation with this primordial power, a confrontation that could perhaps exceed all confrontation hitherto. Certainly, this confrontation is not some leisurely game of scholarly comparison of current views with earlier views, but rather a questioning that is truly necessitated, one that has the task of once again first bringing about a historically spiritual space. This can occur only if such questioning is necessitated from out of the ownmost need of our historical Dasein. How many experience the need and have the courage to know of it is a matter of indifference. The need *is* in any case. It is the need of needlessness, the need of the complete inability to experience the innermost question-worthiness of Dasein.

Anxiety in the face of questioning lies over the Western world. It binds peoples to worn-out and dilapidated paths and drives them back in flight into their decrepit shells. Where a rupture does occur, they do not want to see that something other than a mere variation on internal political affairs is happening there.

Yet the first thing is that we ourselves comprehend this, and do not forget the need of a century overnight, but learn to know that Hölderlin has in advance founded the need pertaining to a new commencement, so that it awaits us. His saying has coined in advance this need in ever-new forms, and only the poetic word itself, not some extensive and yet lame paraphrase, is capable of maintaining its power to awaken. We said earlier (p. 44ff.) that the inner movement of the poetic saying in the poem "Germania" is a turbulence that tears us away to a determinate location. The poet establishes this locale in a sound and robust word in the first three lines of the poem "Mnemosyne" that we have already mentioned several times (IV, 225):

Ein Zeichen sind wir, deutungslos
Schmerzlos sind wir und haben fast
Die Sprache in der Fremde verloren.

We are a sign that is not read
Without pain we are and have almost
Lost our tongue in foreign parts.

Dasein has become foreign to its historical essence, its mission and mandate. Alienated from itself, it remains without vocation, indeterminable and hence "unread." Its vocation remains absent because the fundamental attunement of standing within the essential conflicts is without attuning force, without pain—that is, without the fundamental form of knowing that belongs to spirit, whence "Without pain we are." Where there is no attuning opening up the clefts of beyng, there too there is no need of having to name and say, hence: 'we have almost lost our tongue in foreign parts.' We are "a sign," a beckoning that has ossified, that has been forgotten, as it were, by the gods, "a sign" for which interpreters must first be nurtured again.

> Ein Zeichen sind wir, deutungslos
> Schmerzlos sind wir und haben fast
> Die Sprache in der Fremde verloren.

> We are a sign that is not read
> Without pain we are and have almost
> Lost our tongue in foreign parts.

The poet stands at such a site of metaphysical need. Yet whoever's poetizing, thinking, and saying must hold out at such a locale comprehends solitude as a metaphysical necessity. That is, he must know that in this solitude there prevails precisely the supreme intimacy of a belonging to the beyng of his own people, even though appearances may indicate merely one who stands removed and remains unheard. Because the poet has to bear all of this as a human being, we may not be surprised to hear a frightful word from around the end of his year of great creativity, 1801. It is found in that letter to his friend Böhlendorff from December 4, written shortly before his departure for Bordeaux, from where the poet returned half a year later, destroyed and defeated. I shall deliberately include the part that was cited earlier (p. 30), so as to maintain the overall attunement of the letter (V, 321f.):

> O friend! The world lies brighter there before me than hitherto, and more grave! it pleases me how things are going, it pleases me, just as in summer when "the ancient, holy father by his gentle hand blesses us with the lightning he shakes down from crimson clouds." For of all the things I can behold of God, this sign has become for me the chosen one. Before I could rejoice over a new truth, a better view of that which lies over and around us, now I fear that things may go for me in the end as they did for the ancient Tantalus, who bit off more of the gods than he could chew. But I do what I can, and think, when I see, if I too must take my path the same way as the others, that it is godless and crazy to seek a path that would be safe from *all* danger of attack, and that for death, nature offers no remedy.

And now, farewell, my dear friend, until you hear more from me. I am now full of parting. I have not wept for so long. Yet it has cost me bitter tears, resolving now to leave my fatherland, perhaps forever. For what do I have more precious in the world? But they have no use for me. I wish to, and indeed must, remain German, even if the need of the heart and the need of nourishment should drive me to Tahiti.

"But they have no use for me." How much longer will the Germans fail to hear this frightful word? Unless a great turning in their Dasein makes them lucid, what then can possibly give them ears to hear? It would, however, run counter to the will of the poet if we were to drag this word from this necessarily discrete letter to his friend out into the public eye. The poet has preserved the same word poetically for us.

> . . . Viele sind gestorben
> Feldherrn in alter Zeit
> Und schöne Frauen und Dichter
> Und in neuer
> Der Männer viel
> Ich aber bin allein.

> . . . Many have died
> Generals in ancient times
> And beautiful women and poets
> And in recent times
> Many men
> But I am alone.

("The Titans," IV, 208, lines 7ff.)

The fundamental attunement of Hölderlin's poetizing is a holy mourning, yet in readied distress. In attuning, it must determine for us the locale from which beings as a whole can be experienced anew, can come to power in a structured way, and be conserved in a genuine knowing. The fundamental attunement cannot remain some floating intimation for us. We have already given thought to our own attuned determinacy and to the individuation of attunement. This mourning and this plaint is a mourning and having plaint together with the "waters of the homeland" ("Germania," line 4). The distress is that of the Earth as homeland. For this reason, we must seek out the rivers and the Earth as homeland, and apprehend correctly the poet's telling of them. We shall venture into the sphere of the river poems and select as our first poem the one entitled "The Rhine."

§11. Transitional Overview and Summary: Revisiting the Domains Opened Up Thus Far as a Way of Determining More Precisely the Intent of the Lecture Course

In our previous meeting we accomplished the transition from the poem "Germania" to the poem "The Rhine." What was said in our previous meeting by way of concluding our preliminary interpretation of the poem "Germania" shall not be repeated again here. We shall attempt to undertake the transition through renewed reflection on our overall intent. Such reflection is now necessary in order that we learn to comprehend the properly philosophical sense of our endeavors. And such reflection is also now possible, given that in our interpretation we have covered a certain stretch of our path, such that deliberations on fundamental matters of principle will no longer remain vacuous.

Superficially considered, the titles of the two poems already point to a certain connection: "Germania" as the general and "The Rhine" as a particular in relation to this general. Even if this way of conceiving matters presents the connection in a highly indeterminate and even inappropriate manner, we can nevertheless see in this an indication that we are keeping within the same sphere of poetizing. Admittedly, what we have presented thus far, if it has clarified anything at all, must have made clear to us that the extrinsic form of the poems and the poetizing that belongs to them are altogether divergent, their unity notwithstanding. In terms of the actual poetizing in the two poems, the statement that "The Rhine" represents the particular in relation to "Germania" tells us nothing, and is indeed meaningless, even though it remains correct that the Rhine river constitutes one particular detail of the German land. By this route we shall never become aware of the connection between the poems and the unity of their poetizing.

In order to bring about the correct transition from "Germania" to "The Rhine," we must revisit those domains opened up by our interpretation thus far. Over and beyond a summary that recaps what has been said thus far, we wish thereby to determine more precisely the intent of the lecture course.

It may have been noticeable that we avoided giving an explanation, let alone any justification, of our own manner of proceeding in the interpretation. We did mention right at the outset that our 'procedure in general' was to thoughtfully grasp the poetic, without thereby installing a philosophical system as the standard or even trying to glean such a system from the poetizing. Furthermore, we emphasized that our 'procedure in particular' should avoid a mere process of the ongoing narration of the poet's life and works, but should rather take as its initial point of engagement what in truth should be named last of all: the "fatherland"—that is, the innermost and most far-reaching historical vocation of the people. The goal is thereby set as the highest of all. What we seek to elaborate directly is precisely related to this, yet is by far more provisional.

We first wish to find a point of entry into the domain in which this poetizing unfolds its power, and not, therefore, to become acquainted with many of the different poems so as to construct a world picture from there. Within the domain and power of the poetizing, we must first of all determine the locale from which and toward which the power of the poetizing opens up and maintains its sway. This metaphysical locale of the poetizing is circumscribed by what we set into relief as the fundamental attunement: a holy mourning, yet in readied distress.

a) The Four Essential Components of the Fundamental Attunement

To the extent that we have been able to say something thus far about the general essence of what we are calling 'fundamental attunement,' this has occurred as a negative gesture: (1) Attunement, and especially fundamental attunement, is no mere feeling, not some epiphenomenon of psychic lived experience. (2) Attunement cannot be comprehended at all coming from the perspective of the doctrine of soul and spirit that has been passed down; rather, it is precisely a look into the essence of fundamental attunement that compels us to relinquish the commonplace representation of the kind of being pertaining to the human being, and to ground it more primordially. Why this is so, and how the concept of human existence [*Dasein*] transforms itself starting from here, cannot be indicated here. Presumably, however, with regard to the said fundamental attunement of the poetizing of "Germania," we may provide some pointers for our thinking that can help us to enter the proximity of the concept of a fundamental attunement.

The fundamental attunement of a holy mourning, yet in readied distress, alone places us at once before the fleeing, the remaining absent, and the arriving of the gods—yet not as though the said being of the gods were set before us or represented in the attunement. Attunement does not represent something or set it before us: Rather, it transports our Dasein out into an attuned relation to the gods in their being thus and thus. Insofar as the gods thoroughly govern historical Dasein and beings as a whole, however, the attunement at the same time, from out of this transport, transports us specifically into those relations that have evolved toward the Earth, the countryside, and the homeland. The fundamental attunement is accordingly a transporting *out* toward the gods and a transporting *into* the Earth at the same time. In attuning in this manner, it opens up beings as such in general, and this opening up of the manifestness of beings is indeed so originary that, by virtue of the attunement, we remain inserted into and bound into beings as opened up. This means that we do not first have representations of the gods from somewhere—representations and a representing that we then furnish with affects and feelings. Rather, attunement, as transporting out and transporting into, first *opens up* that realm within which something can first be specifically set before us or represented.

Only on the basis of a certain suppression and blocking of attunement—on the basis of an attempted, apparent forgetting thereof—do we arrive at what we call the mere representing of things and objects. Yet such representation is not what comes first, as though something like a world were built up layer by layer, as it were, by a heaping up and accumulation of represented things. A world can essentially never be opened up or glued together as the subsequent combining of a manifold of perceived things, but is that which is originarily and primordially manifest in advance, within which this or that can first come toward us. The opening up of world occurs in fundamental attunement. The power of a fundamental attunement that transports us out, transports us into, and thereby opens up is thus at the same time *grounding*. That is, it places Dasein into its grounds and before its abysses. The fundamental attunement determines for our Dasein the locale and time of its being, a locale and time that are manifest to Dasein itself. (Locale is not to be taken spatially, nor time temporally, in the usual sense.)

b) Fundamental Attunement as Exposure in the Midst of Beings That Are Manifest as a Whole

By virtue of the power of fundamental attunement, the Dasein of the human being is, in accordance with its essence, *exposure* in the midst of beings that are manifest as a whole, an exposure that Dasein must take on, so as at the same time to take on the preserving of those beings that are manifest as a whole within such exposure. In so doing, Dasein in one way or another conserves within it the possibility of a history—that is, fulfills or squanders this possibility. Dasein is delivered over to beings as such: both to that being that it itself is, and to those beings that it itself is not. Therein lies the distinction of human Dasein: that it not only 'is,' but that all being must be taken up by it in one way or another, sustained and guided by it. Even indifference and forgottenness are merely ways in which Dasein delivers itself over to being as such. This fundamental trait of human Dasein—that it must, insofar as it is, be concerned in one way or another with being—we call *care*. In giving it this name, we are not raising to the level of a metaphysical concept or making into a worldview one of those feelings familiar in the everyday realm—fear, anxiety, care, and the like. Rather, it is the fundamental experience of the essence of the historical Dasein of the human being that in the first instance demands to be named and that, whenever it is accomplished, can be conceived only from out of this origin.

If we ponder the essence of fundamental attunement and its power to transport us out and transport us into, to open up, and to ground, then it immediately becomes clear that attunement is what is least of all subjective or a so-called interior of the human being; for fundamental attunement is, by contrast, the way in which we are originarily transposed into the expanse of beings and the depths of beyng. The human being's going into him- or herself does not here mean staring at or monitoring one's private lived experiences; rather, it means going out into one's exposure to beings as manifest. Only because fundamental attunement originarily transports and transposes us can it also limit Dasein, restricting it to the sphere of those everyday beings that are closest to us, letting Dasein drift along on the surface of beyng. For fundamental attunement is in each case this or that attunement: not some fixed attribute, but a happening. Human Dasein is indeed always attuned, if only in the manner of a bad or disgruntled mood, or in the peculiar manner of that mood that is familiar to us as the dull, vacuous, and dreary lack of attunement, familiar to us in the everyday realm as that which we express in the statement "I'm not up for anything"—the primordial form of boredom, which for its part can unfold into a fundamental attunement. Because Dasein—insofar as it is—is attuned, for this reason an attunement can in each case be changed into a different one only by way of a counter-attunement. And only a fundamental attunement is capable of bringing about a change of attunement from the ground up—that is, a transformation of Dasein that amounts to a complete recreating of its exposure to beings, and thereby to a recoining of beyng.

The fact that, within modern thinking, and already prior to it, attunements are counted as something 'subjective'—as merely accompanying us in each case and as what are least graspable—is no accident, nor a mere inattentiveness or even incapacity on the part of psychological inspection. This is the case if only because experiencing the essence of attunement remains impossible so long as one views the issue psychologically and portrays the human being as a subject that is, in addition, surrounded by so-called objects—though why, one really does not know. As though subject and object were fixed blocks lying present at hand, between which, subsequently and in addition, various threads were stretched, including those of attunements. The opposite is true. It is the originary character and power at any given time of a dominant and prevailing fundamental attunement that first opens up that realm within which the human being can differentiate himself from nonhuman beings, that realm within which the borders can first be drawn between what is to be called subjective and objective—granted that one may still attribute a justified legitimacy to this distinction at all, once the essence of fundamental attunement has been comprehended.

In attunement there occurs the inaugural exposure to beings. This entails at the same time that the Dasein of the human being is in itself already transposed into the Dasein of others: that it *is*, as it is, only in being with others. Dasein is essentially being with one another, being for and against one another. In accordance with the world that is opened up at any given time in a dominant fundamental attunement, and in keeping with the manifestness of that wherein Dasein is grounded, it finds its basis and the realms of its decisions and of the modes of its comportment. This being with one another of Dasein is, in keeping with the fundamental character of Dasein, in itself *historical*, and thereby bound to the powers of history and configured by them.

c) Fundamental Attunement as Truth of a People.
The Three Creative Forces of Historical Dasein

The fundamental attunement dominant at any given time, and the opening up of beings as a whole occurring in it, is the origin that attunes and determines what we are calling the truth of a people. The truth of the people is the manifestness of being as a whole that prevails at a given time, in accordance with which the sustaining, configuring, and guiding powers receive their respective rank and bring about their attuned accord. The truth of a people is that manifestness of being out of which the people knows what it wills historically in willing *itself*, in willing to be itself.

The fundamental attunement—which is to say, the truth of the Dasein of a people—is originarily founded by the poet. The beyng of beings thus unveiled, however, is comprehended and configured and thereby first opened up as beyng by the thinker, and the beyng that has been comprehended in this way is set into the ultimate and preeminent gravity of beings—that is, into a *determinate, attuned* historical truth—by the people being brought to itself as a people. This occurs through the creating of the state accorded the people in its essence— a creating accomplished by the creator of the state. This entire occurrence, however, has its own times, and thereby its own temporal unfolding. The powers of poetizing, of thinking, of the creation of the state—especially in eras of developed history—act in both forward and backward directions, and are not at all calculable. They can act in unrecognized ways over a long period of time, alongside one another without bridges and yet to the benefit of one another, in each case in accordance with the different unfolding of power belonging to poetizing, thinking, and the action of statesmanship, and in different degrees of publicness in each case. These three creative forces of historical Dasein act to bring about that to which we can alone attribute greatness.

d) Historical and Historiographical Truth

Everything great is unique, yet this uniqueness has its own manner of steadfastness—that is, of historically transformed and altered return. 'Unique' here means: precisely not present at hand on one occasion and then past, but rather, having been and thereby prevailing within the constant possibility of a transformed unfolding of its essence, and accordingly within the propensity to be discovered and to become powerful ever anew and in an inexhaustible manner.

What is small has its steadfastness too: It is the blunt obstinacy of the everyday, of the ever-the-same, which is steadfast only because it closes itself off and must close itself off against all transformation. The uniformity of the everyday is as necessary as the uniqueness of essential saying, thinking, and acting. If, however, we take the measures for historical beyng and knowing from the everyday alone, then we must constantly reside in a realm that is completely out of joint. In that case, we never comprehend that Sophocles, for example, can, and indeed must, one day also be interpreted otherwise; that Kant can, and indeed must, be comprehended otherwise; that Frederick the Great can and must one day be portrayed otherwise. Everyday opinion thinks that there must be a Sophocles in himself, a Kant in himself, a Frederick the Great in himself, in the same way as the desk here is a desk and the chalk, chalk. Supposing that there were, for example, an interpretation and depiction of Sophocles' poetizing in itself, and suppose this interpretation could be seen by Sophocles: Then he would have to and indeed would find this interpretation boring in the highest degree. For he did not poetize so that some inconsequential, world-poor imitation could be erected somewhere.

Is there, then, no historiographical truth? This conclusion is premature. There is historiographical truth. Yet in order to comprehend it as such, those who seek to do so must themselves first stand within the power of history. Then they know that a historiographical truth 'in itself'—in the superficial, everyday sense of the correctness of statements—is nonsensical, more nonsensical than a square circle. At most, there could be an objective truth about history in itself for an Absolute Spirit. Yet for such a Spirit, something like this is impossible for a different reason, namely, because historiographical science is superfluous for it and contrary to its essence.

What is great has historical endurance because it is unique. What is great has greatness because, and insofar as, it in each case has something greater beyond itself. Such being able to have something greater beyond itself is the mystery of that which is great. Whatever is small is incapable of this, even though, properly speaking, it most directly and comfortably bears the greatest distance from that which is great. Yet whatever is small wills only itself; that is, it wants to be small, and its mystery is no mystery, but rather a ploy and the irksome deviousness of diminishing and casting suspicion upon, and thereby of assimilating to itself, all that is not of its kind.

e) Awakening the Fundamental Attunement as a Founding of Futural Historical Beyng

The opening up of truth that configures and shapes the historical Dasein of a people occurs in and from out of a fundamental attunement whose originary character, clarity, extent, and binding force are never brought to bear at a single stroke. The fundamental attunement itself, however, must first of all be awakened. For this battle to transform the attunements that still dominate and perpetuate themselves at any given time, the first-born must be sacrificed. They are those poets who, in their saying, ahead of time tell of the futural beyng of a people in their history and, in so doing, necessarily go unheard.

Hölderlin is such a poet. The fundamental attunement of a holy mourning, yet in readied distress, that is awakened in his late and most mature poetizing, founds the metaphysical locale of our futural historical beyng, if indeed it fights its way toward the vocation of its greatness. The flight, absence, and arrival of the gods of the people are opened up in this fundamental attunement. Our historical Dasein is thereby placed into the supreme need and into a decision that lies far before and beyond the question of whether it will be Christendom or not, of whether there is to be a schism in denominations or not; before and beyond all such things because it is the question of whether, and in what way, the people grounds its historical Dasein upon an originarily unitary experience of being bound in return to the gods, and can thus first comprehend and preserve its vocation. The question is not, for instance, that of how a supposedly already-existent people comes to terms with a religion or denomination that has been passed down. What is at issue is the true appearing or non-appearing of the God in the being of the people from out of the need of its beyng, and for such beyng. This appearing must become the fundamental event. Otherwise, all that remains is confusion and the persistent illusion of an equalizing in which nothing occurs.

> . . . wenn aber
> Ein Gott erscheint, auf Himmel und Erd und Meer
> Kömmt allerneuende Klarheit.

> . . . but when
> A God appears, upon heaven and Earth and sea
> Comes all-renewing clarity.
> ("Conciliator, you who never believed . . . ," IV, 162, lines 11ff.)

f) The Conflict of Mourning and Joy within the Fundamental Attunement

Hölderlin knows of the entirely singular character and gravity of the need and vocation that prevail in his fundamental attunement. Cf. "Bread and Wine," strophe VII (IV, 123f., lines 109–124):

> Aber Freund! wir kommen zu spät. Zwar leben die Götter,
> 110   Aber über dem Haupt droben in anderer Welt.
> Endlos wirken sie da und scheinens wenig zu achten,
> Ob wir leben, so sehr schonen die Himmlischen uns.
> Denn nicht immer vermag ein schwaches Gefäss sie zu fassen,
> Nur zu Zeiten erträgt göttliche Fülle der Mensch.
> Traum von ihnen ist drauf das Leben. Aber das Irrsaal
> Hilft, wie Schlummer und stark machet die Noth und die Nacht,
> Biss dass Helden genug in der ehernen Wiege gewachsen,
> Herzen an Kraft, wie sonst, ähnlich den Himmlischen sind.
> Donnernd kommen sie drauf. Indessen dünket mir öfters
> 120   Besser zu schlafen, wie so ohne Genossen zu seyn,
> So zu harren und was zu thun indess und zu sagen,
> Weiss ich nicht und wozu Dichter in dürftiger Zeit?
> Aber sie sind, sagst du, wie des Weingotts heilige Priester,
> Welche von Lande zu Land zogen in heiliger Nacht.

> But friend! we come too late. The gods indeed live,
> 110   Yet over our heads in another world above.
> Endlessly they are at work there and seem little to heed
> Whether we live, so greatly do the heavenly protect us.
> For not always can a weak vessel grasp them,
> Only at times can the human withstand divine fullness.
> Life follows as a dream of them. Yet errancy
> Helps, like slumber, and need and the night make strong,

> Until heroes enough have grown in a cradle of ore,
> Hearts in their strength, as before, approach the heavenly.
> Thundering then they come. Yet often it seems to me
> 120   Better to sleep, than to be thus without companions,
> To wait in such manner and what to do and to say meantime,
> I know not and wherefore poets in time of need?
> Yet they are, you say, like the wine god's holy priests,
> Who journeyed from land to land in holy night.

Here, holy mourning borders on complete hopelessness and despair. Yet at this border there ensues the most profound turnaround; there arises the courage to hold out in the storms of the gods and to await the lightening flash—that is, to sow such ability to wait into the Dasein of the people in foretelling it poetically.

The interpretation we have provided of the fundamental attunement of mourning leaves little room for the misunderstanding to arise that what is at issue here is a passive immersion in some impotent, general melancholy. As a readiness that is an awaiting, mourning is not only altogether remote from such melancholy, but we must pay heed in general to the fact that, in accordance with its intimacy, there lies contained within the essence of the fundamental attunement a counter-attunement. Hölderlin elucidates this on one occasion in an epigram entitled "Sophocles" (IV, 3):

> Viele versuchten umsonst, das Freudigste freudig zu sagen,
> Hier spricht endlich es mir, hier in der Trauer sich aus.

> Many tried in vain to joyfully say the most joyful,
> Here finally it speaks to me, here within mourning.

The counter-attunement of joy, however, is here not just something like the opposite side that also lies present at hand, but is rather that joy that is brought to attune within mourning. More precisely, this attuning that thus oscillates in such conflict is characteristic of fundamental attunement. Such attunement in each case attunes, from the ground up, all essential attunements, and, in its own way in each case, determines and attunes their rank as well.

g) Entering into the Sphere of the River Poems. Transition from "Germania" to "The Rhine"

If, here and now, we endeavor to cultivate the correct hearing for this telling of the poet's, then we do so because the fundamental experience of the need pertaining to modern thinking—of its uncomprehended anxiety in the face of a real questioning after that which is properly worthy of question—opens our eyes to the need of this poet, and does so because one need contains the other within it. It therefore remains superfluous to provide lengthy assurances that what calls upon us to concern ourselves with precisely this poetizing, *in the context of a far-reaching, fundamental task of philosophy,* is neither some particular orientation of aesthetic taste, nor some superficial predilection for the poet and his work, nor even the necessity (which certainly exists) of appropriating this work.

The reflections just provided have been undertaken with a view to helping us to understand the transition from the poem "Germania" to the poem "The Rhine" from out of the sense of the task we have set ourselves. If this transition is to continue this task and to make it more incisive—and this is what it seeks to accomplish—then the selection of the poem "The Rhine" must be intended to intensify and enrich the unfolding of the fundamental attunement that we have initiated—which is to say, however, that it is to bring closer to our comprehension the beyng that is opened up in this attunement.

The poem "The Rhine" belongs to the river poems. Earlier (p. 81ff.>), we already pointed to the sense and significance of the rivers and of the telling of them. "[T]he yearning waters / Of the homeland"[1] assume an essential role in the grounding opening up of the world of historical Dasein. Cf. "The Ister" (IV, 221f., lines 49ff.):

> . . . Umsonst nicht gehn
> Im Troknen die Ströme. Aber wie? Sie sollen nemlich
> Zur Sprache seyn. Ein Zeichen braucht es,
> Nichts anderes, schlecht und recht, damit es Sonn'
> Und Mond trag' im Gemüth', untrennbar,
> Und fortgeh, Tag und Nacht auch, und
> Die Himmlischen warm sich fühlen aneinander.
> Darum sind jene auch
> Die Freude des Höchsten. Denn wie käm er sonst
> Herunter?

> . . . Not in vain do
> Rivers run in the dry. Yet how? Namely, they are
> To be to language. A sign is needed,
> Nothing else, plain and simple, so that sun
> And moon may be borne in mind, inseparable,
> And pass on, day and night too, and

---

1. "Patmos," first version, IV, 190, lines 23f.

> The heavenly feel themselves warm by one another.
> Whence those ones too
> Are the joy of the Highest. For how else would he
> Descend?

The river poems are neither descriptions of nature nor mere symbolic images, say for human existence [*Dasein*]. Both do, indeed, appear to play a role here. Yet there is another meaning and reason for this, and this is the case because the poet's founding telling compels beings as a whole into a new projection: nature, history, and the gods. We shall necessarily go astray with regard to this poetic struggle for an anticipatory configuring that shapes in advance the whole of beyng so long as we take our guiding thread from commonplace views of the world in appropriating this poetizing, or from views that we justify to ourselves by appealing to philosophical systems, such as German Idealism.

What we have here is not an indeterminate confluence of the realms of nature, history, and the gods in some murky pantheism; nor is it an arraying of nature, history, and the gods alongside or on top of one another as circumscribed realms or fields. It is neither a mere renewal of the ancient picture of the world nor the mixing of such a world picture with some indeterminate, Enlightenment Christendom. What we must know here is this: The poet experiences poetically a creative decline of the truth of beyng hitherto, which is to say that in the dissolution thereof, new and youthful powers captivate him and tear him onward. Yet all this happens poetically. We should not, therefore, be of the opinion that such beyng, as shaped in the telling of the poet, could be readily dressed in the cloak of a 'philosophical' discourse, so as to transform the poetic saying into the thinker's knowing by such procedures, and from there into a useful and profitable knowledge of things.

If a task here stands ready for philosophy, then such a task can be determined only from out of philosophy's ownmost necessities— that is, in terms of what is transmitted in the Greco-Germanic mission, from out of which thinking, from its own origin, may enter into an originary dialogue with poetizing and its need. Our interpretation here serves only the poet; it leaves thinking's dimension and its necessities—that is, its need—knowingly unsaid.

PART TWO
"THE RHINE"

Der Rhein[1]

I   Im dunkeln Epheu sass ich, an der Pforte
    Des Waldes, eben, da der goldene Mittag,
    Den Quell besuchend, herunterkam
    Von Treppen des Alpengebirgs,
    Das mir die göttlichgebaute,
    Die Burg der Himmlischen heisst
    Nach alter Meinung, wo aber
    Geheim noch manches entschieden
    Zu Menschen gelanget; so
10 Vernahm ich ohne Vermuthen
    Ein Schiksaal, denn noch kaum
    War mir im warmen Schatten
    Sich manches beredend, die Seele
    Italia zu geschweift
    Und fernhin an die Küsten Moreas.

II Jezt aber, drinn im Gebirg,
    Tief unter den silbernen Gipfeln,
    Und unter fröhlichem Grün,
    Wo die Wälder schauernd zu ihm
20 Und der Felsen Häupter übereinander
    Hinabschaun, taglang, dort
    Im kältesten Abgrund hört'
    Ich um Erlösung jammern
    Den Jüngling, es hörten ihn, wie er tobt',
    Und die Mutter Erd' anklagt'
    Und den Donnerer, der ihn gezeuget,
    Erbarmend die Eltern, doch
    Die Sterblichen flohn von dem Ort,
    Denn furchtbar war, da lichtlos er
30 In den Fesseln sich wälzte,
    Das Rasen des Halbgotts.

III Die Stimme wars des edelsten der Ströme,
    Des freigeborenen Rheins,
    Und anderes hoffte der, als droben von den Brüdern,
    Dem Tessin und dem Rhodanus
    Er schied und wandern wollt', und ungeduldig ihn
    Nach Asia trieb die königliche Seele.
    Doch unverständig ist
    Das Wünschen vor dem Schiksaal.

---

1. IV, 172ff.

40   Die Blindesten aber
        Sind Göttersöhne. Denn es kennet der Mensch
        Sein Haus und dem Thier ward, wo
        Es bauen solle, doch jenen ist
        Der Fehl, dass sie nicht wissen wohin
        In die unerfahrne Seele gegeben.

     IV Ein Räthsel ist Reinentsprungenes. Auch
        Der Gesang kaum darf es enthüllen. Denn
        Wie du anfiengst, wirst du bleiben,
        So viel auch wirket die Noth
50   Und die Zucht, das meiste nemlich
        Vermag die Geburt,
        Und der Lichtstral, der
        Dem Neugebornen begegnet.
        Wo aber ist einer,
        Um frei zu bleiben
        Sein Leben lang, und des Herzens Wunsch
        Allein zu erfüllen, so
        Aus günstigen Höhn, wie der Rhein.
        Und so aus heiligem Schoose
60   Glüklich geboren, wie jener?

     V Drum ist ein Jauchzen sein Wort.
        Nicht liebt er, wie andere Kinder,
        In Wikelbanden zu weinen;
        Denn wo die Ufer zuerst
        An die Seit ihm schleichen, die krummen,
        Und durstig umwindend ihn,
        Den Unbedachten, zu ziehn
        Und wohl zu behüten begehren
        Im eigenen Zahne, lachend
70   Zerreisst er die Schlangen und stürzt
        Mit der Beut und wenn in der Eil'
        Ein Grösserer ihn nicht zähmt,
        Ihn wachsen lässt, wie der Bliz, muss er
        Die Erde spalten, und wie Bezauberte fliehn
        Die Wälder ihm nach und zusammensinkend die Berge.

     VI Ein Gott will aber sparen den Söhnen
        Das eilende Leben und lächelt,
        Wenn unenthaltsam, aber gehemmt
        Von heiligen Alpen, ihm
80   In der Tiefe, wie jener, zürnen die Ströme.
        In solcher Esse wird dann

Auch alles Lautre geschmiedet,
Und schön ists, wie er drauf,
Nachdem er die Berge verlassen,
Stillwandelnd sich im deutschen Lande
Begnüget und das Sehnen stillt
Im guten Geschäffte, wenn er das Land baut
Der Vater Rhein und liebe Kinder nährt
In Städten, die er gegründet.

90 VII Doch nimmer, nimmer vergisst ers.
Denn eher muss die Wohnung vergehn,
Und die Sazung, und zum Unbild werden
Der Tag der Menschen, ehe vergessen
Ein solcher dürfte den Ursprung
Und die reine Stimme der Jugend.
Wer war es, der zuerst
Die Liebesbande verderbt
Und Strike von ihnen gemacht hat?
Dann haben des eigenen Rechts
100 Und gewiss des himmlischen Feuers
Gespottet die Trozigen, dann erst
Die sterblichen Pfade verachtend
Verwegnes erwählt
Und den Göttern gleich zu werden getrachtet.

VIII Es haben aber an eigner
Unsterblichkeit die Götter genug und bedürfen
Die Himmlischen eines Dings,
So sinds Heroën und Menschen
Und Sterbliche sonst. Denn weil
110 Die Seeligsten nichts fühlen von selbst,
Muss wohl, wenn solches zu sagen
Erlaubt ist, in der Götter Nahmen
Theilnehmend fühlen ein Andrer,
Den brauchen sie; jedoch ihr Gericht
Ist, dass sein eigenes Haus
Zerbreche der und das Liebste
Wie den Feind schelt' und sich Vater und Kind
Begrabe unter den Trümmern,
Wenn einer, wie sie, seyn will und nicht
120 Ungleiches dulden, der Schwärmer.

IX Drum wohl ihm, welcher fand
Ein wohlbeschiedenes Schiksaal,
Wo noch der Wanderungen

Und süss der Leiden Erinnerung
Aufrauscht am sichern Gestade,
Dass da und dorthin gern
Er sehn mag bis an die Grenzen,
Die bei der Geburt ihm Gott
Zum Aufenthalte gezeichnet.
130   Dann ruht er, seeligbescheiden,
Denn alles, was er gewollt,
Das Himmlische, von selber umfängt
Es unbezwungen, lächelnd
Jezt, da er ruhet, den Kühnen.

    X Halbgötter denk' ich jezt
Und kennen muss ich die Theuern,
Weil oft ihr Leben so
Die sehnende Brust mir beweget.
Wem aber, wie, Rousseau, dir,
140   Unüberwindlich die Seele,
Die starkausdauernde ward,
Und sicherer Sinn
Und süsse Gaabe zu hören,
Zu reden so, dass er aus heiliger Fülle
Wie der Weingott, thörig göttlich
Und gesezlos sie die Sprache der Reinesten giebt
Verständlich den Guten, aber mit Recht
Die Achtungslosen mit Blindheit schlägt
Die entweihenden Knechte, wie nenn ich den Fremden?

150   XI Die Söhne der Erde sind, wie die Mutter,
Allliebend, so empfangen sie auch
Mühlos, die Glüklichen, Alles.
Drum überraschet es auch
Und schrökt den sterblichen Mann,
Wenn er den Himmel, den
Er mit den liebenden Armen
Sich auf die Schultern gehäufft,
Und die Last der Freude bedenket;
Dann scheint ihm oft das Beste
160   Fast ganz vergessen da,
Wo der Stral nicht brennt,
Im Schatten des Walds
Am Bielersee in frischer Grüne zu seyn,
Und sorglosarm an Tönen,
Anfängern gleich, bei Nachtigallen zu lernen.

XII Und herrlich ists, aus heiligem Schlafe dann
    Erstehen und aus Waldes Kühle
    Erwachend, Abends nun
    Dem milderen Licht entgegenzugehn,
170 Wenn, der die Berge gebaut
    Und den Pfad der Ströme gezeichnet,
    Nachdem er lächelnd auch
    Der Menschen geschäfftiges Leben
    Das othemarme, wie Seegel
    Mit seinen Lüften gelenkt hat,
    Auch ruht und zu der Schülerin jezt,
    Der Bildner, gutes mehr
    Denn böses findend,
    Zur heutigen Erde der Tag sich neiget.

180 XIII Dann feiern das Brautfest Menschen und Götter
    Es feiern die Lebenden all,
    Und ausgeglichen
    Ist eine Weile das Schiksaal.
    Und die Flüchtlinge suchen die Heerberg,
    Und süssen Schlummer die Tapfern,
    Die Liebenden aber
    Sind, was sie waren; sie sind
    Zu Hausse, wo die Blume sich freuet
    Unschädlicher Gluth und die finsteren Bäume
190 Der Geist umsäuselt, aber die Unversöhnten
    Sind umgewandelt und eilen
    Die Hände sich ehe zu reichen,
    Bevor das freundliche Licht
    Hinuntergeht und die Nacht kommt.

XIV Doch einigen eilt
    Diss schnell vorüber, andere
    Behalten es länger.
    Die ewigen Götter sind
    Voll Lebens allzeit; bis in den Tod
200 Kann aber ein Mensch auch
    Im Gedächtniss doch das Beste behalten,
    Und dann erlebt er das Höchste.
    Nur hat ein jeder sein Maas.
    Denn schwer ist zu tragen
    Das Unglük, aber schwerer das Glük.
    Ein Weiser aber vermocht es
    Vom Mittag bis in die Mitternacht

Und bis der Morgen erglänzte
Beim Gastmahl helle zu bleiben.

210   XV   Dir mag auf heissem Pfade unter Tannen oder
Im Dunkel des Eichwalds gehüllt
In Stahl, mein Sinklair! Gott erscheinen oder
In Wolken, du kennst ihn, da du kennest, jugendlich,
Des Guten Kraft und nimmer ist dir
Verborgen das Lächeln des Herrschers
Bei Tage, wenn
Es fieberhaft und angekettet das
Lebendige scheinet oder auch
Bei Nacht, wenn alles gemischt
220   Ist ordnungslos und wiederkehrt
Uralte Verwirrung.

The Rhine

I   In ivy dark I sat, at the portal
    Of the woods, just as the golden midday,
    Visiting the source, descended
    On the staircase of the Alps,
    Those I know as the divinely built,
    The fortress of the heavenly
    According to ancient opinion, yet where
    Much decided comes
    In secret to humans still; thus
10   I apprehended, unsuspectingly,
    A destiny, for scarcely yet
    In the warmth of the shade
    Pondering much, had my soul
    To Italy roamed
    And afar to the coasts of Morea.

II   Now however, within the mountains,
    Deep beneath the silver peaks
    And below the cheerful green,
    Where to him the teeming woods,
20   And the summits of the rocks
    Look down, all day long, there
    In the coldest abyss I heard
    Him pining for deliverance
    The youngster, he was heard, as he raged,
    And accursed the Mother Earth,
    And the Thunderer who had produced him,
    With pity by his parents, yet
    Mortals had fled the locale,
    For frightful, since without light he
30   In his fetters tossed, was
    The fury of the demigod.

III   The voice it was of that most noble of rivers,
    The freely born Rhine,
    He who hoped for something else, as up there from his brothers,
    The Tessin and the Rhodanus,
    He departed and wished to wander, and impatiently
    To Asia he was driven by that kingly soul.
    Yet uncomprehending is
    Wishing in the face of destiny.

40   The blindest however
           Are sons of gods. For well the human knows
           His house and to the animal came, where
           It should build, yet to those ones
           The lack, that they know not whereto
           Is given their untraveled soul.

    IV   Enigma is that which has purely sprung forth. Even
           The song scarcely may unveil it. For
           As you commenced, so will you remain,
           However much need achieves,
50   And discipline, it is birth
           That is capable of most,
           And the ray of light, that
           Meets the newly born.
           Yet where is one,
           To free remain
           His whole life long, and his heart's wish
           Alone to fulfill, from
           Such favorable heights as the Rhine,
           And from so holy a womb
60   Born happy, as that one?

    V   Thus a jubilance is his word.
           Not like other children does he love
           To wail in swaddling wraps;
           For where the banks at first
           Creep to his side, the winding ones,
           And thirstily entwining him desire
           To steer the impudent one,
           And presumably to protect him,
           With his own tooth, laughing
70   He rips apart the serpents and rushes off
           With his prey and if in his hurry
           Someone greater does not tame him,
           Lets him grow, like lightning must he
           Split the Earth, and as though enchanted flee
           After him the woods and mountains collapsing.

    VI   A god however wishes to spare his sons
           A hurried life and smiles,
           When unrelentingly, yet restrained
           By holy Alps, down
80   In the depths, the rivers rage at him, as does that one.
           In such a forge too is

Everything pure then wrought,
And beautiful it is, how then,
Abandoning the mountains,
And tranquilly wandering, he contents himself
In the German land and stills his longing
In good trade, as he builds the land,
Does Father Rhine, and nourishes dear children
In towns that he has founded.

90   VII   Yet never, never does he forget it.
For sooner must habitation pass away,
And order and the human day
Become deformed, before such as he
Might forget the origin
And the pure voice of youth.
Who was it, who first
Spoiled the bonds of love
And made them into ropes?
Then of their own right
100   Certain and of the heavenly fire
Did they defiant mock, then first
Despising mortal paths
Chose reckless
And endeavored to be equal to the gods.

VIII   Yet of their own
Immortality the gods have enough, and if one thing
The Heavenly require,
Then heroes and humans it is
And otherwise mortals. For since
110   The most blessed feel nothing of themselves,
There must presumably, if to say such a thing
Is allowed, in the name of the gods
Another participate in feeling,
Him they need; yet their own ordinance
Is that he his own house
Shatter and his most beloved
Chide like the enemy and bury his father
And child beneath the ruins,
If someone wants to be like them and not
120   Tolerate unequals, the impassioned one.

IX   And so presumably for him, who found
A well-apportioned destiny,
Where recollection of his wanderings still

And, sweetly, of his sufferings
Washes up upon safe shores,
That there and fondly away
He may look to the boundaries
Which at his birth God
Drew for his stay.
130   Then he rests, blissfully humble,
For everything that he wanted,
That is heavenly, of its own accord surrounds
Him uncompelled, smiling
Now that he rests, the bold one.

   X   Demigods now I think
And the dear ones I must know,
For often does their life
So move my longing breast.
Yet he whose soul, like yours,
140   Rousseau, became invincible,
Enduring ever strong,
And in its sense assured
And sweet in its gift of hearing,
Of talking thus, that out of holy fullness he
Like the wine god, foolishly divine
And lawlessly bestows this, the language of the purest,
Understandable for the good, yet rightly strikes
With blindness those who fail to heed
The unrevering slaves, how shall I name the stranger?

150   XI   The sons of the Earth are, like the Mother,
All-loving, so too they receive
Effortlessly, those fortunate ones, everything.
Thus it surprises too
And terrifies the mortal man,
In pondering the heaven, which
He with loving arms
Has heaped upon his shoulders,
And the burden of his joy;
Then often it seems best to him,
160   To be almost entirely forgotten,
Where the ray does not burn,
In the shade of the woods
There by the Bielersee amid the fresh green leaves,
And careless-free of tones,
Like beginners, to learn with nightingales.

XII   And glorious it is, then from holy sleep
      To arise and from the coolness of the woods
      Awakening, at evening now
      To go towards more mellow light,
170   When he, who built the mountains
      And drew the rivers' path,
      Having directed with a smile
      The busy lives of humans,
      Short of breath, guiding their sails
      With his breezes too,
      Now rests and to her, the pupil,
      The creator, finding
      More good than evil,
      To the present Earth the day inclines.

180 XIII Then humans and gods the bridal festival celebrate,
      All the living celebrate,
      And destiny is
      Evened out for a while.
      And those in flight seek asylum,
      And sweet slumber the courageous,
      But lovers are
      What they always were, they are
      At home, where the flower enjoys
      Benevolent warmth and spirit caresses
190   The darkling trees, but those unreconciled
      Are now turned around and hasten
      To extend hands to one another,
      Before the friendly light
      Goes down and night arrives.

XIV   Yet this hurries
      Quickly by for some, others
      Retain it longer.
      The eternal gods are
      At all times full of life; yet until death
200   Can a human being too
      In memory retain what is best,
      And then he experiences the highest.
      Only each one has his measure.
      For difficult to bear is misfortune,
      But fortune more difficult still.
      A wise man, however, was able,
      From midday unto midnight,

And until the morning shone forth,
To stay lucid at the banquet.

210 XV To you on sultry paths beneath the firs or
Shrouded in the dark of oak woods
In steel, my Sinclair! may God appear or
In clouds, you know him, for, in your youth, you know
The force of good, and never is from you
Concealed the smiling of the lord
By day, when
Feverish and chained down the
Living all appear or indeed
By night, when all is mixed
220   Disorderedly and there returns
Primordial confusion.

TRANSITIONAL REMARK

The Question Concerning What Is 'Innermost' in a Poetic Work as a Question of the Opening Up and Founding of Beyng in the Each Time New Prevailing of Its Fundamental Attunement

The poem originated in 1801, the same year as "Germania," and belongs in the sphere of that poetizing that attains its definitive shape in "Germania." Nevertheless, we must seek to understand the poem wholly on its own terms. Its peculiar multifacetedness, to say nothing of the intricacies of its content, already compels us to do so. And yet this initial impression of its ungraspable character, and of the lack of any unified compositional structure, is merely a semblance.

Viewed extrinsically, the poem consists of 15 strophes. Breaking it down into the following five sections can aid us in interpreting the whole: (1) strophe I, (2) strophes II to IX, (3) strophes X to XIII, (4) strophe XIV, and (5) strophe XV. This extrinsic sectioning of the poem can first be understood only in terms of the poetic work, and can therefore find its legitimation only through our interpretation.

Beyond this thoroughly 'extrinsic' division of the strophes, we shall inquire concerning what is 'innermost' in the poetic work: its fundamental attunement and that beyng that is opened up within it and poetically founded. Although we have good grounds for suspecting that the fundamental attunement will be the same, we may not simply assume this as our basis, especially given that sameness of a fundamental attunement does not at all mean simple repetition, but quite the opposite: an unfolding that is each time new. Accordingly, we shall not directly experience in the hymn "The Rhine" anything of what we name a holy mourning in readied distress.

Chapter One
The Demigods as Mediating Middle between Gods and
Humans. The Fundamental Attunement of the Poem.
The Beyng of the Demigods and the Calling of the Poet

The pivot upon which the entire poetic work turns, so to speak, is to
be sought at the beginning of strophe X, in the first four lines. For this
reason, the first major break within the indicated divisions is found
at lines 135ff., following the end of strophe IX:

> Halbgötter denk' ich jezt
> Und kennen muss ich die Theuern,
> Weil oft ihr Leben so
> Die sehnende Brust mir beweget.

> Demigods now I think
> And the dear ones I must know,
> For often does their life
> So move my longing breast.

"Demigods"—frequently in the context of Hölderlin's late poetry we
encounter the naming of the demigods.

> . . . kaum weiss zu sagen ein Halbgott
> Wer mit Nahmen sie [die Himmlischen] sind, die
> mit den Gaaben ihm nahn.

> . . . a demigod scarcely knows how to tell
> Who they [the heavenly] are by name, who
> approach him with their gifts.
>
> ("Bread and Wine," IV, 122, lines 75f.)

Demigods are not entirely gods, yet neither are they mere ordinary humans.

Denn nimmer herrscht er [der Vater] allein.
Und weiss nicht alles. Immer stehet irgend
Eins zwischen Menschen und ihm.
Und Treppenweise steiget
Der Himmlische nieder.

For never does he [the Father] rule alone.
And knows not everything. Always there stands some
One between humans and him.
And on staircases
Descends the heavenly one.

("The Only One," first version, IV, 188, lines 65ff.)

Demigods—these are, therefore, in-between beings. These the poet now 'thinks.' What does 'thinking' mean here? It does not mean thinking of them, nor merely calling them to mind. Above all, it does not mean thinking up such beings, demigods, for 'oneself,' whimsically conjuring them up. Rather the poet thinks them *as the ones* that they are, and only this does he think. He thinks their essence. Thinking the essence, however, is a creative projection, insofar as the essence of beings is not something that we just stumble upon and can pick up in the way that we can pick up particular beings. Such a projection of essence nevertheless has its own constraints and grounds, and does not spring from an unrestrained imagination or from ungrounded notions. Moreover, this thinking remains a thinking of the poet. The projection is not a conceptual one that grasps beyng as such in terms of a concept, but rather a founding one—one that happens in a poetic telling.

Yet even if, as is required, we do not understand thinking in the philosophical sense here, 'thinking' is surely not an attunement, and our questioning, after all, concerns the fundamental attunement. Our hint regarding the lines cited thus seems unable to provide us with what we are seeking. At most we may discern a fundamental stance from them, but not the fundamental attunement. Yet in the end, the two cannot be separated. Our task will be to come to understand this 'thinking of the demigods' in a more determinate and attuned manner. We must ask:

1. What is properly being thought here, and in what sphere of beyng does this thinking move?

2. By what is this thinking compelled and occasioned; in what situation does it occur?

3. In what respect, as what, are the demigods thought? Which beyng is founded here?

4. Which fundamental attunement prevails in this thinking ("Demigods now I think")?

a) The Distinction between Humans and Gods Opened Up in the Question Concerning the Essence of the Demigods as Founding a Realm of Beyng in General

Regarding the first question: Demigods, we said, are in-between beings—not entirely gods, and yet more than humans. These in-between beings can thus only be thought once we are already acquainted with and know, as it were, that which they lie between in their essence: between gods and humans. We can figure out these in-between beings in our thinking, then, by subtracting some attributes from the gods and adding a few to humans. Yet this manner of accounting by means of 'subtraction' and 'addition' can succeed only if we already know the essence of the gods and the essence of humans. If we do not know that, then how are we to think demigods? The fundamental attunement of the poem "Germania" tells us, after all, that the gods have fled from us and are veiled, and that we now intimate only a "wisp" of them (line 25); that we likewise know just as little who we ourselves are, who the people is, and what its vocation is. Given this, how can the poet venture, and want to venture, to think demigods? Yet presumably, in keeping with its innermost kinship to the poetizing of the thinker, the thinking of the poet is fundamentally different from our everyday thinking and opining, which must indeed be conceived as a reckoning with things, a taking into account of circumstances, a counting on such and such conditions—a counting that here occurs entirely without numbers. The Greek word λόγος, from which we obtain 'logic' as the 'doctrine of thinking,' with the increasing development of conscious everyday thinking already comes to mean the equivalent of such 'reckoning.' Yet both poetic and philosophical thinking are fundamentally different from such thinking. The poetic thinking of essence with regard to the demigods is not, therefore, some calculative figuring out of this essence as the result of a reciprocal taking into account of the essence of gods and of humans so as to arrive at an in-between being. Yet what, then, is it?

Demigods are not themselves gods, but beings that point in the direction of the gods, and indeed in a direction that leads over and beyond human beings: *overhumans*, who nevertheless remain beneath the stature of the gods: *undergods*. We are no longer understanding this 'over' and 'under,' however, as indeterminate measurements of the degree of distance, but as directions that in themselves belong together and are one direction, namely, a direction of questioning. Within what questioning? Whenever we really ask concerning the essence of the human, we ask over and beyond the human being, because every genuine question asks over beyond that which is interrogated. Asking concerning the essence of the human, we are always somehow thinking the overhuman. Whenever we really ask concerning the essence of the gods, our question rebounds off their essence as a mystery and falls short. In questioning concerning the essence of the gods, we are always somehow thinking undergods. Overhumans and undergods are, however, the same issue being asked about in the dual question concerning humans and gods. The demigods are this same issue. Whoever thinks them moves within the question concerning the essence of humans, and at one and the same time within the question concerning the essence of the gods. Whoever really asks these questions that intrinsically belong together does so because he knows neither the essence of humans nor the essence of the gods, and, in order to know this, he asks concerning the essence of the demigods.

This question is thus not a belated one that first arises once the essence of gods and humans has been thought and is known, firmly established, so as then to fill in the gap. The converse is the case: Thinking demigods is the decisive questioning, the breakthrough that opens into the direction leading over and beyond humans—a direction that, however, remains only a direction oriented toward the gods, and does not directly attain the gods themselves. Thinking the demigods and their essence strikes open for the very first time the breach that affords access to the realm of questioning within which a sufficiently developed question can be asked concerning the essence of humans and gods.

Questioning concerning the demigods is decisive questioning in the strictest sense of the word, because in it the distinguishing of humans and gods first becomes a question, and thinking within the distinction as such a distinction first gains a foothold (distinguishing = the founding of limit). Thinking demigods—such thinking precisely does not move within an intermediate realm to the exclusion of the remaining realms (humans and gods), but to the contrary: Such thinking founds and breaks open the realm of beyng in general. With this, our first question is answered.

b) The Poet's Being Compelled to Think the Demigods
at the Threshold of the Homeland as a Being
Enjoined Back into Historical Dasein

Now to the second question: By what is this thinking of the poet compelled and occasioned? In what situation does it occur? The poet says at the beginning of strophe X: "Demigods now I think." When, now? The beginning of the poem, the first strophe, gives us the answer:

I   Im dunkeln Epheu sass ich, an der Pforte
     Des Waldes, eben, da der goldene Mittag,
     Den Quell besuchend, herunterkam
     Von Treppen des Alpengebirgs,
     Das mir die göttlichgebaute,
     Die Burg der Himmlischen heisst
     Nach alter Meinung, wo aber
     Geheim noch manches entschieden
     Zu Menschen gelanget; so
10   Vernahm ich ohne Vermuthen
     Ein Schiksaal, denn noch kaum
     War mir im warmen Schatten
     Sich manches beredend, die Seele
     Italia zu geschweift
     Und fernhin an die Küsten Moreas.

I   In ivy dark I sat, at the portal
     Of the woods, just as the golden midday,
     Visiting the source, descended
     On the staircase of the Alps,
     Those I know as the divinely built,
     The fortress of the heavenly
     According to ancient opinion, yet where
     Much decided comes
     In secret to humans still; thus
10   I apprehended, unsuspectingly,
     A destiny, for scarcely yet
     In the warmth of the shade
     Pondering much, had my soul
     To Italy roamed
     And afar to the coasts of Morea.

However, this gives more the locale from where the poet sees that which he thinks, and not the time. Yet neither can be separated from the other, and the situation in which he experiences being compelled to think the demigods is determined by both. Admittedly, the locale can initially be grasped more readily. It can even be geographically determined with accuracy. The poet sees the mountain range of the Alps as the golden midday descends upon it. He sees it in the South from the vantage point of the North, from the banks of the lake of the homeland, the Swabian sea, as Lake Constance is also called. Hölderlin has poetically portrayed the landscape of Lake Constance and of the foothills of the Alps in the poem "Homecoming," dedicated to his relatives (IV, 107ff.). This poem, which stems from the same period as "The Rhine," depicts Hölderlin's return home from one of the last positions he held as a private tutor, in Hauptwyl in the vicinity of St. Gallen. We take note, above all, of the third and fourth strophes of the poem, in which the crossing from the Swiss bank of the lake to Lindau is depicted (IV, 108f.):

3

Vieles sprach ich zu ihm, denn, was auch Dichtende sinnen
Oder singen, es gilt meistens den Engeln und ihm;
Vieles bat ich, zu lieb dem Vaterlande, damit nicht
40   Ungebeten uns einst plözlich befiele der Geist;
Vieles für euch auch, die im Vaterlande besorgt sind,
Denen der heilige Dank lächelnd die Flüchtlinge bringt,
Landesleute! für euch, indessen wiegte der See mich,
Und der Ruderer sass ruhig und lobte die Fahrt.
Weit in des Sees Ebene wars Ein freudiges Wallen
Unter den Seegeln und jezt blühet und hellet die Stadt
Dort in der Frühe sich auf, wohl her von schattigen Alpen
Kommt geleitet und ruht nun in dem Hafen das Schiff.
Warm ist das Ufer hier und freundlich offene Thale,
50   Schön von Pfaden erhellt, grünen und schimmern mich an.
Gärten stehen gesellt und die glänzende Knospe beginnt schon,
Und des Vogels Gesang ladet den Wanderer ein.
Alles scheinet vertraut, der vorübereilende Gruss auch
Scheint von Freunden, es scheint jegliche Miene verwandt.

4

Freilich wohl! das Geburtsland ists, der Boden der Heimath,
Was du suchest, es ist nahe, begegnet dir schon.
Und umsonst nicht steht, wie ein Sohn, am wellenumrauschten
Thor' und siehet und sucht liebende Nahmen für dich,
Mit Gesang ein wandernder Mann, glükseeliges Lindau!
60   Eine der gastlichen Pforten des Landes ist diss,
Reizend hinauszugehn in die vielversprechende Ferne,
Dort, wo die Wunder sind, dort, wo das göttliche Wild,
Hoch in die Ebnen herab der Rhein die verwegene Bahn bricht,
Und aus Felsen hervor ziehet das jauchzende Thal,

Dort hinein, durchs helle Gebirg, nach Komo zu wandern,
Oder hinab, wie der Tag wandelt, den offenen See;
Aber reizender mir bist du, geweihete Pforte!
Heimzugehn, wo bekannt blühende Wege mir sind,
Dort zu besuchen das Land und die schönen Thale des Nekars,
70   Und die Wälder, das Grün heiliger Bäume, wo gern
Sich die Eiche gesellt mit stillen Birken und Buchen,
Und in Bergen ein Ort freundlich gefangen mich nimmt.

3

Much I spoke to him, for, whatever poets ponder
Or sing, it concerns mostly angels and him;
I requested much, for love of the fatherland, lest
40   Spirit should suddenly befall us unbidden one day;
Much for you too, who are troubled in the fatherland,
To whom holy thanks, smiling, brings those who flee,
Countrymen! for you, meantime, the lake swayed me
And the rower sat calmly and praised the journey.
Far out on the surface of the lake there was a joyful surge
Beneath the sails and now the town blossoms and brightens
There in the dawn, and from the shadows of the Alps
The ship is guided in and rests now in the harbor.
Here the shore is warm, and open valleys,
50   Resplendent with beautiful paths, grow verdant and shimmer
        invitingly.
Gardens stand in close company, and the glistening bud breaks
        already,
And the bird's song invites the traveler in.
All seems familiar, the passing greeting too
Appears to be a friend's, every face seems related.

4

Yes, indeed! it is the land of our birth, the soil of the homeland,
What you seek is close by, comes to meet you already.
And not in vain, like a son, at the gate embraced by the wash
Of the waves, stands a traveling man and looks
And seeks loving names for you, with song, blessed Lindau!
60   One of the welcoming portals of the land this is,
Enticing the guest into all that the distance promises,
There where the wonders are, there where the creature, wild
        yet divine,
The Rhine, from on high blasts his reckless path down into the
        plains,

> Extracting from rocks the jubilant valley,
> Through the sunlit mountain range, making for Como,
> Or down toward the open lake, as the day drifts on;
> Yet you entice me more, consecrated portal!
> To go home, where familiarly blossoming paths await me,
> To visit there the land and the Neckar's beautiful valleys,
> 70   And the woods, the green of sacred trees, where gladly
> The oak communes with silent birches and beech trees,
> And surrounded by mountains a locale makes me its captive
>   friend.

Twice the poet names this locale: "One of the welcoming portals of the land" (line 60); "Yet you entice me more, consecrated portal!" (line 67). This emphatic use of the word "portal" indicates that in our poem "The Rhine" the expression "portal / Of the woods" (lines 1f.) does not refer to just any exit from or entrance to the woods; rather, "portal" here is the entrance to the woods of the homeland, from where the poet's view is drawn away from the homeland, across the lake to the "mountain range of the Alps" (line 4). The poet sits at the threshold of the Earth as homeland: 'there' he thinks the demigods. Yet why here, precisely? This question cannot be answered directly. Yet we know that the gods are always the gods of the people; in them, the historical truth of the people reveals and fulfills itself. Standing at the threshold of the homeland has the dual meaning that from there the poet's longing can range into the foreign and remote, and that there, at the threshold, the gods that belong to the homeland must also be received for it. The poet must take up residence at the threshold so that whatever is happening can happen to him. Decisions fall only at thresholds—decisions that always concern thresholds or limits, or the lack thereof.

Pondering the distant gods, the poet is torn back "unsuspectingly" (line 10), so as to apprehend, and in so doing to think, something quite other. This thinking befalls him: It is not forcibly brought about in an artificial or capricious manner. (Cf. "Patmos," first version, IV, 190f., strophe II.) The thinking and knowing of beyng cannot be taken from the gods by cunning, and the most supreme acumen remains an empty delirium, if it is not mastered in a thinking that has sprung forth in a truthful manner. Yet the manner in which this thinking befalls the poet is not accidental either. The poet is prepared and ready, in that he "feels / The shadows of those who once have been" ("Germania," lines 27f.). It is within our being transported to that which has been, and in such transport alone, that something un-suspected is possible. Only one who suspects [*vermutet*], whose sensibility and courage [*Mut*] and mind [*Gemüt*] are really directed toward something, can be struck and befallen by something un-suspected [*Un-vermutetes*]. As the poet thinks out beyond the homeland, beyond the human being and human existence [*Dasein*] and in the direction of the gods of old, he stands in an orientation from which this unsuspected thing can now strike him. Cf. in this regard, the conclusion to the poem "The Journey" (IV, 171, lines 110ff.):

> Die Dienerinnen des Himmels
> Sind aber wunderbar,
> Wie alles Göttlichgeborne.
> Zum Traume wirds ihm, will es Einer
> Beschleichen und straft den, der
> Ihm gleichen will mit Gewalt.
> Oft überrascht es den,
> Der eben kaum es gedacht hat.

> The servant girls of the heavens
> Are a wonder to behold,
> Like everything divinely born.
> A dream it becomes for him who would
> Approach it by stealth, and punishes him
> Who would equal it with force.
> Often it surprises one
> Who indeed has scarcely thought it.

This poem likewise belongs within the sphere of the poetizing that we are endeavoring to understand. "The servant girls of the heavens"—the divinely born takes flight and slips away and becomes destructive if someone seeks to approach it by stealth, with cunning and in a calculative manner, as though it were some tangible thing. Or else, if, instead of cunning, someone uses force and wants to grab hold of the divine, he will be punished. Neither compulsive force nor surreptitious contriving will work here. What is called for here is not any kind of making, but only a readiness that, secure in itself, grows and yet remains inconspicuous to itself. Being compelled to think the demigods grows from out of that 'scarcely thinking' the divine at the threshold of the homeland. This 'scarcely thinking,' however, needs the entire strength that belongs to readiness. That which befalls the poet casts his roaming soul back to the homeland and its proximity. His view is deflected by the Alpine range, turned back toward the Rhine valley, and enjoined into his own historical Dasein. It is there that the poet must think demigods. *What* does he think, in thinking *them*?

c) Destiny as the Fundamental Word of the Poem.
A Preparatory Discussion of Destiny as
the Beyng of the Demigods

Now to the third question: As what are the demigods thought? What is the beyng that is founded in this thinking, insofar as such thinking is poetic? What does the poet apprehend when, unsuspectingly, he is torn away from his pondering that which has been, that which is remote, and is torn back and around into the thinking of his own homeland? The first strophe tells us (lines 9ff.):

. . . so
Vernahm ich ohne Vermuthen
Ein Schiksaal,

. . . thus
I apprehended, unsuspectingly,
A destiny,

With the word "destiny" we hit upon the fundamental word of this poem, and with this we grasp the key to what it poetizes. "Destiny"— this is the name for the beyng of the demigods. According to what we have already said, the thinking of such beyng must open up a realm that is broad and deep enough to be able to think both the beyng of the gods and that of humans. It is therefore no accident that, as we follow this poetizing, "The Rhine," we repeatedly come across the word "destiny" at essential points and in different contexts. For the moment, we shall simply cite these places by listing them in a cursory manner:

. . . so
Vernahm ich ohne Vermuthen
Ein Schiksaal,

. . . thus
I apprehended, unsuspectingly,
A destiny,

(Strophe I, lines 9ff.)

Doch unverständig ist
Das Wünschen vor dem Schiksaal.

Yet uncomprehending is
Wishing in the face of destiny.

(Strophe III, lines 38f.)

Drum wohl ihm, welcher fand
Ein wohlbeschiedenes Schiksaal,

And so presumably for him, who found
A well-apportioned destiny,

(Strophe IX, lines 121f.)

Und ausgeglichen
Ist eine Weile das Schiksaal.

And destiny is
Evened out for a while.

(Strophe XIII, lines 182f.)

The word shows a characteristic multiplicity of meaning, even quite apart from what it signifies in terms of its own content: Destiny as (1) a determinate, governing power, (2) a way of being, and (3) a being that is on each occasion determined by the manner of such beyng, that stands under such power. All three meanings are contained in the lines just cited. What "destiny" means here is to be told poetically in thinking through the beyng of the demigods, and the beyng thus revealed is thereby, shrouded in the word, to be placed into the truth of the people, thus into its knowing willing, that is: such beyng is thereby to be founded. This is the inner will of this poem.

By way of anticipation, and merely to ward off misapprehension, we can say what, from the outset, cannot be referred to by this word. The poet is not thinking "destiny" in the sense of a 'fatum' or 'fatality,' by which we represent beyng in the sense of a will-less, unknowing progression amid the perpetual unfolding of some impassive fatality within the totality of beings that remain enveloped within themselves. Precisely this Asiatic representation of destiny, as we may call it, is creatively overcome in Hölderlin's thinking. The first overcoming of the Asiatic sense of *fatum* was accomplished by the Greeks in an overcoming that, in the manner of its accomplishment, remains unrepeatable, and that occurred in unison with the emergence of this people through poetry, thinking, and statesmanship. Through the Greeks' knowing of μοῖρα and δίκη as such, what is thus named stands in the light of a beyng that exceeds them. It loses its blind, exclusive character, and at the same time first takes on the aspect of that which is extraordinary, of an apportioning and determining that sets limits. The fundamental experience in this is the experience of death and the knowing of death. For this reason too, no concept of beyng is adequate that has not set itself the task of thinking death.

We must not, however, equate Hölderlin's knowing of destiny with the Greek one. We must learn to use this essential German word to name an essential beyng in its true German content, and to do so in an essential manner, which also means: seldom.

Over and beyond our warding off such misapprehensions concerning how that beyng that is named by the word "destiny" is to be determined, it is also possible and necessary to say in which perspective we must think in Hölderlin's poetizing in general in order to come to a correct understanding. What is thought under destiny is the beyng of the demigods—a beyng that is at the same time above the human and beneath the divine, and indeed in such a way that precisely human being and divine being in each case correspond in their own way to such being as destiny; that is, each has its own relationship to it. Only if beyng in the sense of destiny speaks to us is a correspondence possible that is appropriate to being, whether a correspondence to the human or to the gods (co-respondence in "dialogue").

By contrast, beyng in the sense of destiny does not directly impart any correspondence to, for instance, the being of a boulder, of a rose, or of an eagle. We do indeed directly experience stone, plant, and animal as being. Yet who, when asked, would presume to say how things stand concerning the beyng of such beings? Does the boulder 'have' its beyng, just as it 'has' its extension, heaviness, hardness, and color? And where, then, does such beyng 'reside'? And correspondingly in the case of the rose and the eagle: We can say one thing only, and that only on the basis of a very difficult argument: stone, plant, and animal are—but their 'own' beyng remains closed off to them as such beyng, and indeed in a different way each time for each of these beings. It is even precipitous to say that they have their 'own' beyng.

For us humans, by contrast, our beyng—that we are and how we are—is manifest to us in a certain way, yet not only, and not primarily, by our having knowledge of such beyng as something already established that we can ascertain, in the way that, for instance, we can take note of the fact that a tower stands on the Feldberg. Something like that does not affect us. But our beyng does affect us: we cannot be at all without our being affected by such being. Our being, however, is not that of an individuated subject, but rather, in accordance with what was said earlier (p. 126), it is historical being with one another as being in a world. That such being of the human being is in each case mine does not mean that such being is 'subjectivized'—confined to the isolated individual and determined starting from him—but means only that in the first and last instance, and always, this historical being with one another of the human being must pass through decisions that no one can ever take from another.

We are indeed of the opinion that we are the ones who entirely direct our being and dispose over it. In a certain sense this is true, yet in a certain sense it is equally untrue, for we have neither bestowed such beyng upon ourselves, nor can we take away such beyng from ourselves. Even in the freest act of suicide—assuming we are able to know what 'free' is supposed to mean here—we can indeed take away such beyng from ourselves, yet we can never take it from *ourselves* and thereby, as it were, rid ourselves of beyng, because with this annihilation of beyng we annihilate ourselves, so that precisely he is lacking who could now 'be' (!) rid of his beyng. Precisely here the unique relationship of the human being, as a being, shows itself as a relationship to the being of this being.

Our being is one into which, as we say, we are thrown, without knowing the trajectory of this throw, and without, proximally and for the most part, our explicitly taking up this thrownness into our Dasein, because we have unknowingly always already avoided it for all sorts of reasons. Yet in one way or another, we must take responsibility for the being [*Sein*] to which we are delivered over. That is to say: Our being is not only *thrownness,* it is at the same time *projection:* a projection in which, in one way or another, the trajectory of the throw of our thrownness opens itself up or closes itself off and becomes contorted, and does so as a mission or mandate. That beyng that exceeds the human—in accordance with which a human being is not just simply a human being—will therefore be such as to take up, in a supreme way, being as something that has come over it: to truly suffer it—in a suffering that is quite remote from all wretchedness and from every mere dejected putting up with. In that suffering [*Leiden*] is the origin of what we must truly comprehend as *passion* [*Leiden-schaft*]. Such being, which by its essence is a *suffering of itself,* can therefore also only appropriately be experienced by someone who is capable of such suffering—that is, is capable of being equal to the magnitude of a need. This suffering, in which beyng becomes manifest as destiny, is not, however, a mere capability to simply receive, as it were, a destiny that lies before it. Rather, this suffering is creative. It discloses and unfolds the need.

Only in such suffering can a destiny take hold of us, a destiny that never simply lies present before us, but that is a sending—that is, is sent to us—and in such a way that it sends us toward our vocation, granted that we ourselves truly send ourselves into it, and know of what is fittingly sent, and, in knowing it, will it. The concept and word for 'fittingly sent or destined' [*das Schickliche*], frequently used by Hölderlin, holds an essential meaning for him, and an intrinsic relation precisely to the renewal and transformation of human being, in the sense of a being out beyond what is merely habitual and everyday. Cf. in this respect the letter to his friend Dr. Ebel, the personal physician of the Frankfurt family for whom Hölderlin worked as a private tutor. The letter was written from Homburg toward the end of 1799, shortly after Hölderlin fled from Frankfurt. We shall cite the whole letter, because in its attunement and in its content it is as though ready made to shed light on the question we are now considering (III, 458ff.):

Dear Friend!

As much as I feel greatly obliged to you on account of your gracious promise to perhaps in the future participate in my literary endeavors, still, the real joy that your letter gave me was a different one. In reading it I felt, more than I am able to say, how much you meant to me from the first moment, and how much I have been deprived of since I have no longer seen you.

The more I learn to understand and to tolerate and to love human beings in their various forms of suffering, the more deeply and unforgettably those who excel among them remain etched in my mind; and I must confess to you that I know of few with whom I am able to follow my conscience with such certainty as I do whenever I think of you and speak of you, and this happens not infrequently. Would that we lived closer, for my sake; for you have no, or at any rate less, need of me, and I do not know whether I would still mean as much to you as I once seemed to. Many experiences that almost inevitably had to happen to me, given my way of thinking, have so greatly shaken my confidence in practically everything that especially gave me joy and hope, in an image of human beings and their lives and their essence; and the ever-changing circumstances of both the wider and narrower world in which I see myself, now terrify me, as I am once again somewhat freer, to a degree that I can confess only to you, because you understand me. Habit is such a powerful goddess that no one, presumably, can rebel against her without being punished. The accord with others that we so readily attain when we remain attentive to whatever is simply there, this harmony of opinions and of customs, appears in its full significance only when we have to live without it; and our heart will most likely never again find proper peace once we have abandoned those former ties. For forging new ties is so little up to us, especially with regard to those that are more refined and excellent. Admittedly, the human beings who have elevated themselves into a new world of what is fitting [*des Schiklichen*] and good then keep together all the more inseparably.

How readily would I like to have given you a full account of my leaving the house that was and remains so precious to both you and me. But there is so infinitely much I would have to tell you! I would rather have made an appeal to you, and would still like to do so. Our noble lady friend, whom I have once again found, despite many a difficult trial, to be only still more independent and in the best state of life, only still more refined on account of bitter and unfortunate circumstances, nevertheless appears to me, if she is not in the end to fall into deep sadness, to be in great need of a clear and reliable word, reassuring her of her inner worth and of her own path of life with regard to the future; and it has been made almost impossible for me to communicate with her with ease. It would be greatly appreciated, dear friend, if you could possibly do this. One's own reflection, or a book, or whatever else one might turn to, are surely good, but the word of a true friend, who is familiar with the person and their situation, will have a more beneficial effect and be less likely to lead astray.

Your judgment about Paris was very upsetting to me. If someone else had told me the same thing, someone with a less broad perspective and without your clear and unprejudiced eye, I would have been less disturbed by it. I can well comprehend how a powerful destiny that was able to cultivate so magnificently human beings who are strong and grounded tends only to tear apart those who are weak; I can comprehend it all the more, the more I see that even the greatest owe their greatness not simply to their own nature, but also to the fortunate position from which, in their life and work, they can enter into a relation to their time; but I cannot comprehend how many great and pure forms, both individually and together, are so unable to heal or to help, and it is this especially that frequently makes me so quiet and humble in the face of almighty and all-governing need. If such need is once decided, and has a more pervasive effect than the effectiveness of purely independent human beings, then it must end tragically and in a deadly manner for many or for individuals who live through it. We are fortunate indeed if any other hope remains for us! And how do you find the new generation, with regard to the world that surrounds them?– – –

In addition to what is fittingly destined, the poet speaks also of that which is unfitting. Cf. the letter to his brother, already cited several times, of January 1, 1799 (III, 370f.):

I would now like to see whether I can bring out something more of what I wanted to say to you earlier concerning poetry [*Poësie*]. Poetry, I said, does not unite people as does a game; it unites them when it is genuine and has a genuine effect, together with all the manifold suffering and happiness, and striving and hoping and fearing, with all their opinions and shortcomings, all their virtues and ideas, with everything great and little that is found among them, uniting them increasingly into a living, intimate whole, articulated in a thousand ways, for this it what poetry itself is meant to be, and as the cause, so the effect. Is it not true, dear brother,

that the Germans could indeed use such a panacea, even after a political
and philosophical cure; for discounting everything else, a philosophical-
political education already has the intrinsic inconvenience that it indeed
links human beings to the essential, inevitably necessary states of affairs,
to duty and law, yet how much then is left with regard to human harmony? The foreground and background that is drawn according to the
rules of perspective is not by a long way the landscape that would in any
case seek to present itself alongside the living work of nature. Yet the best
of the Germans are for the most part still of the opinion that everything
would be accomplished if only the world were pleasingly *symmetrical.*
O Greece, with your genius and your piety, what have you come to? Even
I, with all good intention, in my deeds and my thinking merely falter
along after these human beings who were unique in the world, and in
what I do and say, I am often so very clumsy and out of tune because, like
a flat-footed goose, I stand in modern waters and lack the ability to soar
upward into the Greek skies. Do not take this metaphor amiss. It is unfitting, yet true, and we can still allow such a thing between us, if I may
indeed say so myself.

Cf. also Fragment 14, lines 12ff. (IV, 247):

O wär es möglich
Zu schonen mein Vaterland

Doch allzuscheu nicht,
                          lieber sei
Unschiklich und gehe, mit der Erinnys, fort
Mein Leben.

O were it possible
To spare my fatherland

Yet not too timidly
                          let rather
Unfittingly, and with the Erinys, proceed
My life.

Because destiny is the beyng of the demigods, they, and they alone
in each case, must experience such being "in accordance with suffering," become transformed in such experience, and in this transformation bring such being to fulfillment. In being in such a way the ones
that they are—demigods—their being is in itself an *intimating directedness toward the gods* themselves; yet at the same time, in the direction
of the human being, they are the *incitement of human beyng,* an incite-

ment in which and through which human beyng is first awakened in its impassioned character and placed into the possibilities that provide a measure. What we have thus now said by way of anticipation and hinting concerning destiny as exceptional beyng may suffice for the purposes of understanding, at least approximately, the last part of a fragment from Hölderlin's later poetizing. See Fragment 14, lines 18–27 (IV, 247f.):

> Denn über die Erde wandeln
> Gewaltige Mächte,
> 20   Und es ergreiffet ihr Schiksaal
> Den der es leidet und zusieht,
> Und ergreifft den Völkern das Herz.

> Denn alles fassen muss
> Ein Halbgott oder
> 25   Ein Mensch, dem Leiden nach,
> Indem er höret, allein, oder selber
> Verwandelt wird, fernahnend die Rosse des Herrn,

> For over the Earth range
> Powerful forces,
> And their destiny seizes
> 20   The one who suffers it and looks on,
> And seizes the heart of the peoples.

> For everything must
> A demigod grasp or
> 25   A human being, in accordance with suffering,
> As he hears, alone, or himself
> Is transformed, intimating from afar the sovereign's steed,

Our third question, concerning the respect in which the poet thinks the demigods, is thereby adequately answered within the framework of this preparatory consideration. Admittedly, this still does not provide us with a concept of destiny, and poetizing neither seeks, nor is able, to provide such a concept. Yet what has been said served the purpose of letting us intimate in general the sphere of beyng with respect to which this word properly has the force of its naming.

These three questions—(1) In what sphere does the thinking of demigods move in general? (2) By what is this thinking compelled? (3) In what respect are the demigods being thought?—we shall now bring together in the fourth question: Which fundamental attunement prevails in this thinking?

d) The Founding and Grounding of Beyng out of the
Fundamental Attunement of Suffering-with
the Suffering of the Demigods

If we inquire in this way concerning the fundamental attunement, then we must now keep to the concept of such attunement that was developed in a preliminary way. Earlier we listed as the most essential points that attunement is (1) a transporting out into beings as a whole, (2) a transporting into the Earth, (3) an opening up of beings, and (4) a grounding of beyng.

We heard that the thinking of demigods leads precisely as such out into the realms of human and divine beyng, realms that are reciprocally related to one another. And it does so in such a way that it seeks to attain these realms in their relatedness as such and not, for instance, simply to settle *between* them as unrelated extremities. The inner trait of such thinking of the demigods accordingly maintains itself precisely in the domain of an *essential transport out into divine and human beyng itself.* What this tells us is that the determinative domain within which this thinking maintains itself coincides with that which opens up and is held open in the attunement of a holy mourning, yet in readied distress.

From our answering of the second question, however, we learned this: The poet is befallen by this thinking and by that which he thinks in it. Being thus befallen brings him back to the Earth of his homeland—that is, transports him into historical Dasein and its Earthly rootedness in a landscape. Being transported in this way does not, however, arise from just some arbitrary appreciation for the homeland and for autochthony that just happens to suggest itself. Rather, this being enjoined back into the Earth of his homeland, and thereby into the poetic founding and freeing of the powers that prevail there, happens precisely in and from out of his being transported out into the beyng of the demigods, and that means: into the middle of divine-human beyng. The unsuspected transition to thinking the demigods is in itself the turning back and turning in toward the homeland and toward that historical people in connection to whom there is a telling of the gods.

Now it might be objected: Certainly in terms of thinking the demigods here and with regard to the fundamental attunement of "Germania" on the other hand, there is each time a correlation in terms of 'content' between the domains to which the poet is transported out and transported back: the gods and the Earth of the homeland in the relatedness of their being. Yet from this—from their correlation with respect to content—it is not by any means demonstrated that their fundamental attunement is the same, since being transported out and back into those realms could surely accomplish itself in a different fundamental attunement each time. The way in which beyng is opened up, and the grounding of beyng, can be configured differently.

Our response to the third question, however, told us: The beyng of the demigods is a suffering of beyng, and suffering can be experienced in turn only by suffering, in a suffering-with, one that, certainly, is as far removed from mere pity, from weakly giving in to a sense of compassion, as is mere pain from that suffering from which passion arises.[8] The poet, therefore, can think and experience in advance the demigods, that is, their beyng, only because and insofar as he suffers along with such beyng as a suffering of beyng, and thus himself stands within the necessity of such suffering. The way in which the beyng of the demigods—the middle of beyngs as a whole—thus opens itself up, is suffering. This great and singular, essential suffering, however, can prevail through a given Dasein only as that attunement in which the fleeing and approaching, overwhelming power of the divine and the readied need of human being open themselves up at the same time, the attunement of a holy mourning in readied distress. This mourning, as we can only now see more clearly, is no longer 'a feeling' among others, but belongs to the suffering of beyng, that fundamental attunement in which in an exceptional, that is, here exclusive sense, destiny—the beyng of the demigods—can be experienced. That the poet, however, stands within the necessity of a suffering-with the suffering of the demigods—this he says explicitly at the decisive point (strophe X, lines 135f.):

> Halbgötter denk' ich jezt
> Und kennen muss ich die Theuern,

> Demigods now I think
> And the dear ones I must know,

The "And" means: This thinking, however unsuspectedly it may come over me precisely now, nevertheless corresponds to my innermost and most far-reaching beyng. It simply cannot, therefore, be otherwise than that this beyng of the demigods is familiar to me. I must be familiar with it, it must already have encountered me, and I must in every case have at my disposal the conditions for determining it. This 'must,' however, also has a second meaning here, and is therefore ambiguous. It not only means: The beyng of the demigods cannot be foreign to me, but at the same time says: I am not permitted to retreat from the task of thinking it. The poet is not permitted to evade the suffering-with that experiences this beyng. He must withstand the need of this suffering. Why?

> Weil oft ihr Leben so
> Die sehnende Brust mir beweget.

> For often does their life
> So move my longing breast.

(Strophe X, lines 137f.)

The poet's own being stretches out toward this beyng of the demigods and is ready for them, and this not just from time to time, but "often." The attunement is not an occasional one; rather, this need and this necessity comprise the constancy of his Dasein. The attunement is a fundamental attunement.

In the poetizing of "The Rhine," however, the fundamental attunement unfolds a unique, determinative power. It specifically determines and attunes the poet to proceed into the task of thinking the middle of being, from which beings as a whole—gods, humans, Earth—are to open themselves up anew: the task of thinking the beyng of the demigods. Earlier (p. 34), we heard Hölderlin's word:

> . . . dichterisch wohnet
> Der Mensch auf dieser Erde.

> . . . poetically
> Humans dwell upon this Earth.

("In beautiful blue . . . ," VI, 25, lines 32f.)

This is to say: The historical Dasein of the human being is, from the ground up, sustained and guided by that beyng which the poet has experienced in advance, shrouded in the word for the first time, and thus placed into the people. We capture this entire occurrence in saying that the poet founds [*stiftet*] beyng. This founding of beyng was accomplished for the Dasein of the Western world in Homer, whom Hölderlin names the "poet of all poets."[1]

Insofar as the being of the demigods is a suffering, the founding of such beyng can only be a suffering with them. Yet insofar as this founding contains that which is unprecedented and provides a measure, such suffering is always necessarily a suffering in advance [*Vor-*

---

1. "On Achilles," Fragment 2, III, 247.

leiden]. Thus has Hölderlin's work established itself, like a leap ahead that has solidified itself within the Dasein of our people: a veiled, poetic grounding of our beyng.

Given the singular uniqueness of our world-historical situation—and in general—we cannot predict or plan how Hölderlin's poetizing as a whole will come to word and to work in the accomplishing of our historical vocation. Only this may be said: The historical Dasein of the Western world is unavoidably and irrevocably one of *knowing*. The stages of knowledge, which are never to be ordered in a sequence of progress, can change. Even where knowledge is subject to restriction, it unfolds knowingly, out of a knowing that merely does not yet know itself. Because our Dasein is a knowing one—which is not to be taken as synonymous with rational calculation—there can, therefore, no longer be a *purely poetic* becoming of Dasein for us; neither can there be one *purely of thinking*, nor one of *action alone* either. What will be demanded of us is not to simply arrange convenient, ongoing compromises between the powers of poetizing, thinking, and acting, but to take seriously their individual uniqueness, as though of concealed mountain peaks, and to experience in this the mystery of their originary belonging together, shaping it in an originary manner into a new, previously unheard of configuration of beyng. Cf. "The Only One" (later version, IV, 234, lines 78ff.):

> . . . Himmlische sind
> Und Lebende beieinander, die ganze Zeit. Ein grosser Mann,
> Im Himmel auch, begehrt zu einem, auf Erden. Immerdar
> Gilt diss, dass, alltag, ganz ist die Welt. Oft aber scheint
> Ein Grosser nicht zusammenzutaugen
> Zu Grossen. Die stehn allzeit, als an einem Abgrund, einer neben
> Dem andern.

> . . . The heavenly and
> The living are by one another, the entire time. A great man,
> In the heavens too, craves to become one, on Earth. Evermore
> This holds, that, ever, whole is the world. Yet often a great man
> Appears not to be worthy of being together
> With greats. They stand forever, as at an abyss, one next
> To the other.

It must now have become clear, through our answering of the four questions posed: The thinking of the demigods is a founding, determined by the fundamental attunement of distress, readied in holy mournfulness, a founding of that beyng from out of which, as the determinative middle, both the being of the gods towering over it and the being of humans that falls short in relation to it become manifest. Here, thinking is not the empty operation of the intellect in making distinctions and connections, setting to work on some pre-given material, but rather is the suffering, anticipatory understanding of that beyng that is experienced as the destiny of the demigods—suffering as a suffering that sustains [*Er-leiden*]—a suffering that accomplishes and creates. Yet the poet is here far removed from a 'metaphysically speculative,' conceptual grasping of the essence of destiny as such. Moreover, the poet says (strophe I, lines 9ff.):

> . . . so
> Vernahm ich ohne Vermuthen
> Ein Schiksaal,

> . . . thus
> I apprehended, unsuspectingly,
> A destiny,

We take two things from this: First, what is at stake is not something like destiny in general, but rather something singular—the destiny of the Rhine, "that most noble of rivers" (line 32), befitting of a "kingly soul" (line 37). This singular destiny is also not conceived as an individual instance of a general essence of destiny; rather, this singularity has its own essential character that is *historical*. It is only a prejudice of the intellect and of its logic to maintain that essence must always be that of the universal and of genus. Second, this unique, singular destiny is apprehended. What this initially conveys is that the thinking of the demigods—as an apprehending, accepting, and receiving—is a *suffering*. In what sense, must now be further clarified by our interpretation.

§13. Strophe I: The Point of Departure for the Telling,
and the Composure through Which It Is
Experienced. The Apprehending of a Destiny

I   Im dunkeln Epheu sass ich, an der Pforte
    Des Waldes, eben, da der goldene Mittag,
    Den Quell besuchend, herunterkam
    Von Treppen des Alpengebirgs,
    Das mir die göttlichgebaute,
    Die Burg der Himmlischen heisst

             Nach alter Meinung, wo aber
             Geheim noch manches entschieden
             Zu Menschen gelanget; so
    10   Vernahm ich ohne Vermuthen
             Ein Schiksaal, denn noch kaum
             War mir im warmen Schatten
             Sich manches beredend, die Seele
             Italia zu geschweift
             Und fernhin an die Küsten Moreas.

      I In ivy dark I sat, at the portal
             Of the woods, just as the golden midday,
             Visiting the source, descended
             On the staircase of the Alps,
             Those I know as the divinely built,
             The fortress of the heavenly
             According to ancient opinion, yet where
             Much decided comes
             In secret to humans still; thus
    10   I apprehended, unsuspectingly,
             A destiny, for scarcely yet
             In the warmth of the shade
             Pondering much, had my soul
             To Italy roamed
             And afar to the coasts of Morea.

According to our division of the hymn into five sections, the first
strophe taken by itself constitutes the first section. In clarifying the
fundamental attunement and fundamental will of this poetizing, we
have already referred to this strophe on a number of occasions. It transposes us to the threshold of the Earth of the homeland, tells of how the
meditative longing of the poet is torn around, torn out of its roaming
off into what has been and toward the apprehending of a destiny. It is
in the lucidity of this new desire to know and the necessity of knowing that the poet's apprehending is first opened up to what is happening over in the mountains of the Alps in view of the homeland—and
now affecting the homeland itself. So it is not as though, for instance,
a so-called lived experience of nature—the Alps, the source of the
river Rhine—motivates the poet to poetically 'exploit' these conditions and occurrences, using them as an image for some other occurrence. And how could that be the case? Unless this occurrence were
already known in advance, and were guiding and binding for expe-

riencing the spirit of the river belonging to the waters of the homeland!

Taken as a whole, the content and the task in the first strophe—the point of departure for the telling, and the composure through which it is experienced—is clear. Our response to the preliminary questions has already clarified the main content of strophe I. Yet we must still take note of a few 'details' that ultimately remain quite decisive poetically and that first accord this strophe, in its composition, its distinctive significance at the beginning.

a) Dionysos as Witness of Divine and Human Beyng

For one thing, our attention is immediately drawn to the first line of the first strophe, and thereby of the entire poem: "In ivy dark I sat." Why ivy? Surely, it is quite certain that this has no special relation to the landscape in question or to the homeland of the poet. Ivy—the dark, entangled thrust of its stems, the green of its leaves, constantly choking life and yet cool and refreshing—is the favorite plant of Greek peasants. And still today the peasant farmers in the Black Forest have in their cabins the ever-fresh shoots of ivy that convey life and growth, and they take silent pleasure in the force of life when outside nature is encased in snow and ice and long nights.

"Ivy" is the chosen favorite of Dionysos, that demigod whom Hölderlin likes to name the "wine god."[1] "Ivy" in Greek is κισσός; Dionysos is called ὁ κισσοφόρος (Pindar: Second Olympian Ode, line 31[2]), even directly invoked as κισσός. In the poetic work "Bread and Wine," eighth and ninth strophes, lines 139–148 (IV, 125), Hölderlin says that the God has chosen the crown of ivy, and at the same time he also provides here an essential determination of that beyng that is named by the name Dionysos:

> Darum denken wir auch dabei der Himmlischen, die sonst
> 140   Da gewesen und die kehren in richtiger Zeit,
> Darum singen sie auch mit Ernst die Sänger den Weingott
> Und nicht eitel erdacht tönet dem Alten das Lob.

> 9

> Ja! sie sagen mit Recht, er söhne den Tag mit der Nacht aus,
> Führe des Himmels Gestirn ewig hinunter, hinauf,
> Allzeit froh, wie das Laub der immergrünenden Fichte,
> Das er liebt, und der Kranz, den er von Epheu gewählt,

---

1. "The Rhine," IV, 177, line 145; "Bread and Wine," IV, 124f., lines 123 and 141.
2. *Pindari carmina cum fragmentis selectis.* Ed. Otto Schroeder. Leipzig, 1908, 13.

Weil er bleibet und selbst die Spur der entflohenen Götter
Götterlosen hinab unter das Finstere bringt.

Wherefore we give thought to the heavenly too, who once
140   Were there and at the right time return,
Wherefore too the singers sing earnestly the wine god
And devoid of pretense, praise for the ancient one rings out.

9

Yes! rightly so they say, he reconciles day with night,
Eternally guides the heaven's star downward, upward,
Ever cheerful, like the foliage of the ever-verdant spruce,
That he loves, and the crown that he chose to make of ivy,
Because it endures, and he himself brings the trace of the gods
      who have fled
Down to the godless amid the gloom.

Dionysos brings the trace of the flown gods down to the godless. To
bring the trace—that passing on the beckonings of the gods to human beings, that being in the middle between the beyng of humans
and of gods. Hölderlin comprehends the essence and calling of the
poet starting from this being in the middle—beyng in the manner of
the demigods. It points to a deep connection between the beyng of
the demigods (destiny) and the calling of the poet that we find in the
penultimate strophe of that poem from which we earlier learned the
task of the poet, "As when on feast day . . ." (IV, 153, final strophe;
see p. 296), the following decisive reference to Dionysos (IV, 152f.,
lines 43–55):

Des gemeinsamen Geistes Gedanken sind
Still endend in der Seele des Dichters.

Dass schnellbetroffen sie, Unendlichem
Bekannt seit langer Zeit, von Erinnerung
Erbebt, und ihr, von heilgem Stral entzündet,
Die Frucht in Liebe geboren, der Götter und Menschen Werk
Der Gesang, damit er von beiden zeuge, glükt.
50   So fiel, wie Dichter sagen, da sie sichtbar
Den Gott zu sehen begehrte, sein Bliz auf Semeles Haus
Und die göttlichgetroffne gebahr,
Die Frucht des Gewitters, den heiligen Bacchus.

Und daher trinken himmlisches Feuer jezt
Die Erdensöhne ohne Gefahr.

Thoughts of communal spirit are
Quietly ending in the poet's soul.

That swiftly struck, long since
Familiar to the infinite, it quivers
With recollection, and, kindled by the holy ray,
Its fruit born in love, the work of gods and humans,
Its song, bearing witness to both, succeeds.
50   And thus, as poets tell, since she
Desired to see visible the God, his lightning fell on Semele's
    house
And she, by divinity struck, gave birth,
The fruit of the thunderstorm, to holy Bacchus.

And now therefore the sons of the Earth
Without danger drink heavenly fire.

Dionysos is the son of a mortal woman, Semele, one of the four daughters of Cadmos, king of Thebes. His mother was consumed by the lightning flash of father Zeus before she gave birth to her son, and the father protected him from the searing flames with cooling vines of ivy. Thus engendered by the God in a mortal woman, Dionysos bears witness to the beyng of both: he *is* this beyng in a primordial unity. Dionysos is not just one demigod among others, but the distinctive one. He is the Yes that belongs to life at its wildest, inexhaustible in its creative urge, and he is the No that belongs to the most terrifying death and annihilation. He is the bliss of magical enchantment and the horror of a crazed terror. He is the one in being the other; that is, in being, he at the same time is not and in not being, he is. Being, however, for the Greeks means 'presence'—παρουσία. In presencing, this demigod is absent, and in absencing he is present. The symbol of the one who is absent in presencing and present in absencing is the mask. The mask is the distinctive symbol of Dionysos—that is, understood metaphysically in a Greek way: the originary relatedness to one another of being and non-being (presence and absence). Conversely, precisely this symbol, as Dionysos, is decisive evidence for the truth of our interpretation of the Greek experience of being.

The myth and cult of Dionysos has recently been portrayed by Walter F. Otto in his fine and valuable book *Dionysos* (1933). Otto has also incorporated into his book—although without touching upon the decisive metaphysical connections—the preceding interpretation of Dionysos as the being of the mask, an interpretation that I suggested to him on the occasion of his lecture on Dionysos that he presented here a few years ago (pp. 85ff.³). See also the author's more comprehensive work, *The Gods of Greece*.⁴

Dionysos: the demigod pure and simple—that beyng that, as such, is essentially non-being, and vice-versa; this God who is named the bearer of ivy. "In ivy dark I sat," begins the poetic work in which the beyng of the demigods is to be thought and founded. It becomes clear that this talk of "ivy" here is no accident: The thinking and telling of the poet is, as it were, entwined and interwoven through and through with the beyng of Dionysos as the demigod.

Yet the importance of pondering the start of this poem, its first line, goes still further. The poem ends with the lines:

. . . und wiederkehrt
Uralte Verwirrung.

. . . and there returns
Primordial confusion.

This is the beyng of night, the reign of confusion, sinister violence, and fury—the kingdom of Dionysos and his priests, of whom, as we know (cf. p. 129f.), Hölderlin says at the end of strophe VII of "Bread and Wine" (IV, 124, lines 123f.):

Aber sie [die Dichter] sind, sagst du, wie des Weingotts heilige Priester,
Welche von Lande zu Land zogen in heiliger Nacht.

Yet they [the poets] are, you say, like the wine god's holy priests,
Who journeyed from land to land in holy night.

The first line and the last lines thus enclose the entire poetic work and raise its telling into the fundamental realm of that beyng named by the name Dionysos/Dionysian. We know that the last Western interpretation of beyng, that of Nietzsche, one that simultaneously prepares what is to come, also names Dionysos.

b) The Nearness of the Alpine Range as Nearness of the Origin

The further point that must be heeded in the first strophe of our poem concerns the depiction of the Alpine range. We may not approach it as a scenic 'panorama' that can be seen from the shore of Lake Constance. The Alpine range stands in the neighborhood of the homeland; it is the "hearth of the house," the determining middle of the Earth

---

3. Third edition, Frankfurt 1960, 80ff.
4. *Die Götter Griechenlands,* first edition, 1929; second, unaltered edition, 1934.

of the homeland, the locale of origin—of that most noble of German rivers. "Alpine range"—its nearness is the nearness of the origin, of that essential dimension of beyng to which the poet wants to remain bound. Cf. the beginning of "The Journey" (IV, 167):

> Glükseelig Suevien, meine Mutter,
> Auch du, der glänzenderen, der Schwester
> Lombarda drüben gleich,
> Von hundert Bächen durchflossen!
> Und Bäume genug, weissblühend und röthlich,
> Und dunklere, wild, tiefgrünenden Laubs voll,
> Und Alpengebirg der Schweiz auch überschattet,
> Benachbartes dich; denn nah dem Heerde des Hausses
> Wohnst du, und hörst, wie drinnen
> 10   Aus silbernen Opferschaalen
> Der Quell rauscht, ausgeschüttet
> Von reinen Händen, wenn berührt
>
> Von warmen Stralen
> Krystallenes Eis und umgestürzt
> Vom leichtanregenden Lichte
> Der schneeige Gipfel übergiesst die Erde
> Mit reinestem Wasser. Darum ist
> Dir angeboren die Treue. Schwer verlässt
> Was nahe dem Ursprung wohnet, den Ort.
> 20   Und deine Kinder, die Städte,
> Am weithindämmernden See,
> An Nekars Weiden, am Rheine,
> Sie alle meinen, es wäre
> Sonst nirgend besser zu wohnen.

> Blissful Suevia, my mother,
> You too, like the more sparkling, sister
> Lombarda over there,
> By a hundred streams traversed!
> And trees aplenty, blossoming white and reddish,
> And darker ones, wild, full of deeply verdant foliage,
> And the Alpine range of Switzerland casts its shadows too
> Over you, neighboring one; for near the hearth of the house
> You dwell, and hear, how within
> 10   From silver sacrificial vessels
> The source rushes, splashed out
> By pure hands, when touched

By warm rays
Crystalline ice and overturned
By gently stimulating light
The snowy peak overflows the Earth
With purest water. Whence
Your inborn fidelity. Reluctantly that which
Dwells near the origin abandons the locale.
20   And your children, the towns,
By the distant shimmering lake,
By Neckar's pastures, by the Rhine,
They all say there could be
No better dwelling place.

"Reluctantly that which / Dwells near the origin abandons the locale."
(lines 18f.). This truth is, at the same time, the inner bridge that draws
the poem "The Journey" into the circle of poems we are concerned
with. This word contains an essential fulfillment of that thought of
origin that we shall encounter in what follows. (Cf. "The Rhine," line
46: "Enigma is that which has purely sprung forth.") The originary
belonging is the ground for a fidelity to beyng. Fidelity to beyng is the
presupposition for all comportment that unfolds and is thus and thus.
Conversely, whoever readily abandons the locale demonstrates that he
has no origin and is just present at hand like other things.

The Alpine range is here not meant to serve as an illustrative image
or embellishment, but rather is a realm that belongs to the homeland.
At the same time, however, it is conceived as "fortress of the heavenly"
("The Rhine," line 6). With this, the poet points in advance toward
that beyng that is to be told of in the poetic work: first, the beyng of
the gods—their fortified enclosure and self-sufficiency; second, we
are told of the "staircase of the Alps" (line 4). This ascending and descending "on a staircase" occurs within the realm of that beyng whose
measure the demigods fathom and inhabit (cf. "The Only One," IV,
188, lines 68f.: "And on staircases / Descends the heavenly one"), that
beyng that in itself is a "trace,"[5] a hint left behind concerning the direction of the path and of being within the entire contexture of beings.

Beyng within the 'realms' of the gods, demigods, and humans
can admittedly never be attained or regarded by perceiving events
or qualities that can be encountered here or there, but only ever insofar as such beyng springs from decision and preserves decidedness
within it; insofar as it is a passage through a need and in every instance the withstanding of a struggle. The origin that secretly preserves such beyng in safekeeping is the 'divinely built fortress'—"yet

---

5. "Bread and Wine," IV, 125, line 147.

where / Much decided comes / In secret to humans still" ("The Rhine," lines 7ff.), not as decided in the sense that humans could simply receive it without decision and employ it in their Dasein, but something decided that can in turn only ever be comprehended in each case in a decisive taking up of beyng with regard to its truth. Thus, the poem "Patmos" tells of the disciples of the Lord, after the Lord has taken leave of them (IV, 193, lines 91ff.):

> Doch trauerten sie, da nun
> Es Abend worden, erstaunt,
> Denn Grossentschiedenes hatten in der Seele
> Die Männer,

> Yet they were mournful, now that
> Evening had come, astonished,
> For the men had something great and decided
> Within their souls,

Only if we heed all of this may we succeed in grasping in its fullness the essential content of the first strophe in its pointing ahead, and thus of preparing our comprehension for the transition into what is to follow.

§14. Strophes II and III: The River Rhine as Destiny. Hearing Its Origin and Assuming Its Vocation

The second section that we marked out was strophes II through IX. Our access to the whole poetic work depends on an understanding of this section, as indeed does our elucidation of the major section that follows, strophes X through XIII and its reciprocal relationship to strophes II through IX, and thereby our elucidation of its position within the poem as a whole.

We wish to remain clear from the beginning, however, about the fact that our interpretation, in its telling, has the task of following and accompanying a poetic telling in which the beyng of the demigods is to be shaped: a beyng that in itself, as a mediating middle, is directed in a twofold manner, toward gods and humans; a beyng that accordingly, despite its own essential uniqueness, is precisely discordant. This continually gives rise to obstacles and impediments to our understanding for our habitual, everyday thinking, starting from which one might initially seek to understand the poetic work.

The first thing that must strike us is that we do not encounter a self-contained, unfolding presentation of an image of the river and its course. Even strophe II, the beginning of strophe III, strophe V, and strophe VI, which are specifically concerned with and depict the river Rhine, are not descriptive. In general, it presents difficulties and in the end is thoroughly mistaken if we seek to introduce a distinction between strophes that are descriptive and those that are explanatory. For even the strophes that forgo supplying any image relating to the river (the second part of strophe III and strophes VII, VIII, and IX) are not some kind of philosophical elaboration of what has been told by way of images in the preceding strophes. Rather, what we have in each case is an ongoing telling or, better, a telling that goes back and forth, and that in itself presents the fact that what is to be told is, in its essence, manifold.

a) On the Distinction between a Poetic Understanding of Nature and the Scientific Representation of Nature

We know that the rivers are not simply images of something, but are intended to be taken for themselves, and together with them the Earth of the homeland. Yet the Earth is not a domain of land, water, plants, animals, and air belonging to our planet, a domain that is somehow circumscribed in the manner of the field of objects for the natural sciences extending from geology to astrophysics—it is not at all 'nature' in the modern sense. For precisely the metaphysical sense of nature, *natura,* φύσις in the primordial naming force of the word—a naming force pertaining to the commencement—is already an essential interpretation of being that does not have the slightest thing to do with natural science. Primordial nature, disclosed and brought to word by the Greeks, later came to be *denatured* by way of two alien powers: on the one hand, by Christendom, through which nature was first demoted to something 'created,' and at the same time brought into a relationship with a supra-nature (the realm of grace); and then by modern science, which dissolved nature into domains of power belonging to the mathematical ordering of world commerce, industrialization, and technology, which in a special sense is machine technology. Events that in turn came to impact our view of science in general, and not only the natural sciences, and that led to what we have today: science as the organized business of procuring and transmitting knowledge. Whether this business is kept in operation in the stance taken by so-called liberal objectivity, or in one that merely rejects that stance, alters nothing with regard to the shape of contemporary science as such. This purportedly new science is new only by virtue of the fact that it does not know how antiquated it is. It has nothing whatsoever to do with the inner truth of natural science.

If, therefore, we today set for ourselves the task of bringing about a transformation 'of science' as a whole, then we must first come to know one thing: Science as a whole can never be transformed through science, and still less through measures that are concerned merely with altering the business of its teachings, but only through another metaphysics—that is, a new fundamental experience of beyng. Such an experience entails, first, a transformation in the essence of truth; and second, a transformation in the essence of labor. This fundamental experience will have to be more original than that of the Greeks, which expresses itself in the concept and word φύσις.

Whenever we hear talk of the river and of waters here, we must therefore set aside our contemporary representation of nature, insofar as we still have one at all. Earth and homeland are meant historically. The river is historical. For this reason, it is not, for instance, a mere sensuous image borrowed from nature that symbolizes the beyng of the demigods, but the reverse: The poetic thinking of such beyng first of all creates, in an anticipatory manner, the condition for experiencing river and homeland in what they are—that is, historically. The poet, therefore, not merely can, but must tell alternately of the river and of destiny. In so doing, he means by river not a visual image, and by destiny not an accompanying abstract concept; he means one and the same thing by both. The river Rhine *is* a destiny, and destiny comes to be only in the history of this river. Every attempt to separate out image and concept here necessarily misses the poetic truth.

Our interpretation will now follow the sequence of strophes. The last strophe of this section (IX) will then of its own accord compel us to provide a retrospective summary.

b) Strophe II: Hearing the Origin

II   Jezt aber, drinn im Gebirg,
      Tief unter den silbernen Gipfeln,
      Und unter fröhlichem Grün,
      Wo die Wälder schauernd zu ihm
20   Und der Felsen Häupter übereinander
      Hinabschaun, taglang, dort
      Im kältesten Abgrund hört'
      Ich um Erlösung jammern
      Den Jüngling, es hörten ihn, wie er tobt',
      Und die Mutter Erd' anklagt'
      Und den Donnerer, der ihn gezeuget,
      Erbarmend die Eltern, doch
      Die Sterblichen flohn von dem Ort,
      Denn furchtbar war, da lichtlos er
30   In den Fesseln sich wälzte,
      Das Rasen des Halbgotts.

    II Now however, within the mountains,
        Deep beneath the silver peaks
        And below the cheerful green,
        Where to him the teeming woods,
20   And the summits of the rocks
        Look down, all day long, there
        In the coldest abyss I heard
        Him pining for deliverance
        The youngster, he was heard, as he raged,
        And accursed the Mother Earth,
        And the Thunderer who had produced him,
        With pity by his parents, yet
        Mortals had fled the locale,
        For frightful, since without light he
30   In his fetters tossed, was
        The fury of the demigod.

According to strophe I, the poet is called back unsuspectingly from
losing himself in what has been and the gods that come to presence
there. At the threshold between his unfolding turning away from
such remoteness and the barely awakening question, Whereto now?,
there occurs a profound unsettling of his Dasein, an unsettling that
is historical in a metaphysical sense. With this, that which remained
unfulfilled and indeterminate within his concealed seeking comes
to power and makes its claim. An expansive looking around oneself
arises, a surveying that is ready for itself, and that means, for its vocation. Dasein opens itself to its sought-after vocation, to that beyng re-
served for it, which must be encountered originarily in the word and
is therefore apprehended in a hearing. See lines 16ff.:

Jezt aber . . . dort
Im kältesten Abgrund hört'
Ich um Erlösung jammern
Den Jüngling,

Now however . . . there
In the coldest abyss I heard
Him pining for deliverance
The youngster,

α) Customary Ways of Hearing. The Gods' Hearing
with Pity and Mortals' Not Wanting to Hear

What kind of a hearing is that? Is it, for instance, a purely receptive
taking note of something accessible through our ears? For example,

we hear bells ringing because the sound penetrates our ear. Or is it a hearing in the sense of the kind of hearing that lets what is audible pass by more or less indifferently, and that itself ceases to hear once what is audible has passed? Or is this hearing of the poet's the kind of listening out for something, a listening out that belongs to curiosity, a hearing that would seek to apprehend by stealth what has hitherto gone unheard and remains unheard of, whatever is surprising and unfamiliar to others? Or is this hearing much more the kind of hearing that immerses itself in what is heard, and, fulfilled and captivated by it, lets itself be lulled into losing itself therein? Neither these nor other customary ways of hearing are meant here. Yet which hearing, then?

" . . . I heard / Him pining for deliverance / The [imprisoned] youngster," (lines 22ff.) This indeed tells us *what* is heard, yet not how, not the *kind* of hearing. Yet why are we becoming fixated on determining more precisely the kind of hearing? Is it not quite sufficient that we learn *what* the poet hears? Certainly, we could let things go at ascertaining what is heard if we were dealing here with points communicated by some arbitrary ear-witness who happened to hear some arbitrary incident. Here, however, we are dealing with a hearing that belongs to the poet. In this poetic work, moreover, in which the poet tells of his hearing, he is not even the only one hearing: " . . . he was heard . . . / With pity by his parents" (lines 24ff.) The parents of the youngster hear his accursing and raging, and they hear him "with pity." The hearing of these hearers is thereby even directly determined. Pity is, at any rate, a kind of partaking—indeed, a superior partaking. A poetic hearing, by contrast, would merely be a listening to his pining without partaking in it, a listening that would not be equal to it. Those hearing—the poet on the one hand and the parents on the other—in any case hear 'the same.' No other hearers are named. There are "the mortals," indeed (line 28), but they are said precisely to have "fled." Yet is this 'fleeing' not also a hearing? Indeed, it is even a distinctive kind of hearing: namely, a not wanting to hear and not being able to hear. There are thus three kinds of hearer: the gods, the mortals, and the poet. The kind of hearing belonging to the gods and that belonging to mortals are determinate; that belonging to the poet is indeterminate or, more precisely, still concealed from us.

β) The Poet's Hearing That Stands Firm (Suffering) as
Apprehending the Originary Origin in Its Springing Forth

Given all that has been said thus far concerning the poet and concerning gods and humans, may we suspect that the poet, with his own kind of hearing, stands between the gods and humans, at the locale of the demigods? If this is the case, however, then we cannot indeed figure out what kind of hearing this poetic hearing is in terms of the hearing of the gods and that of humans—as an in-between kind of hearing, as it were. Rather, the poet's hearing must let itself be determined in its own terms, and in such a way that starting from there we can first determine how gods and mortals hear in this context. Manifestly, the kind of hearing belonging to the poet must come to light through the poetizing as a whole. Nevertheless, our interpretation must already seek to indicate this kind of hearing in advance so that we are in a position to accompany the poet in his hearing in the right manner, for hearing and hearing are not the same thing. Many people hear a lot, and listen around everywhere, and eke out their existence [*Dasein*] in terms of what they hear said, yet without ever bringing themselves to hear anything in the process; for the human being must be graced by the ability to hear, or at least must be brought up so as to be able to hear.

How may we now already determine more precisely the kind of poetic hearing in question? A makeshift measure suggests itself. Manifestly, the hearing that belongs to the gods, to mortals, and to the poet is directed toward the pining, accursing, and raging of the youngster—that is, of the river; toward the frightful tossing, the fury of the demigod, deprived of light (end of the second strophe). The poetic hearing can be neither that of the gods, nor that of human beings, both of which are opposed to one another in the extreme. The gods hear "with pity" (line 27), but the mortals flee, turn away, leave the demigod in the lurch, as it were. The poet's hearing is neither pitying nor flight. Yet this determines his hearing in a merely negative way, by saying what it is not. If we failed to have some intimation of the positive nature of this hearing, from out of the poetizing as a whole, then we would never attain our goal by way of this merely negative characterization. What we shall now indicate positively does not, therefore, derive from our figuring out, by way of negation, some kind of hearing that lies in between hearing with pity and a hearing that takes flight (not hearing). Rather, it comes from an anticipatory view of the entire, authentic truth of the poetizing. We shall, however, intentionally retain the form of a negative delimitation.

The gods hear "with pity" (line 27); this we call an *acquiescent hearing* [*Erhören*]. Mortals hear as not being able to hear; their hearing is a *failure to hear* [*Überhören*] and an unwillingness to hear. Acquiescent hearing consists in giving a place to that to which it grants a hearing; that is, the one raging in his fetters is released. The gods release the origin that is initially fettered within itself and, with this, the origin as such is left to itself. The failure to hear, however, turns away from the fettered origin and thus from the origin in general. Mortals flee before the origin, want to forget it, avoid its frightfulness, and keep only to that which *has sprung forth*, without giving thought to this having sprung forth as such. If they do give thought to what has sprung forth, then they do so in such a way that they explain the origin in terms of that which has sprung forth from it. Success and usefulness becomes the measure of the origin. The origin is worth only the same—that is, fundamentally less and less—as whatever emerges from it here. Such remains the sole acquaintance of everyday thinking with the origin.

This acquiescent hearing from the side of the gods and this failure to hear from the side of mortals are two fundamentally different ways in which the origin is heard. Yet what they have in common is that both leave the origin to itself, albeit in different ways: The one sets it free; the other forgets it and pushes it away. Both, in their own way, let the origin go. The gods assist it in springing forth. Mortals 'let it go'—that is, give it up, fail to turn toward it, and turn away.

The poet, however, since he is not a god, cannot set free the origin; his hearing cannot be an acquiescent hearing. Yet the poet, since he is also no mere human being, in the sense of an everyday human being, also cannot hear in the manner of mortals; that is, he cannot *want to fail to hear* the origin. His hearing stands firm before the frightfulness of the fettered origin. Such hearing that stands firm is suffering. Suffering, however, is the being of the demigod. Cf. Fragment 14, lines 23ff. (IV, 248):

Denn alles fassen muss
Ein Halbgott oder
Ein Mensch, dem Leiden nach,
Indem er höret, allein,

For everything must
A demigod grasp or
A human, in accordance with suffering,
In that he hears, alone,

In this hearing that stands firm as suffering, there thus also occurs that apprehending that alone remains appropriate to that which is to be apprehended—"Demigods now I think" (line 135)—destiny as suffering. The hearing of the origin—a hearing that stands firm—is, therefore, a hearing of the origin that does not yet spring forth, of the origin that is fettered precisely in its readiness to spring forth, and thus remains entirely with itself as an origin: the originary origin. This the poet hears. His hearing as standing firm is therefore an originary apprehending of what the origin then is as such. It is this hearing that stands firm that first apprehends the fact that an originary being [*Sein*] prevails here. The hearing that stands firm itself grants a hearing to the fettered origin as such. The hearing that stands firm in this way thus 'sets' out for the first time what is really happening there: what in the first instance 'is.' This hearing that sets out and sets forth brings for the first time what is heard into the sounding of the word. It founds, as does telling, and this because telling and hearing essentially belong together and sustain the possibility of a dialogue, of that dialogue that we know constitutes the fundamental trait of our Dasein (cf. p. 62ff.).

The hearing that stands firm is an abiding on the part of our inner ear. An abiding with what? With the origin, with its springing forth as such—that is, with what and how it authentically *is*. The hearing that stands firm does not hear this or that as a particular thing, but hears, rather, that which authentically has substance in what is to be heard and comprises its substance [*Bestand*]. This is what its hearing discerns in advance, over and beyond everything contingent. As this hearing that discerns in advance, the hearing that stands firm is a *po-etizing* hearing. What the poet hears, and the way in which he hears in this hearing, first unfolds itself as beyng and brings itself to word in such standing firm, to the word that henceforth stands within the people. This word shelters within it the truth concerning the origi-nary origin. Yet just as the origin that has merely sprung forth is not the origin, neither is the merely fettered origin. Rather, the entire es-sence of the origin is the fettered origin in its springing forth. Yet the springing forth itself first comes to be what it is as the river runs its entire course; it is not limited to the beginning of its course. The en-tire course of the river itself belongs to the origin. The origin is fully apprehended only as the fettered origin in its springing forth as hav-ing sprung forth.

It is this entirety that the poet hears. If, in their acquiescent hear-ing, the gods release the origin in letting it go, then the poet's hear-ing as standing firm is, by contrast, a hearing that partakes in and lets resonate the leap [*Sprung*], a hearing in which the entire being of the river is experienced in an originary manner. As standing firm, how-ever, it is at the same time that hearing and telling that will one day become uncircumventable for those human beings who initially do not want to hear, and that in the end will compel them to listen to it.

With this, it should have become sufficiently clear in what manner the poet hears. Yet together with this, we have also arrived at some-thing essential regarding *what* the poet apprehends. From strophe I, we know this: His thinking and telling is the 'apprehending of a destiny'—destiny as the beyng of the demigods. Now it has become clear that what is decisive for an apprehending that understands such beyng is a *hearing knowing of the originary origin in its springing forth.* The question concerning the essence of the destiny is essentially, if not exclusively, a question concerning the essence of the origin as such. No wonder that we are repeatedly told of the origin in the course of the poetizing. Admittedly (strophe IV, lines 46f.):

> Ein Räthsel ist Reinentsprungenes. Auch
> Der Gesang kaum darf es enthüllen.

> Enigma is that which has purely sprung forth. Even
> The song may scarcely unveil it.

Yet it is the song—the poetizing—that indeed comes closest to doing so. It is more a telling that veils than one that unveils, and is thus anything but a progressive narrative and description. The form of the telling in this poetizing—the inner construction of the sequence of strophes—must count as one of the greatest creative accomplishments of the poet. This telling can be accompanied only through the stance of an originary hearing, and vice-versa.

Strophe II tells: The parents heard him, the raging demigod, with pity, that is, they let him go. He now 'is' sprung forth. What the poet heard 'was' the pining of the as-yet fettered river, of the origin before its leap, yet pressing forward in its readiness to leap.

c) Strophe III: Origin, Self-Will, Destiny.
Assuming One's Vocation

III Die Stimme wars des edelsten der Ströme,
         Des freigeborenen Rheins,
         Und anderes hoffte der, als droben von den Brüdern,
         Dem Tessin und dem Rhodanus
         Er schied und wandern wollt', und ungeduldig ihn
         Nach Asia trieb die königliche Seele.
         Doch unverständig ist
         Das Wünschen vor dem Schiksaal.
40   Die Blindesten aber
         Sind Göttersöhne. Denn es kennet der Mensch
         Sein Haus und dem Thier ward, wo
         Es bauen solle, doch jenen ist
         Der Fehl, dass sie nicht wissen wohin
         In die unerfahrne Seele gegeben.

III   The voice it was of that most noble of rivers,
       The freely born Rhine,
       He who hoped for something else, as up there from his brothers,
       The Tessin and the Rhodanus,
       He departed and wished to wander, and impatiently
       To Asia he was driven by that kingly soul.
       Yet uncomprehending is
       Wishing in the face of destiny.
40   The blindest however
       Are sons of gods. For well the human knows
       His house and to the animal came, where
       It should build, yet to those ones
       The lack, that they know not whereto
       Is given their untraveled soul.

Now that the river has sprung forth, its entire flowing also already lies present before our gaze. Seen from the perspective of this present, the origin appears as something past. Accordingly, the past tense is used to speak of it: The voice it "was" (line 32); he who "hoped" (line 34); he "departed" (line 36); he "was driven" by his soul (line 37).

α) The Appropriation of Its Authentic Beyng in the Turning of the River's Direction

The originary thrust, previously fettered and now unfettered, is surveyed with regard to the direction it assumes when set loose. The shape that the river's direction takes now manifests something decisive. The direction, in its commencement pointing toward the East, suddenly breaks off at the present-day locale of Chur and proceeds toward the German land in the North. This break is a sudden turning away from what, from the very origin, has stood in the thrust of the river's will: toward the East. Asia, Asia Minor, Ionia, Greece: It was the entire ancient world from which its soul—its restless, magnificent and superior soul, thinking in the direction of being as a whole; that is, its kingly soul—hoped for fulfillment. This was something other than what comes to be assigned him through this turning in direction. That which, from the very origin, stands in his originary will here is not the East as East, but as that beyng that the river in its origin alone had to regard as appropriate to its own kingly character, as that which alone could grant him the fulfillment of his essence. Moreover, this 'other,' toward which the impatiently wandering one was driven, was not even foreign, for according to the poet's opinion, the German race had already migrated there in ancient times. Cf. "The Journey," strophe III (IV, 167f.):

Ich aber will dem Kaukasos zu!
Denn sagen hört ich
Noch heut in den Lüften:
Frei sei'n, wie Schwalben, die Dichter.
Auch hat mir ohnediss
30   In jüngeren Tagen Eines vertraut,
Es seien vor alter Zeit
Die Eltern einst, das deutsche Geschlecht,
Still fortgezogen von Wellen der Donau,
Dort mit der Sonne Kindern
Am Sommertage, da diese
Sich Schatten suchten zusammen
Am schwarzen Meere gekommen;
Und nicht umsonst sei diss
Das gastfreundliche genennet.

I, however, am bound for the Caucasus!
For I heard it said
Just today in the breezes:
Free, like swallows, are the poets.
And someone, moreover,
30   In earlier days confided to me
That back in ancient times
Our parents, the German race,
Carried off silently on waves of the Donau,
Arrived there with children of the sun
On a summer's day, when they
Sought shade together
Down by the Black Sea;
And not for nothing is this one
Named the hospitable one.

The Greeks themselves: a people of related lineage, the same intrinsic primal drive to the origin, to where the originary is driven, to the same beyng. The Greeks: long since the people who established measure and rank, without whom Western history cannot be thought, yet to whom our contemporary historical Dasein can no more return than can the river return into its origin. This originary direction of the river itself becomes broken off. Yet the break does not become a shattering for that which has sprung forth. The break would have to become a shattering if that which had sprung forth merely became set in its initial direction and thereafter let itself be thrust into a pure recalcitrance of the will. Such recalcitrance of the will would be its becoming fixated into mere wishing, which not only remains futile, but which above all is deceptive with regard to appropriating one's authentic beyng.

> Doch unverständig ist
> Das Wünschen vor dem Schiksaal.

> Yet uncomprehending is
> Wishing in the face of destiny.

(Lines 38f.)

That is to say: Merely persisting in wishing, that is, in a striving devoid of all actualization, or in one that does not itself engage in such actualization, is incapable of assuming destiny as such and altogether fails to understand what has come over it there. Such wishing indeed seems in fact to retain our originary vocation, but that is mere semblance. Such wishing is precisely that turning away from destiny that remains unequal to it. It is that small-minded obstinacy, the illusion of true steadfastness, that keeps our destiny at bay. For such destiny to be taken up as beyng, and for our very being to be transformed thereby into suffering, neither wishing that remains set on a particular wish, nor merely restricting ourselves by way of renunciation to a limited, calculative action, is sufficient.

β) The Blindness of the Demigods as Excess of Vocation

> Die Blindesten aber
> Sind Göttersöhne.

> The blindest however
> Are sons of gods.

(Lines 40f.)

Initially one might be inclined to understand this word in terms of what has preceded it: namely, that they are the most uncomprehending in the face of destiny and therefore remain the most set in mere wishing, and thus remain most thoroughly excluded from the possibility of assuming a destiny as the fundamental trait of their beyng—of being in a destinal manner. Yet the opposite is the case. Precisely the Rhine—this demigod—is a destiny. "The blindest however / Are sons of gods" cannot, therefore, mean that they are entirely uncomprehending—those who, accordingly, become entirely and exclusively caught up in themselves in the manner of an empty wishing. Precisely the sons of gods do not have this way of being. This in no way excludes the possibility, however, that they assert their origin in a uniquely decided manner. Line 40, "The blindest however . . . ," therefore necessarily begins a new and indeed disconcerting thought, one that, rather than continuing on from and applying what has preceded it, sets itself over against what has preceded by the word "however," and does so in the following sense: The blindest are admittedly, however, sons of gods. Yet this with the still unexpressed, transitional thought in the background: yet nonetheless are no mere wishers. This new thought is connected with the following line, line 41:

> . . . Denn es kennet der Mensch
> Sein Haus und dem Thier ward . . .

> . . . For well the human knows
> His house and to the animal came . . .

Human beings' knowing their way about and the assuredness with which animals behave, each within their own sphere, turn out to be the kind of beyng that can have no destiny. From this it becomes clear: The thought, "The blindest however / Are sons of gods," does not mean to say: therefore they are least of all in a position to assume their destiny as such, but the reverse. The blindest, "however," are precisely those for whom destiny becomes their beyng. Such excess of blindness is not a shortcoming, but the superiority that consists in a richness of vocation. The higher the origin, the less does keeping to the origin devolve into the mere wretchedness of an arbitrary obstinacy and mere wishing that never gets beyond incomprehension. The higher the origin, the more originary—and the more far-reaching and comprehensive—must be our self-will [*Eigenwille*]. However, the latter alone can offer resistance and, in the recalcitrance of its will, create the realm for a collision and thus the sphere of a danger and, in so doing, the precondition for taking up into its counter-willing whatever runs up against it. Which is to say, it alone can take on the suffering of a beyng and thus in each case fit itself into a destinal sending and be a destiny.

Only that which is in itself originarily great has destiny. It is indeed broken by the turn that the direction of its path takes, but not destroyed. In this break and divergence in its direction, it assumes its vocation and is alone able to assume it and to endure it by virtue of its origin. For if the origin were not to constantly spring forth as the origin that it is, then the river that has diverged from its initial course would be unable to flow and to be a river.

The demigods know not whereto. This not knowing whereto has nothing in common with mere wishing, for such wishing indeed knows what it wishes, but it does not know what it wills or whether it wills. The not knowing of the demigods, by contrast, does not spring from an empty cluelessness, from the barrenness and exhaustion that belong to a nonwilling, but from an excess of vocation, the measurelessness of an as-yet untamed power. Their will is *excess of will* [*Überwille*].

For the demigods, it is too trivial a matter to cheat their way through by means of small-minded calculations or attempts to outwit. They do not know the kind of petty ambition that each day satiates itself with daily successes and, through its skillfulness, procures new needs that renew its hunger. They are not content to share the desire to make history with the little people and to outdo the littlest. They do not seek to master ruse and subterfuge. They are unfamiliar with all those things that are necessary, and indeed essentially necessary, in order to initiate those everyday affairs that are uncircumventable and to bring them into their appropriate order. Their soul is "untraveled" (in the realm of figuring out and securing on a daily basis the unrestricted process of getting through and moving on). For the demigods take their goals and their willing and sustaining from their originary origin, but not from the habitual course of things, those things swimming on the surface that can be seized upon by everyone. Their doing and suffering can never at all be confirmed by whatever lies present at hand; for the latter always speaks against them. The truth of their being never finds any appropriate confirmation at all, because whenever such confirmation arises, then their being has already been extracted from its superiority; it has become run of the mill and made trivial.

That wishing that remains uncomprehending in the face of destiny is characteristic of those who are concerned with surveying and figuring out everything, and who bring their being into the security of the unquestionable. All questioning is a kind of disturbance for them, and therefore false from the outset. Answers are more comfortable and therefore true, even if they are answers to questions that merely bear the semblance of being questions. Such wishing and contentedness with the fulfilled wish—which amounts to the same as wishing—is uncomprehending in the face of destiny; it fails to understand such destiny. It can be understood only in being willed as a task, in a willing whose origin remains an excess of will. So much toward our initial clarification of the third strophe.

γ) The Demigods' Lack from out of Abundance

Certainly, we now need to explicitly elucidate a word from the end of the third strophe, a word that seems from the beginning to demolish our interpretation. For Hölderlin names this 'not knowing whereto'—this supreme blindness—a "lack" (line 44), a lack given to the demigods in their untraveled soul. Yet "lack" here is no mere defect or flaw or weakness. This word, which Hölderlin uses on a number of occasions, indeed means a kind of missing the mark, yet one that always springs from strength, fullness, and abundance, not from weakness or wretchedness. Cf. "The Only One" (IV, 188, lines 70ff.):

> Es hänget aber an Einem
> Die Liebe. Diesesmal
> Ist mir vom eigenen Herzen
> Zu sehr gegangen der Gesang,
> Gut will ich aber machen
> Den Fehl, mit nächstem
> Wenn ich noch andere singe.
> Nie treff ich, wie ich wünsche,
> Das Maas.

> Yet love clings
> To One alone. This time
> Too much from my own heart
> The song has come,
> Yet I want to make good
> The lack, with what lies nearest
> When others still I sing.
> Never do I hit, as I wish,
> The measure.

The poet here tells of the God of the Christians, and tells of him as though he were "The Only One" (as the title says). Yet he is not, so the poet, in keeping with his vocation, must 'sing others still' and in this way make good the lack.

It has recently become fashionable to portray Hölderlin's apparent turn away from Greece as a turning toward the homeland and as a turn to Christendom. This is completely erroneous, as this excerpt alone already attests, and belongs within apologetics, which today has become so adept that it now speaks only in the language of Nietzsche. Thus there is talk in the pulpits today of Christ as the Führer, which is not only an untruth, but worse still, a blasphemy toward Christ. The true and in each case sole Führer in his beyng indeed points into the realm of the demigods. To be a Führer—a leader—is a destiny, and therefore finite beyng. For ecclesiastical dogmatics, however, in keeping with the decision by the Council of Nicea, Christ is *deus verus ex deo vero—consubstantialis patri*—ὁμο / οὐσιος τῷ πατρί, equal in essence to the Father, not ὁμοιούσιος, not merely similar in essence. This is just a passing remark in order to orient the increasing conceptual confusion to be found amid the contemporary thoughtlessness.

To tell only of the God of the Christians is, according to the poet, a lack: lack in the sense of not hitting the measure, due to excess and excess of will. This should also be compared with the last two strophes of "Poet's Calling" (IV, 147):

> Noch ists auch gut, zu weise zu seyn. Ihn kennt
> Der Dank. Doch nicht behält er es leicht allein,
> Und gern gesellt, damit verstehn sie
> 60   Helfen, zu anderen sich ein Dichter.

> Furchtlos bleibt aber, so er es muss, der Mann
> Einsam vor Gott, es schüzet die Einfalt ihn,
> Und keiner Waffen braucht's und keiner
> Listen, so lange, bis Gottes Fehl hilft.

> Nor is it good to be too wise. Thanks
> Knows Him. Yet a poet cannot easily hold on to it,
> And is fond of the company of others,
> 60   So they understand how to help.

> Fearless, however, as he must be, the man remains
> Solitary before God, simplicity protects him,
> And no weapons are needed, and no
> Cunning, until God's lack is of help.

The issue is once again the telling of the poet, who has the most intimate kinship with the being of the demigods. The poem also names Dionysos at the start, and bears an essential relation to "The Rhine" that has yet to be discussed.

" . . . until God's lack is of help." What is that supposed to mean? At any rate, the "lack" is here something that is God's, and is even meant to help and to be of assistance. From this dual determination we can already perceive that "lack" once again does not signify a shortcoming or mere incompleteness. Nevertheless, the sense of the word is not clear without further ado. In a draft, the poet says (IV, 332) "And no honors are needed, and no weapons, so long as the God is not lacking"; following that: "so long as the God remains near to us." That is clear, yet sheds no light on the final version, which appears to say precisely the opposite. What is said in the draft is that God's not lacking, his remaining near, is of help;[9] now "God's lack" is supposed to help. Von Hellingrath wants to understand the point as follows: Now— in the period around 1801–1802, the period of the poetizing we are considering—the poet is helped more if the divine does not press too insistently upon him (IV, 331, top). Now that he "bit off more of the gods than he could chew" (Letter to Böhlendorff of December 4, 1801, V, 321), the lack of the gods is of more "help" than their presence; thus, "lack" = absence (cf. p. 209f.). I consider this interpretation incorrect and impossible, for the following two reasons.

First, for Hölderlin "lack" does not mean the same as lacking in the sense of being absent, but, as both the aforementioned citation and that from "The Rhine" unequivocally say, not being able to hit the mark. Second, however, von Hellingrath's interpretation falls entirely outside of the intrinsic context of the final two strophes and, above all, of the poem as a whole. The poet says: "Nor is it good to be too wise" (line 57); that is, what is needed is an excess of knowing that is different and superior not simply in 'amount,' for instance, but in kind compared to that knowing of which we are told:

> Zu lang ist alles Göttliche dienstbar schon,
> Und alle Himmelskräfte verscherzt, verbraucht,
> Die Gütigen, zur Lust danklos ein
> Schlaues Geschlecht und zu kennen wähnt es,

50
> Wenn ihnen der Erhabne den Aker baut,
> Das Tagslicht und den Donnerer, und es späht
> Das Sehrohr wohl sie all und zählt und
> Nennet mit Nahmen des Himmels Sterne.

> Too long already has everything divine been servile,
> And all heavenly powers discarded, used up,
> The good-natured ones, thanklessly for the pleasure
> Of a cunning race that thinks it knows,

50
> When the Exalted One tills the soil for them,
> Daylight and the Thunderer, and the
> Telescope claims to spy them all and counts and
> Designates with names the heaven's stars.

("Poet's Calling," IV, 146f., lines 45ff.)

Chapter Two
A More Incisive Review.
Poetizing and Historical Dasein

We interrupted our engagement with Hölderlin's poetry during our interpretation of the third strophe of his poem "The Rhine." Our task is to take it up again where we left off. Yet in order that we may find our way back there in the right manner, three things are necessary:

1. Our proper task must once again be brought before our inner gaze.

2. The fundamental approach in which our interpretation of the poetizing moves must reconfirm itself for us.

3. The discussion that we ended with and left standing must be directly re-engaged.

In short, and to put it formulaically, we must become reacquainted with (1) the general approach of the whole lecture course, (2) the particular points made as the lectures progressed, and (3) the details of the last lecture. We cannot at this point provide a complete review of what was said; nor do we want to give an abbreviated report. Instead, we shall draw out what is essential, by way of a more free-flowing presentation that can stand on its own.

§15. The Task of the Lecture Course: Entering the Domain in Which Poetry Unfolds Its Power, and the Opening Up of Its Actuality

It remains the goal of the lecture course to first create once again in our historical Dasein a space and locale for what poetizing is. This can only happen through our bringing ourselves into the domain in which an actual poetizing unfolds its power and by opening ourselves up to its actuality. Why do we choose Hölderlin's poetry for this task? This choice is not some arbitrary selection made from among available poets. This choice is a historical decision. Of the essential grounds for this decision, we may name three: (1) Hölderlin is the poet of poets and of poetizing. (2) Hölderlin is, together with this, the poet of the Germans. (3) Because Hölderlin plays this concealed and difficult role of being the poet of poets as poet of the Germans, he has not yet become a force in the history of our people. Because he is not yet such a force, he must become such. In this process, we must keep in mind 'politics' in the highest and authentic sense, so much so that whoever accomplishes something here has no need to talk about the 'political.'

a) Founding the Essence of Poetizing and Grounding Dasein upon It. Poetizing as the Primordial Language of a People

Yet in what does the essence of the poet consist? Hölderlin himself gives the answer in the last line of his hymn "Remembrance" ["*Andenken*"] (IV, 63):

Was bleibet aber, stiften die Dichter.

Yet what remains, the poets found.

That which remains is that which is: a being, and it is this through its beyng. The poet is the founder of beyng. 'Founding' and 'to found' mean something intrinsically twofold here: On the one hand, 'to found' means to project in advance for the first time and in its essence that which is not yet. Insofar as such founding as poetizing is a telling [*Sagen*], it also means bringing this projection into the word—as a telling and as something said, to place it as a *myth* [*Sage*] into the Dasein of a people, and thus to bring this Dasein to a stand for the first time, to ground it (cf. "Voice of the People," IV, first version, 139ff., second version, 142ff.). On the other hand, 'founding' means to deposit and save, as an enduring remembrance of the essence of beyng thus opened up, whatever has in this way been foretold and grounded, as it were—a remembrance to which a people must think its way ever anew.

Beyng as in this way founded in poetizing, however, always embraces beings as a whole: the gods, the Earth, human beings, and humans in their history—as history, that is, as a people. Instead of now going into more detail and talking about the essence of poetizing as founding, we want to hear how what we have said is depicted by the poet himself. To this end, we have chosen an excerpt from Hölderlin's *Empedocles*. This poetic work has remained a fragment. We possess several stages of its development. The excerpt we shall cite comes from stage two of the first version of *The Death of Empedocles* (III, 78f.). Panthea and Rhea, the two priestesses of Vesta, are in Empedocles'

garden in Agrigento on the island of Sicily (his home), and they begin
a dialogue about Empedocles, the thinker and poet.

PANTHEA: Ich sinn ihm nach—wie viel ist über ihn
        Mir noch zu sinnen? ach! und hab' ich ihn
        Gefasst, was ists? Er selbst zu seyn, das ist
        Das Leben und wir andern sind der Traum davon.—
        Sein Freund Pausanias hat auch von ihm
        Schon manches mir erzählt—der Jüngling sieht
        Ihn Tag vor Tag, und Jovis Adler ist
        Nicht stolzer, denn Pausanias—ich glaub' es wohl.

RHEA: Ich kann nicht tadeln, Liebe, was du sagst,
        Doch trauert meine Seele wunderbar
        Darüber, und ich möchte seyn, wie du,
        Und möcht' es wieder nicht. Seid ihr denn all
        Auf dieser Insel so? Wir haben auch
        An grossen Männern unsre Lust, und Einer
10   Ist izt die Sonne der Athenerinnen,
        Sophokles! dem von allen Sterblichen
        Zuerst der Jungfraun herrlichste Natur
        Erschien und sich zu reinem Angedenken
        In seine Seele gab. – – – – –
        – – –jede wünscht sich, ein Gedanke
        Des Herrlichen zu seyn, und möchte gern
        Die immerschöne Jugend, eh' sie welkt,
        Hinüber in des Dichters Seele retten,
        Und frägt und sinnet, welche von den Jungfern
20   Der Stadt die zärtlichernste Heroide sei,
        Die seiner Seele vorgeschwebt, die er
        Antigonä gennant; und helle wirds
        Um unsre Stirne, wenn der Götterfreund
        Am heitern Festtag ins Theater tritt,
        Doch kummerlos ist unser Wohlgefallen,
        Und nie verliert das liebe Herz sich so
        In schmerzlich fortgerissner Huldigung.-

PANTHEA: I ponder him—how much of him
        Have I yet to ponder? Alas! and if I have
        Grasped him, what of it? To be him himself, that is
        Life and we others are the dream thereof.—
        His friend Pausanias has also already
        Told me many a thing about him—the youth sees

Him day after day, and Jovis's eagle is
Not prouder than Pausanias—well I believe it.

RHEA: I cannot rebuke, my dear, what you say,
        Yet my soul is amazingly mournful
        Over it, and I would like to be like you,
        And then again would not. Are you then all
        like this upon this island? And we do
        Take pleasure in great men, and one
10   Is now the sun of Athenian women,
        Sophocles! To whom of all mortals
        The most magnificent virgin nature first
        Appeared and gave herself to pure commemoration
        In his soul. $----$ –
        $---$ each desires to be
        A thought of the magnificent, and well would like
        Ever-beautiful youth, before it withers,
        To be taken into rescue in the poet's soul,
        And wonders and ponders which of the city's
20   Virgins is the most tender-serious heroine
        That appeared before his soul, the one he
        Named Antigone; and bright it becomes
        Around our brows, when the friend of the gods
        On a bright day of celebration enters the theater,
        Yet worriless is our pleasure,
        And never does the beloved heart lose itself so
        In painfully transported homage. –

Sophocles the poet apprehended for the first time the radiant shining of 'nature,' φύσις, the beyng of the Athenian virgins. Poetically he set in place a projection of this essence and, through the precedent of the image thus configured, saved this essence for enduring remembrance, founded this beyng forever. Yet the poetic work of Sophocles named *Antigone* is, as a poetic work, a founding of the entire Greek Dasein, for the poetic work as a projection (taking root and saving) of beyng grounds the Dasein of human beings upon the Earth in the face of the gods. As founding, poetizing first brings about the ground of the possibility for human beings to settle on the Earth in the first place, between the Earth and the gods—that is, to become historical, which means to be able to be a people. Whatever the human being may then undertake and procure, once settled on such a ground, may be attributed to him as of merit. Yet his authentic beyng—to be settled in the first place, to be steadfast upon the soil—this dwelling is grounded in and through poetizing; that is, it is "poetic." For this reason, Hölderlin, in that poem from the period of his so-called madness that begins, "In beautiful blue with its / metal roof the church tower blossoms," says the following regarding the beyng of the human being (VI, 25, lines 32f.):

> Voll Verdienst, doch dichterisch wohnet
> Der Mensch auf dieser Erde.

> Full of merit, yet poetically
> Human dwell upon this Earth.

For common understanding, its tangible everyday is whatever is at hand—that is, beings, that which is real. Poetizing, by contrast, is just something poetized, poetically invented, something unreal. For the one who knows, however, and who truly acts, the converse is the case. Poetizing as founded is what is real, and so-called reality is the unreal that is continually disintegrating.

That commonplace perversion and misrepresentation of the essence of poetizing that necessarily and repeatedly takes hold has its proper ground nowhere else, however, than in poetizing itself, for poetizing is a telling founding. Hölderlin recognizes language, however, as "that most dangerous of goods."[1] In it, beyng first opens itself up to humans and in this way transports them into the realm of a threatening of beyng in general. As a founding, the poet's originary telling is not some whimsical inventing, but his placing himself under the thunderstorms of the gods, capturing in the word and in the becoming of the word their beckonings, the lightning flash, and so placing the word—together with its entire, concealed rupturing force—amidst the people.

This same language, however—and therein lies its additional dangerousness—can remain at the level of something merely said, and become impoverished as mere idle talk and perpetuate its corrupted essence as drivel. Poetizing then appears as the creation of linguistic constructions, manifesting itself as the "most innocent of all occupations." This is what Hölderlin calls poetizing—deliberately maintaining such appearances—in a letter to his mother[2] (cf. p. 32). Yet viewed with respect to its essence, language is in itself the most originary poetizing, and that which is poetized in language, in the narrower sense—that which we specifically call 'poetry'—is the originary

---

1. Fragment 13, IV, 246.
2. January 1799, III, 377.

language of a people, which then disseminates itself as prose and becomes leveled out in such dissemination, so that poetry appears to be a deviation and exception.

If we were to reflect philosophically still further back here regarding the essence and origin of language as originary poetizing, we would have to recognize that language itself has its origin in silence. It is first in silence that something such as 'beyng' must have gathered itself, so as then to be spoken out as 'world.' That silence preceding the world is more powerful than all human powers. No human being alone ever invented language—that is, was alone strong enough to rupture the sway of that silence, unless under the compulsion of the God. We humans are always already thrown into a spoken and enunciated discourse, and can then be silent only in drawing back from such discourse, and even this seldom succeeds. Insofar as we stand within existence [*Dasein*], we ourselves are only a dialogue, and in such dialogue experience something like a world. Cf. p. 62:

Viel hat erfahren der Mensch.
Der Himmlischen viele genannt,
Seit ein Gespräch wir sind
Und hören können voneinander.

Much have humans experienced.
Named many of the heavenly,
Since we are a dialogue
And can hear from one another.

(Fragment from "Conciliator, you who . . . ," IV, 343)

The few excerpts that we have cited up to now from various poems of Hölderlin's already confirm that he is not only a poet, but the poet of the poet, and that he founds anew the essence of poetizing itself. One could be of the opinion that a poet who, as it were, poetizes 'about' poetizing must be a latecomer—that he belongs in an era from which all creative immediacy has vanished, where an unhealthy reflexivity becomes widespread even in poetizing, to the point where the latter now only poetizes about poetizing and thus constantly turns around itself. Such considerations are supremely modern. But everything modern is always already out of date before it has even seen the light of day.

In truth, Hölderlin is the poet of the poet not because he belatedly reflects upon himself and makes his poetizing into an object for himself, but because he retrieves poetizing, and thereby himself, back into its originary essence, letting the power of this essence be experienced and, in newly founding it, casting it in turn far ahead of his time. Hölderlin poetizes the poet not on account of a lack of other, more worthy objects for his creative activity, but from the overflowing necessity of first grounding existence [*Dasein*] once more upon poetizing before all else. As poet of the poet, he is no latecomer, but a forerunner. As such, he is always too far ahead, he comes still too early for us today. Whatever is of the present day in each case speeds right on by him and is reassured in its complacency, in which everything counts as already decided. As the one who comes too early, this poet therefore always comes too late. Cf. the elegy "Bread and Wine," strophe VII (IV, 123f.):

> Aber Freund! wir kommen zu spät. Zwar leben die Götter,
> 110 Aber über dem Haupt droben in anderer Welt.
> Endlos wirken sie da und scheinens wenig zu achten,
> Ob wir leben, so sehr schonen die Himmlischen uns.
> Denn nicht immer vermag ein schwaches Gefäss sie zu fassen,
> Nur zu Zeiten erträgt göttliche Fülle der Mensch.
> Traum von ihnen ist drauf das Leben. Aber das Irrsaal
> Hilft, wie Schlummer und stark machet die Noth und die Nacht,
> Biss dass Helden genug in der ehernen Wiege gewachsen,
> Herzen an Kraft, wie sonst, ähnlich den Himmlischen sind.
> Donnernd kommen sie drauf. Indessen dünket mir öfters
> 120 Besser zu schlafen, wie so ohne Genossen zu seyn,
> So zu harren und was zu thun indess und zu sagen,
> Weiss ich nicht und wozu Dichter in dürftiger Zeit?
> Aber sie sind, sagst du, wie des Weingotts heilige Priester,
> Welche von Lande zu Land zogen in heiliger Nacht.

> But friend! we come too late. The gods indeed live,
> 110 Yet over our heads in another world above.
> Endlessly they are at work there and seem little to heed
> Whether we live, so greatly do the heavenly protect us.
> For not always can a weak vessel grasp them,
> Only at times can the human withstand divine fullness.
> Life follows as a dream of them. Yet errancy
> Helps, like slumber, and need and the night make strong,
> Until heroes enough have grown in a cradle of ore,
> Hearts in their strength, as before, approach the heavenly.
> Thundering then they come. Yet often it seems to me
> 120 Better to sleep, than to be thus without companions,
> To wait in such manner and what to do and to say meantime,
> I know not and wherefore poets in times of need?

Yet they are, you say, like the wine god's holy priests,
Who journeyed from land to land in holy night.

b) Hölderlin as the Poet of Future German Beyng

As this poet of the poet, Hölderlin has a unique historical position and mission. We can comprehend it in saying: He is the poet of the Germans. Yet Klopstock and Herder, Goethe and Schiller, Novalis and Kleist, Eichendorff and Mörike, Stefan George and Rilke are surely German poets also; they too belong to the Germans. But this is not what we mean. 'Poet of the Germans' is meant not as *genitivus subiectivus,* but as *genitivus obiectivus:* the poet who first poetizes the Germans. Yet did not the other poets too sing and tell of the German essence in their own way? Certainly—and yet, Hölderlin is in an exceptional sense the poet—that is, founder—of German beyng, because he has projected such beyng the farthest. That is, he has projected it out ahead into the most distant future. He was able to open up this supremely futural expanse because he brought forth the key from his experience of the most profound need of the withdrawal and approach of the gods.

It is well and good that people everywhere today point to the topic of the fatherland in Hölderlin's poetry, and in this way come to recommend the poet. But this is not the issue. When regarded in this way, the topic of the fatherland remains merely one particular aspect among others in his poetry. It is correct, furthermore, when people emphasize how Hölderlin allegedly turned away from an overly exclusive glorification of the Greek world, and from an apparent vilification of the German, toward the Germanic. But this too is not the issue. Especially not if people thereby want to have us believe that this certain turning away from the Greek world is a turning toward Christendom. For precisely that late poem entitled "The Only One" (IV, 186ff. and 231ff.), which is a reference to Christ, wants to say that Christ is not the only one. The task, rather, is to take seriously the flight of the gods that has long since begun and, from out of such seriousness, to open up an intimation of their coming anew, to contribute to their return, and in this way to creatively transform the Earth and the land. It is not the fatherland as a singled-out content of the poetry that is the issue, but rather the historical truth of our people; the issue is what kind of status this people will conquer for itself amid the pressing distress of our Dasein, that it should once again venture the gods, so as in this way to create a historical world.

All oppositions of Christendom and paganism and the like fail to think far enough here and are incapable of retrieving what Hölderlin has poetically cast ahead of them as the essence of the Germans. For this reason too, every attempt to accommodate Hölderlin's poetizing within Classicism or Romanticism or between the two must fail. As poet of the poet, Hölderlin is the poet of the future Germans and, as such, is singular.

For this reason too, there exists a unique kind of necessity to let this poet and his poetizing become a force in our historical Dasein. The issue is something altogether different from, say, making the too-little-known poet more well known, rescuing from obscurity someone who is not recognized, or directly ascribing a political value to him—all things that, now that the humanities have been brought into line [Gleichschaltung], will certainly be extensively promoted in the coming years.

Hölderlin's poetry is neither for everyone nor for aesthetes. Hölderlin is a herald and proclaimer for those concerned: those who are themselves directed to the calling of builders building a new world. This historical world can come about only if poetizing first becomes a force within its essence, and this poetizing takes the form of a severity and definiteness of a thoughtful, questioning knowing.

However, we are still without poetizing. Yet that is the lesser concern [Not]. The greater concern lies in the fact that instead of poetizing, we possess a well-tended literature here and there: that people can write good novels and sometimes compose a successful poem, and even in such a way that the content is timely for the era. It is precisely this that bars our entrance to the domain in which poetry unfolds its power. We then think we have poetry and that we can have such a thing in the same way that we have, say, artificial silk and the like. We think that such a thing happens of its own accord with time, without a people first venturing back into the innermost need [Not] of its Dasein, so as to first create the space and the possibility of a resonance for its poetry. We think that one day genuine poetry will be delivered to us, without our first delivering ourselves over to the horrors and devastation that threaten the existence [Dasein] of the West on all sides (despite Christendom and churches) and that keep it hovering at the edge of the abyss.

We must press ahead into that domain in which Hölderlin's poetry unfolds its power, if only there to first arm ourselves to bring about a preparedness for this poetry as such—as an essential power of every great, historically spiritual world.

What we have said hitherto may suffice to clarify why, in our thoughtful and philosophical endeavor to empower the power of the essence of poetry, we have chosen Hölderlin. Yet within the domain of this choice we have made a further choice: We have restricted ourselves to the hymns of the late and great period, and begun straightaway with our interpretation of the hymn "Germania." Thus, in reflecting upon general considerations we come to consider the particular, and do so with the intention of securing for ourselves once more the fundamental approach within which our interpretation moves.

§16. The Fundamental Approach in Which Our Interpretation Moves, Taking "Germania" as Our Point of Departure

a) The Essence of Fundamental Attunement. The Thinking and Pondering of the Man in "Germania" as Configured in the Poetic Work "The Rhine"

Our task was, as we said, to determine and to attain the 'metaphysical locale' from where the poet poetizes his telling, and to do so through an interpretation of the first two and a half strophes of "Germania" (lines 1–38). Entailed within this task was the unfolding of the fundamental attunement of the poetizing. The essence of fundamental attunement must be kept free from any psychological misconstrual, from every kind of sophistic reduction to a mere so-called feeling. The essence of fundamental attunement was delimited for us in positive terms according to four aspects:

1. The fundamental attunement transports us to the limits of beings and places us in a relation to the gods, whether as turning us toward or turning us away.

2. The fundamental attunement thrusts us out, and in transporting us at the same time thrusts us into the relations that have evolved toward the Earth and the homeland. The fundamental attunement always transports us out and into at the same time. As such, it opens up

3. beings as a whole as a domain through which it prevails, as the unity of a world.

4. The fundamental attunement in this way delivers our Dasein over to beyng, so that it must take up beyng, configure it and sustain it.

The fundamental attunement that transports us out and transports us into, opening up and delivering us over, attunes the poet's telling projection; this telling, thus attuned, determines in turn the exposure of Dasein that has occurred in the midst of beings.

We considered the hymn "Germania" as the middle of Hölderlin's late hymnal poetry and oriented everything from this period around it. The fundamental attunement of this poetizing is a *holy mourning, yet in readied distress.* Mourning—we grasped this as the lucid superiority of the simple goodness of a grave pain. It is 'holy'—that is, in Hölderlin's sense, purely disinterested. It does not ossify into despair, it does not lose itself in merely hanging on, without any hold, to what has vanished. Holy mourning is a distress that opens itself. It turns toward the gods that have fled, preserves their flight, and awaits the gods to come. The distress is grounded in a readiness to receive those who are coming as the truth of the Earth and of the homeland.

The third strophe of "Germania" begins as follows (IV, 182, lines 33ff.):

> Schon grünet ja, im Vorspiel rauherer Zeit
> Für sie erzogen das Feld, bereitet ist die Gaabe
> Zum Opfermahl und Thal und Ströme sind
> Weitoffen um prophetische Berge,
> Dass schauen mag bis in den Orient
> Der Mann und ihn von dort der Wandlungen viele bewegen.

> Already nurtured for them, the field indeed grows verdant,
> Prelude to a harsher time, the gift is readied
> For the sacrificial meal and valley and rivers lie
> Open wide around prophetic mountains,
> So that into the Orient may look
> The man and from there be moved by many transformations.

We interrupted our interpretation of the poem at this point (line 38). We have attained the position of the man—he is the poet himself, who is moved by many transformations there. Our task, before proceeding with the interpretation of this poem, was to experience more clearly the pondering and thinking of the man, to raise to the level of knowledge *what and how this man thinks* who experiences the flight of the old and the approach of the coming gods.

The poem "The Rhine," which already by its title announces a direct connection to "Germania," tells of this thinking of this man. Or better, the poem in its telling configures this very thinking—yet not in the manner of merely giving a poetic-pastoral description of some particular thing, a river in the German land. "The Rhine"—this poem belongs to Hölderlin's 'river poetry.' The rivers are the "waters of the homeland" ("Germania," line 4), with whose flowing "The heart's love has plaint" (line 5). The rivers create paths and limits upon the originally pathless Earth. Since the flight of the gods, the Earth has been pathless. The human being cannot find the way, nor do the gods point the way directly. Yet in the rushing, self-assured course of the river, a destiny fulfills itself, land and Earth are given limits and shape, and the homeland comes into being for humans and thereby truth for the people. It is no accident that a poem entitled "Voice of the People,"

which exists in two versions, takes up the thought of the river at its
beginning (IV, 139 and 142; the first strophes are identical):

> Du seiest Gottes Stimme, so glaubt ich sonst,
> In heilger Jugend; ja und ich sag es noch!
> Um unsre Weisheit unbekümmert
> Rauschen die Ströme doch auch, und dennoch
>
> Wer liebt sie nicht? und immer bewegen sie
> Das Herz mir, hör ich ferne die Schwindenden
> Die Ahnungsvollen, meine Bahn nicht
> Aber gewisser ins Meer hin eilen.
>
> Denn selbstvergessen, allzubereit den Wunsch
> 10   Der Götter zu erfüllen, ergreifft zu gern
> Was sterblich ist und einmal offnen
> Auges auf eigenem Pfade wandelt,
>
> Ins All zurük die kürzeste Bahn, so stürzt
> Der Strom hinab, er suchet die Ruh, es reisst
> Es ziehet wider Willen ihn von
> Klippe zu Klippe den Steuerlosen
>
> Das wunderbare Sehnen dem Abgrund zu,
> Und kaum der Erd' entstiegen, desselben Tags
> Kehrt weinend zum Geburtstort schon aus
> 20   Purpurner Höhe die Wolke wieder.

> You are God's voice, thus I once believed
> In holy youth; yes and I say so still!
> Unconcerned with our wisdom
> The rivers still rush on, and yet
>
> Who loves them not? And always do they move
> My heart, when afar I hear them vanishing
> Full of intimation, hastening along not
> My path, yet more surely seaward.
>
> For self-oblivious, all too ready to fulfill
> 10   The wish of the gods, does what is mortal
> And now with open eyes once walking
> Its own path, too readily take
>
> The shortest course back into the All, thus does
> The river plunge downward, seeking peace,

> Against its will, from cliff to cliff,
>   The rudderless one is torn, is pulled
>
> By a mysterious longing toward the abyss,
>   And scarcely arisen from the Earth, the same day
>   Weeping the cloud returns from crimson heights
> 20   Back to the place of its birth.

b) The Thinking of the Demigods

Yet why, from among Hölderlin's river poems, did we select "The Rhine" precisely? The beginning of strophe X of this poem tells us the reason: "Demigods now I think" (IV, 176, line 135). With this word we encounter the pivot upon which the entire poem turns. Our concern was therefore to clarify in advance, before a detailed interpretation, what the poet means and wants when he says "Demigods now I think." This thinking does not just begin with strophe X; rather this is merely one resting point of that thinking that the poetizing of the entire poem comprises. We attained clarity by way of answering four questions and a preliminary question.

Preliminary question: What kind of thinking is this in general? Manifestly, a thinking of the poet, an originarily projective founding. Demigods are not freely thought up here, nor are they discovered lying present at hand somewhere and then considered with a view to their attributes. Their essence is poetically projected, opened up, and said. In such telling, the original belonging together and identical need of the thinking poet and of the poetizing thinker announces itself.

First question: In what realm does the thinking of the poet move here? "Demigods"—these are, we might say, 'in-between beings', between humans and gods. Yet their essence precisely cannot be deduced in a calculative manner starting from these two poles, for the gods have fled, and who the human being is, we know not. In questioning who the human being is, however, we are asking beyond the human, and are thus necessarily thinking what is over the human. In questioning concerning the gods, our questioning always falls short of them: Here we think what is beneath the gods. That which lies over the human and beneath the gods is the same. Truly decisive questioning encounters this one and the same. Such questioning is decisive because it first of all creates the scission that institutes measure between humans and gods and opens up the rupture. To think demigods means to think toward the Earth and out to the gods, from out of the originary middle.

Second question: By what is this thinking of the demigods occasioned and compelled? The poet stands at the threshold of the homeland. From there, his mind runs into the distance, and from out of this turning away he is unsuspectingly called back to the Earth of his homeland. The need of the homeland and of the Earth gives rise to the nature and direction of his thinking, which is concerned solely with finding the truth of the people. It is in the poem that Earth first becomes Earth and landscape first becomes landscape.

Third question: In what respect are the demigods thought? With respect to their beyng, and that is "destiny." "Destiny" is thus the fundamental word of this poetizing, and is encountered on numerous occasions at decisive places. In keeping with the fullness that the essence of this word embraces, it means many things. Our interpretation should let us see things more clearly in this regard. One fundamental trait of beyng in the sense of destiny is suffering [*Leiden*], in the sense of creative suffering as the origin of all great passion [*Leidenschaft*].

Fourth question: Which fundamental attunement prevails in this thinking of the poet? We saw that it is the same as that in "Germania," but poetically the same—that is, in an originarily new configuration, not in superficially carrying it over. In the poet's 'thinking demigods,' he thinks "a destiny" (line 11), not as an individual, isolated case, but as singular, in its singularity, and precisely thereby he hits upon its essence.

We are accustomed to think, under the long dominance of a quite specific 'logic,' that the essence is everywhere the 'universal': the rule and law. Among the confusions of the nineteenth century was the view that in order to be a proper science (i.e., like mathematics and natural science), historiography, which has as its object, after all, the unique course of history, had to seek out the universal and whatever followed given laws. Spengler, for example, and all 'morphologies' and 'typologies' of history, think entirely in this direction. The object of historical knowledge is neither what is individual as individuated, nor the universal and the rule, but that which is individual as singular. Singularity is the essence of what is great, yet also the corrupted essence of what is lowly and fallen. Singularity is the configuration and objective character belonging to the essence of history. To experience and inquire concerning singularity is in itself an altogether singular stance on the part of knowing. The kind of togetherness pertaining to the singular, its worldly character, is solitude. Solitude does not close off or exclude, but carries and extends into that originary unity that no community ever attains. All too frequently we continue to think all history in the categories of the natural sciences, in particular biology and the sociology that is determined from there.

That the individual character of the individual is ruptured and grounded otherwise by community is necessary. Yet both community and individuals remain in error if they do not seek singularity as their truth and anchor their will in this. The singularity of historical Dasein is destiny. This the poet thinks in his poem "The Rhine."

This preliminary sketch of the fundamental orientation of the poetic telling must now be filled out and made determinate through our interpretation in its individual details.

§17. The Interpretation in Detail. The River Rhine as Demigod

a) Strophe I: Reference to Dionysos. The Alps.
Strophe II: The River Rhine in Its Origin

Our task is to proceed directly from what was discussed in our previous meeting. Before undertaking the interpretation in detail, we divided the poem "The Rhine" into sections. We proposed five sections: (1) strophe I, (2) strophes II to IX, (3) strophes X to XIII, (4) strophe XIV, and (5) strophe XV.

Our interpretation of the first strophe has been carried out. First, the poet names ivy, "the bacchantic leaf" (Stutgard, IV, 116, line 52). A pointer to Dionysos is found in the first line; the last line, "primordial confusion," recalls the same thing. This connection to the raging demigod and his mask-like nature, for whom death is life and life is death, embraces the entire poetizing. Second is the reference to the "Alps" (line 4): not some imaginative depiction of a landscape, but a descending upon elevated stairs, the fortress of the gods, its peaks towering up into the light, sheltering the dark clefts of rock deep within their womb.

Strophes II to XIII constitute the decisive section, upon whose interpretation our understanding of the whole depends. Strophe II thinks the river in its origin. "Origin" (line 94)—an essential determination of beyng as destiny. Gods, humans, and the poet apprehend the origin and stand in relation to it in three ways: The gods let the one raging in his fetters spring forth, and in letting him spring forth they abandon him to this origin and to the ongoing vocation within it. The humans are unable to listen to this raving and raging, and they flee. Beyng as destiny is the uncanny, the excess of greatness that remains ever burdensome to all that is small and calculative.

The poet alone is able to accomplish that hearing that holds out at the origin and, in holding out, hears out the essence of the origin and shelters what has been heard within that which remains of the poetic word. Yet this hearing that stands firm before the origin in its poetizing thinks the origin not only in its springing forth, but at the same time as something that has sprung forth. This is why in the third strophe the entire directional flow of the river that has sprung forth is surveyed in looking ahead and something essential is caught sight of: essential for the beyng of the demigods that is now to be founded.

b) Strophe III: The Demigods as the Blindest.
The Lack of the Demigods

The directional orientation of the river—proceeding from its origin toward the East, oriented toward the land of the Greeks—suddenly breaks off toward the North, the German land, as Hölderlin tells of in another river hymn, "The Ister" (the lower Danube) (IV, 221, lines 48f.):

> Der Rhein ist seitwärts
> Hinweggegangen.

> The Rhine has departed
> Sideways.

In its thus being forced away from its original direction, there arises in the river something like a counter-will, with which it must come to terms. "Yet uncomprehending is / Wishing in the face of destiny." (lines 38f.) That is to say: Mere wishing closes itself off before such beyng. Mere wishing can perhaps bring about obstinacy, but not that willing in which alone a counter-will can be comprehended and engaged.

"The blindest however / Are sons of gods." (lines 40f.) These lines do not continue or bring to completion what has just been said, as though it were the sons of gods who most of all merely wish. The "however" in line 40 brings a contrast to what has gone before. The sons of gods are indeed still more blind in the face of destiny than those who are merely caught up in the vacuity of wishing. They are the blindest not on account of some shortcoming, however, but from an excess of willing. They know not whereto, because their excessive will cannot be directly measured by what lies at hand. What they will can never be confirmed in terms of what lies at hand, for what lies at hand always speaks against them. Run-of-the-mill human beings know their way around in the everydayness of all that they do. The animal likewise acquires through instinct the assuredness of its behavior, an assuredness that constantly exceeds it. But to the demigods, the blindest, is given that lack in their untraveled soul.

We asked: What does "lack" (line 44) mean here? To help elucidate it, we appealed to the last two strophes of the poem "Poet's Calling" (IV, 147):

Noch ists auch gut, zu weise zu seyn. Ihn kennt
Der Dank. Doch nicht behält er es leicht allein,
Und gern gesellt, damit verstehn sie
60   Helfen, zu anderen sich ein Dichter.

Furchtlos bleibt aber, so er es muss, der Mann
Einsam vor Gott, es schüzet die Einfalt ihn,
Und keiner Waffen braucht's und keiner
Listen, so lange, bis Gottes Fehl hilft.

Nor is it good to be too wise. Thanks
Knows Him. Yet a poet cannot easily hold on to it,
And is fond of the company of others,
60   So they understand how to help.

Fearless, however, as he must be, the man remains
Solitary before God, simplicity protects him,
And no weapons are needed, and no
Cunning, until God's lack is of help.

And yet these lines appear to be still more obscure. Von Hellingrath, appealing to a draft of these lines, understands "lack" here as 'missing' in the sense of not being there, of 'absence.' We asserted that this interpretation is incorrect and at the same time untenable. Our task is to show this (cf. p. 191ff.).

We pointed already (p. 193) to the place in "Poet's Calling" where it is said (IV, 146f., lines 45ff.):

Zu lang ist alles Göttliche dienstbar schon,
Und alle Himmelskräfte verscherzt, verbraucht,
Die Gütigen, zur Lust danklos ein
Schlaues Geschlecht und zu kennen wähnt es,

Wenn ihnen der Erhabne den Aker baut,
50   Das Tagslicht und den Donnerer, und es späht
Das Sehrohr wohl sie all und zählt und
Nennet mit Nahmen des Himmels Sterne.

Too long already has everything divine been servile,
And all heavenly powers discarded, used up,
The good-natured ones, thanklessly for the pleasure
Of a cunning race that thinks it knows,

When the Exalted One tills the soil for them,
50   Daylight and the Thunderer, and the

> Telescope claims to spy them all and counts and
> Designates with names the heaven's stars.

This knowing is based upon cunning and calculation. It is purely re-sourceful, and finds only whatever is of use to it and promotes its own enterprises. It becomes widespread as a knowing that, when it wants to know, takes refuge in standards and numbers, in machines and apparatus, which it inserts between itself and the things. And yet despite the telescope and the most sophisticated mechanisms of distance vision, it sees in the end nothing more than its own cleverness, before which it grovels. The folly of this knowing, for all its success, remains a kind of impotence; for all the fawning amazement over what is each day supposed to be something unprecedented, it remains a kind of delusion.

> . . . denn es gilt ein anders,
> Zu Sorg' und Dienst den Dichtenden anvertraut!

> . . . for something different is the task,
> Entrusted to the poets' care and calling!

> ("Poet's Calling," IV, 145, lines 12f.)

Cf. "The Titans" (IV, 210, lines 62ff.):

> Ihr fühlet aber
> Auch andere Art.
> Denn unter dem Maasse
> Des Rohen brauchet es auch
> Damit das Reine sich kenne.

> Yet you also feel
> A different kind.
> For under the measure
> The unrefined is needed too
> For the pure to know itself.

The poet must persevere in this other knowing and telling—that is, in one that is different in kind and in its standards: He must be "Fearless" ("Poet's Calling," line 61) and "Solitary" (line 62) before the God. No kind of cunning or weapons are needed there. His singular protection is simplicity—that is, a superiority with regard to the many different things that merely accrue, a simple assuredness in occupying the single direction of his calling, which always exceeds him in mea-

sure. It is this not deviating from a simple not being able to do otherwise. Yet such simplicity is admittedly what is most difficult. "Yet a
poet cannot easily hold onto it" (line 58). The poet remains within
the assuredness of this simplicity so long as his telling—and that also
and necessarily means his hitting or missing the mark—comes from
the excess of divine vocation ("as he must be," line 61) "until God's
lack is of help" (line 64). What is to be emphasized is not God's *lack*,
but *God's* lack. That is to say, insofar as the lack is a lack of the God.
With this, it becomes clear what "God's lack" means here. Not absence
of the God, but presence—the fact that the vocation imposed by the
God is not suspended. Such vocation is, in its being taken up, always
lack and missing the mark—not out of weakness, but out of having
to bear the overpowering. Yet precisely "until"—that is, insofar as—
the lack is one coming from the God, the fidelity to this calling persists, even if it falls short in the work.

> . . . Vieles aber ist
> Zu behalten. Und Noth die Treue.

> . . . Yet much is
> To be retained. And fidelity needed.
>
> ("Ripe, bathed in fire . . . ," IV, 71, lines 13f.)

The lines mean exactly the opposite of what von Hellingrath wants
to read in them. His interpretation of lines 61 through 64 would result in the following incoherent reading: The man, the poet, is fear-
lessly "Solitary before God" so long as the God is absent. Yet—one
might counter—is not our reading supremely strange? Above all, the
lines from the draft that von Hellingrath cites (IV, 332) surely say unequivocally the opposite of what we want to read in the final version:
"so long as the God is not lacking," and specifically "so long as the
God remains close to us." It is incontestable that this is clearly said in
the draft. And yet we know from our earlier remarks (p. 51f.) (and
shall shortly see this clearly again), how far apart, even opposed to
one another, draft and final version are in Hölderlin. The draft is frequently only a pointer, and the final version is then raised up and
into the poetic, and this is always something strange. Compare this
to the impetus behind the reworking of the poem "The Blind Singer"
(IV, 57ff.) into "Chiron" (IV, 65ff.). Neither what appears strange, nor
the appeal to the lines in the draft, can be objections to our reading,
quite the contrary.

We turn back to our poem "The Rhine." It tells of the "lack" (line
44) that is "given" to the demigods in their untraveled soul. Von Hel-

lingrath's interpretation of the word in the sense of 'absence' could make no sense whatsoever here. At the same time, this line now confirms: The lack is, for the demigods, a divine one, not a mistake that they make or commit, but the endowment of their origin—that is, *God's lack.*

The third strophe thus tells of the divergence of the river's path, of the initial willing of the demigods. Such willing is no mere unbroken flowing in an unbroken self-will; rather, precisely the brokenness creates resistance, the possibility of lack, the necessity of mastering it in suffering and sustaining the origin.

The strophe provides a look ahead into the essential moments of destiny as the beyng of the demigods. Such beyng remains inaccessible to the understanding that characterizes everyday thinking. Such thinking wants to have everything on one common denominator. Wherever there are fetters and rupture, it immediately sees only shortcoming. But for beyng in the manner of destiny, such things are its mark of distinction and the condition of its greatness.

c) A Sustaining Suffering of Beyng through the Irruption of a Counter-Will

The third strophe is the prelude within the poetic thinking of the demigods. The event proper begins with strophe IV and extends to strophe IX inclusive. Placed into sharp relief, and immediately seizing upon what is decisive, the fourth strophe begins (IV, 173):

Ein Räthsel ist Reinentsprungenes. Auch
Der Gesang kaum darf es enthüllen.

Enigma is that which has purely sprung forth. Even
The song may scarcely unveil it.

That which "has purely sprung forth" is an enigma in its origin, and for this very reason in its entire beyng, as that which has sprung forth then is. The scope of the mystery extends also to that which has sprung forth, not to the 'whence' taken by itself, which we cannot account for from anywhere else. A mystery is that which "has purely sprung forth." And only in the latter itself *is* the origin in each case fully as origin. The origin is not abandoned and left behind as a beginning that stands by itself; what emanates from the river in its flowing—what the river at every point of its flowing is—is the origin.

. . . und wie die Quelle dem Strome folgt,
Wohin er denkt,

> . . . and as the source follows the river,
> To where he thinks,
>
> ("The Blind Singer," IV, 58, lines 34f.)

For this reason, the place where the river breaks off is also not some isolated locale, not the event of a mere alteration in the superficial direction of the river that is in turn immediately left behind, but the irruption of a counter-willing, counter to the originary will of the river. Only with this counter-willing does the origin enter its need and thereby come to itself. Were it not for the counter-will that made the self-will back up and flow steadfastly back into itself, then there would remain a mere flowing out and draining of the source, a running away from it. Only in the origin that has sprung forth having to cut its path in relation to this resistance does the being of the river become a destiny: a suffering in the sense of suffering that sustains. This does not refer to a merely being passively afflicted by something else, but rather to a sustaining suffering as *first actively contesting and creating beyng in the process of suffering.* Beyng as destiny does not have its origin behind it as something once imposed or assigned, as a merely inalterable 'lot,' or as a vocation that simply unfurls over and beyond everything that follows; rather, beyng as destiny is marked by surviving this rupture and willing to return from out of this into the origin. All of this, however, belongs as part of the mystery of that which has purely sprung forth. The task is to unveil the mystery of such beyng.

Whoever simply pushes the enigma aside into the 'irrational'—as that which is, so to speak, ungraspable—not only fails to solve it, but also fails to conceive and grasp it as an enigma. In thus pushing it aside, there indeed arises the appearance of not touching it, of a reverence in the face of the mystery. Yet in truth it is an indifference, one that trivializes the mystery and makes it accessible to undisciplined guessing and to the arbitrariness of whatever opinion happens to arise. As against this, it is the task of the song—of the poetizing—to unveil that which has purely sprung forth. If the poetizing is great and genuine, then it will necessarily fall short in this process. In this way, however, in the supreme passion of the most rigorous will to say, it precisely manages to run up hard against the unsayable. It is granted this poetizing only "scarcely" (line 47) to grasp what has purely sprung forth in its unconcealment, for the sake of need only, and from out of need. Yet this is the reason why it is poetizing, precisely, that must effect this unveiling—in such a way, indeed, that this unveiling becomes its primary and ultimate task.

Yet why can only song unveil this beyng of the demigods?

§18. *Interim Reflection on the Metaphysics of Poetizing*

We initially concluded our interpretation focusing on the third strophe. Our task was to arrive at a correct reading of the word "lack." Cf. "The Departure" (IV, 30, line 9):

Aber anderen Fehl denket der Weltsinn sich

Yet the world's meaning thinks a different lack

"Lack" does not here mean 'lacking' in the sense of absence; nor does it mean 'mistake' in the sense of a mere shortcoming or defect. "Lack" means missing the mark. This entails wanting to hit the mark, thus an overarching binding oneself in advance to that which provides the target. Yet this missing the mark is not a failure to attain in the sense of non-arrival—of falling short in relation to the target—but rather missing the mark in the sense of an overshooting, of an excessive thrust, and not just on one occasion, but as a disposition. "Lack" is missing the mark on account of overfullness and exceeding the measure, befalling the demigods as coming from the gods. The lack can therefore be named: God's lack, a missing the mark that overshoots out of an excess of vocation stemming from the gods. It was possible not only to demonstrate this sense of the word "lack" on the basis of other poems, but it will be substantiated above all on the basis of our poem "The Rhine" in its entirety.

Admittedly, when we refer to this entirety, then this is like the attempt to elucidate what is obscure by way of what is still more obscure. For we might repeatedly despair of our actually accomplishing a true entry into the domain where this poetizing unfolds its power. Indeed, we must do so. If the grounds for our falling short were merely extrinsic, concerning our inability and lack of preparation on the one hand, and the lack of transparency and complexity of the poem's content on the other hand, then these are things that could readily be remedied one day by others. But the reason for our falling short is an essential one: namely, that the issue is not the poem, but poetizing; that we are not familiar with the metaphysical locale of this poetizing, but that this poetizing seeks to open up a new space for poetizing within the whole of being, and thereby the possibility of a where and a there [*Dort*] where poetizing happens is first said and heard.

It is not that we continually make false moves and fail to attain it, but that from the outset we stand in an erroneous relation to the poetizing—indeed do not at all stand, but *wander in errancy:* This is what then prevents us from even being able to interpret correctly our falling short. What is most genuine is therefore willingness to despair concerning the possibility of access, for in this way we preserve a distance and remoteness and do not fall prey to the semblance of true nearness. Nearness to the work, to power, and to gods does not consist in closeness, familiarity, or imposing oneself. The degree of nearness is not measured in terms of the shortness of distance, but in terms of the expanse of the remove and in terms of the pure transparency of this expanse. We can bring to a stand only that which we are able to release into such a remove. The fact that we are so seldom capable of accomplishing such release is the reason we retain so little and most things simply whirl around us in an economy of perpetual change.

Insofar as the poetizing "The Rhine" 'thinks' the beyng of the demigods, poetically founds such beyng, it thoughtfully poetizes the essence of poetizing. Yet insofar as the beyng of the demigods is destiny, then what is destinal must also determine the beyng of the poetizing and of the poet.

If the essence of poetizing initially delimited itself for us as a founding of beyng, then the full essence of poetizing and of that which is founded in it will first open up as the beyng of such founding becomes manifest—that is, in creatively grounding the ground of the beyng of poetizing. Such beyng, however, which itself essentially prevails as a founding of beyng, can only be grounded within the essence of being as a whole. To the essence of beyng as such, however, there belongs its being cast back upon itself in the manner of founding. Beyng lets poetizing spring forth, so as to originarily find itself within it, and thus within it to open itself up in closing itself off as mystery.

In this poetizing of the beyng of the demigods—that is, of the middle of beyng, between gods and humans—beyng as a whole must unveil itself to us.

Chapter Three
That Which Has Purely Sprung Forth as Strife in the Middle of Beyng

§19. Strophe IV: The Enigma of What Has Purely Sprung Forth and the Origin of Poetizing

IV   Ein Räthsel ist Reinentsprungenes. Auch
     Der Gesang kaum darf es enthüllen. Denn
     Wie du anfiengst, wirst du bleiben,
     So viel auch wirket die Noth
50   Und die Zucht, das meiste nemlich
     Vermag die Geburt,
     Und der Lichtstral, der
     Dem Neugebornen begegnet.
     Wo aber ist einer,
     Um frei zu bleiben
     Sein Leben lang, und des Herzens Wunsch
     Allein zu erfüllen, so
     Aus günstigen Höhn, wie der Rhein.
     Und so aus heiligem Schoose
60   Glüklich geboren, wie jener?

IV   Enigma is that which has purely sprung forth. Even
     The song scarcely may unveil it. For
     As you commenced, so will you remain,
     However much need achieves,
50   And discipline, it is birth
     That is capable of most,
     And the ray of light, that
     Meets the newly born.
     Yet where is one,
     To free remain
     His whole life long, and his heart's wish

Alone to fulfill, from
Such favorable heights as the Rhine,
And from so holy a womb
60   Born happy, as that one?

Our interpretation pauses at the beginning of the fourth strophe. "Enigma is that which has purely sprung forth. Even / The song scarcely may unveil it." The resonance of the words in these two lines is already unusual with respect to their linguistic formation. "Enigma"—how this word leaps into prominence after what has gone before; "is that which has purely sprung forth"—how in this one word all that has gone before is suddenly condensed. "Even"—how this word stands nakedly into the open at the end of the line. "The song scarcely"—how these words are paired together and rise; "may unveil it"—how these fall and ebb away in unassuming peacefulness. Yet every line of Hölderlin's is like this, so long as we do not look for a canvas of sounds, but hear each line out of the fullness of its truth, where sound and meaning are not yet torn asunder.

Just as the beginning of the tenth strophe, "Demigods now I think," in the midst of the telling thrusts its intention and claim into the light, so the beginning of the fourth strophe enunciates the entire space of this poetizing. For this reason, all further preoccupation with this poetizing is immediately superfluous unless we venture the effort, from the position now attained, to secure a perspective on the whole by way of an interpretation that reaches ahead. Earlier I provided, by way of anticipation and as an external aid, an internal structural articulation in terms of a few sentences (p. 215f.). They are meant to guide the following interpretation and to seek their fullness therein.

"Enigma is that which has purely sprung forth. Even / The song scarcely may unveil it." (lines 46f.) Four things are named here and woven into an inner structural relation: (1) that which has purely sprung forth, (2) the latter as mystery, (3) the song (that is, the poetizing), and (4) the latter as a scarcely being allowed to unveil the mystery of what has purely sprung forth. This is a hint regarding the fact that the telling of the poetizing itself is simultaneously interwoven into this poetizing that is concerned with the "river." We shall unfold the poetic truth of these two lines as we carry out our interpretation with the aid of the four aforementioned points.

a) The Determinative Powers of Origin and Having Sprung
Forth and Their Enmity within the Essence
of What Has Purely Sprung Forth

It is important that from the outset we retain the full concept of that which has purely sprung forth. It comprises two things in one: (1) the origin as such (that is, that from which there springs forth that which springs forth), and (2) that which has sprung forth itself, the way it *is* as that which has sprung forth. Within what has purely sprung forth, both the origin and having sprung forth must unfold in the untarnished appearance of their determinative powers. Yet insofar as these powers, in accordance with their essence, intrinsically enter into conflict with themselves, such conflict, as pure, must unfold into supreme enmity. Because, however, enmity [*Feindseligkeit*] as blessedness [*Seligkeit*] constitutes the *unity* of one beyng, this unity too must attain or, better, maintain *supreme purity*.

That to what has purely sprung forth there belongs origin as such and having sprung forth can readily be demonstrated from the poetic work we are considering, both from what precedes the passage we have now discussed and also from what follows it. What precedes, apart from the introductory strophe, are the second and third strophes. The second concerns the origin as such; named there are the "parents" (line 27), namely, Mother Earth and the Thunderer (Zeus). There follows in the third strophe the telling of the river as that which has already sprung forth. Its beyng is determined by its having broken off from the direction in which it commenced. Because in this divergence of its direction a counter-will prevails counter to that which springs forth, that which springs forth thereby shows itself as not knowing whereto, not from mere impotence, but by virtue of the overwhelming power of the origin.

The same doubling into origin as such and having sprung forth is also named in the telling of strophe IV, which directly follows the passage we have discussed. Here, however, the origin is viewed not only in itself, but more essentially with regard to that which has sprung forth. "As you commenced, so will you remain" (line 48). The pure origin is not that which simply releases something other from itself and abandons it to itself, but rather that commencement whose power constantly leaps over what has sprung forth, outlasts it in leaping ahead of it, and is thus present in the grounding of that which remains. It is present not as something that merely has a residual effect from earlier, but as that which leaps out ahead, that which, as commencement, is thus at the same time the determinative end—in other words, is authentically the destination.

α) Conflict of the Powers of Pure Origin: Birth and Ray of Light

Such an origin, therefore, as that which in advance encompasses all that has sprung forth, "is capable" of the most (lines 50ff.):

    . . . das meiste nemlich
    Vermag die Geburt,

Und der Lichtstral, der
Dem Neugebornen begegnet.

. . . it is birth
That is capable of most,
And the ray of light, that
Meets the newly born.

To the origin as such there belong *birth and ray of light.* "Birth" here
means provenance from the concealed darkness of the womb, "Mother
Earth" (strophe II, line 25). We recall here the passage in "Germania,"
the poetic work from which we set out and at which we wish to arrive:
"Mother of all" (line 76)—"Otherwise named the Concealed One by
humans" (line 77). She is the concealed one in the original sense, because she is concealment itself, the enveloping closure of the womb.
Hence Hölderlin's extraordinary word concerning her, enunciated in
an explicitly poetic way: she is the one who "carries the abyss" (line
76). (This word, which von Hellingrath rightly adopts from version
a, is missing in the Reclam edition and also in the Insel edition of
Zinkernagel.)

Birth—this means: The origin as the grounding abyss is not altogether the origin, however, but only one power of the origin; the
other is the "ray of light" (line 52). In it there prevails the opposite direction of provenance, in its coming to meet the newly born. The "ray
of light" refers here not just to any light or brightness in general, as
opposed to darkness, but as "birth" corresponds to "Mother Earth" in
strophe II, so "ray of light" corresponds to the "Thunderer." The ray
of light is the lightning flash. Thunder, lightning, and storm are for
Hölderlin not merely that wherein something divine announces itself, but that wherein the essence of the God manifests itself. Cf. the
Letter to Böhlendorff of December 4, 1801 (V, 321):

> O friend! The world lies brighter there before me than hitherto, and more
> grave! it pleases me how things are going, it pleases me, just as in sum-
> mer when "the ancient, holy father by his gentle hand blesses us with the
> lightning he shakes down from crimson clouds." For of all the things I can
> behold of God, this sign has become for me the chosen one.

In the ray of light, that which springs forth receives the possibility of
the illuminating look—that is, of that look into the essence in which
the excessive fullness of a great willing presses toward the emergence

of figure. Figure, however, is both inner delimitation bringing itself to a stand and entry into the dark, into which it closes itself off as into the gravity that has been overcome. What is dark, by contrast, itself does not lose its unfettered character in the configuring light of delimitation, but lets it become conspicuous. Cf. "The Titans" (IV, 210, lines 68ff.):

> Und in die Tiefe greifet
> Dass es lebendig werde
> Der Allerschütterer, meinen die
> Es komme der Himmlische
> Zu Todten herab und gewaltig dämmerts
> Im ungebundenen Abgrund
> Im allesmerkenden auf.

> And into the depths reaches
> That things may come alive
> He who shakes all, they say
> The Heavenly One comes
> Down to the dead and violently light irrupts
> Within the unfettered abyss
> In which all becomes conspicuous.

The powers of origin, Earth—Thunderer (birth—ray of light) are those of the *pure* origin; precisely for this reason they can least of all ever be separated out individually—a view one might have, were one to think Earth in isolation and gods in isolation. But the truth lies in the opposite direction: The purer these powers, the more essential, and that means, the more necessary, is their reciprocal relation. This pure origin is, after all, the origin of the demigods, in whose beyng the arc spanning their provenance and future does not stay fastened halfway or remain a mixture of the two. Certainly, in the realm of habitual humankind too we still see a pale reflection of the necessary reciprocal relation between birth and ray of light. There too mere birth remains dim and obdurate and a mere seething, without the illuminating look and the law-giving of that which accords with the essence and that which opposes the essence. Likewise, the ray of light remains fragile and empty, fluttering and playful without the pressing force of birth that in turn closes off. The more pure the origin, the more pure and unconditional is the conflict in the powers of the origin. The originary character of the conflict is all the more genuine the more such conflict conceals itself.

β) The Counter-Striving of Need and Discipline in Having
Sprung Forth. Outline of the Essential Structure of
What Has Purely Sprung Forth

What has purely sprung forth, however, is not determined solely by
the origin, which is in itself doubly directed, but also by the manner
in which its having sprung forth remains. The origin is indeed what
comes first—to the extent that, on the one hand, without it there
would be nothing that had sprung forth at all, and on the other hand,
within the pure origin the commencement embraces that which is
coming by seizing it in advance. Birth and ray of light are indeed capable of "most" (line 50); yet "much" (line 49) is also effected by *need
and discipline*. To these there corresponds all that is referred to in the
third strophe in terms of the diverting of the river's original direction.

In *need* there lies on each occasion compulsion, constraint, impossibility of escape, and constriction, in such a way that need thereby
compels a decision, or else a refraining from decision, an avoidance
that necessitates pressing forward upon new paths. Sprung forth in
the sense of being-in-having-sprung-forth means withstanding such
need. Seen in terms of the origin, need is something that falls to us
[*ein Zufallendes*]—yet not accidentally [*zufällig*]—for need, as necessi-
tating, always creates a turning in each case for that which has sprung
forth, thereby lending determinacy to its attempt to merely flow away.
Need [*Not*] is the ground of necessity [*Notwendigkeit*],[10] provided that
we comprehend it in general in its essential belonging to that which
has purely sprung forth. Need, however, turns not only against one
of the powers of the origin each time, but always against the origin
itself, against both powers in the unity of their own proper conflict.

Within having sprung forth, there operates—together with need—
discipline. In contrast to need as compulsion and constraint, discipline
brings an inner harnessing and binding into the very figuration that
effects and creates. Like need, discipline too comes to encounter the
origin, yet it does not necessitate, as does need, but precisely frees the
excessive will of the origin in enjoining it into the law and in explicitly assimilating such law to itself as what is indeed its ownmost.

Discipline too runs counter to the origin in its entirety. Yet just as
the powers of the origin intrinsically strive counter to one another, so
also do need and discipline, provided we comprehend need as outer
discipline and discipline as inner need, where 'outer' refers to that
which is without freedom and untethered, and 'inner' to that which is
free and provides binding. Such birth and ray of light—need and discipline that intrinsically strive counter to one another—are, however,
in conflict with one another within the entire being of that which has

purely sprung forth. In the crossing over that belongs to this counter-striving, there prevails the originary hostility, yet one that, because it is no breaking apart of oppositions, but rather their originary unification, has the character of a blessedness [*Seligkeit*]—'blessed enmity' [*Feind-seligkeit*]—if we may be permitted to attribute to this word this counter-turning sense of against and toward one another.

By this path of analysis, we can create for ourselves a sketch of the essential structure of what Hölderlin names that which has purely sprung forth, wherein lies contained the beyng of the demigods, that beyng which the poem "The Rhine" poetically thinks.

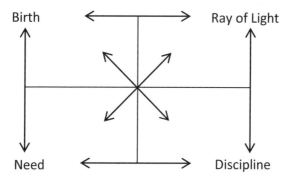

Yet that which has purely sprung forth is an "enigma." With this, we approach what has purely sprung forth as a mystery. In its grounds, however, the mysterious character pertaining to that which has purely sprung forth is not an additional aspect; rather, the enigmatic belongs to the inner essence of what has purely sprung forth. Therefore, we shall not be able to surmise, or ever to explain, such beyng by means of the sketch we have just drawn (birth—ray of light—need—discipline) and, above all, we should from the outset never wish to explain it, precisely if we understand such beyng.

In the commonplace view regarding cognition and knowing, explaining and understanding are conflated as being the same thing. That which has been explained is counted as having been made comprehensible and understood. Occasionally, a difference of degree is inserted between explanation and understanding, and one conceives of explanation as being the understanding of what is thing-like and corporeal, whereas understanding, by contrast, is regarded as that explaining directed toward the psychic and spiritual. By contrast, I take understanding to be the opposite in essence to explanation, and regard explanation as the necessary un-essence [*Un-wesen*] of understanding. To explain something means to bring it back to something that is clear to us—that is, in this context, to whatever is handy and manageable. All explanation is always this escape into what is commonplace for us, that wherein we appease ourselves on a daily basis, that which we immediately have at our disposal at all times, that with which we are already familiar. This is why the discovery of an explanation is always satisfying, in the sense of providing the peacefulness and undisturbedness of an effortless possessing and having. This is why explanation always has that insulting aspect, because it brings that which is explained back to the level of what is readily familiar to everyone. (Cf. also from his perspective: Hegel, *Phenomenology of Spirit*, p.128.[1]) Where something has been explained, there there is nothing more to understand. But that means, strictly speaking, that understanding has no place there and no right to be there. Understanding is authentically—regarded in its originary essence— knowledge of the inexplicable, not as though it would explain the latter and thus eliminate what had been explained; rather, understanding precisely lets what is inexplicable stand as such. Understanding an enigma, therefore, does not mean solving the enigma, but the converse: releasing the enigma as that concerning which and with regard to which we have no known counsel in the sense of our everyday, calculative means of disposal. The more originarily we understand, the further that which is unexplained and inexplicable extends and becomes unveiled as such.

Summary: We are attempting an interpretation of the two lines with which the fourth strophe begins. Their illumination casts a path of light through everything that follows in the poem. We named four things: (1) that which has purely sprung forth, (2) the latter as mystery, (3) the song (that is, the poetizing), and (4) the latter as a scarcely being allowed to unveil the mystery of what has purely sprung forth. Insofar as we are told of the poetry itself here, poetizing itself is poetized, entwining itself in this poetry that tells of the "river."

1. Concerning that which has purely sprung forth: It is essential to grasp it in its full concept from the outset. This entails: first, the origin as such, from where that which springs forth springs forth; second, that which has sprung forth itself in its having sprung forth. This dual aspect can be documented from the two strophes directly preceding. Strophe II concerns the origin as such; the parents are named: Mother Earth and the Thunderer (Zeus). Strophe III tells of the river as already sprung forth, of the breaking off from the direction in which it commences. These two aspects are taken up again and brought together

---

1. *Phänomenologie des Geistes.* Fourth edition, 136. Hegel, *Werke,* Jubiläumsausgabe. Edited by H. Glockner. Volume 2, Stuttgart, 1964.[11]

in strophe IV. Origin in general: "As you commenced, so will you remain" (line 48).

The commencement leaps over what has sprung forth, and in leaping ahead outlasts that which remains, embraces the latter coming from its end, and thus, at the same time, becomes the destination for that which remains. Such an origin is capable of the most. To it there belong birth and ray of light. Birth means provenance from out of the closedness of the womb. Yet this is only one power of the origin; the other is the ray of light: not some arbitrary brightness, but the lightning flash—the God, that look into the essence that pertains to a great willing that wills the emergence of figure. A reciprocal relation between these is necessary.

Yet this is only one, initial aspect of that which has purely sprung forth: namely, that which is capable of most. Much too is effected by need and discipline. Need—compulsion—the impossibility of escape compels decision, or refraining from or avoiding decision. It works against the two powers of the origin. Discipline—as distinct from the compulsion that restricts—is the harnessing and binding that proceeds from the inside, assimilation of law. It too directs itself against the entire origin.

Just as birth and ray of light intrinsically strive counter to one another, so too do need and discipline. Thus there prevails a counterstriving that crosses over itself within that which has purely sprung forth, an originary hostility, and accordingly an originary unity that has the character of blessed enmity.

2. Concerning the enigma: This we shall not explain by means of the sketch of the beyng of the demigods that we have drawn, but rather understand it, release it as the mystery. We regard explaining and understanding as opposite in essence. To explain means to bring back to what is commonplace and familiar to us, to fit it back into this. Where something has been explained, there is nothing more to be understood; everything already has the semblance of being understood. Explaining is the corrupted essence of understanding. Understanding the enigma, therefore, is not equivalent to solving it, but means precisely holding fast to that which is inexplicable and thus attaining a manner of authentic knowing.

b) "Intimacy" as the Originary Unity of the Powers of What
Has Purely Sprung Forth, and as the Mystery of Such Beyng

The sketch we have drawn of that which has purely sprung forth does not explain the latter, but the converse: It merely brings us to the nearest and most extreme edge of understanding. Understanding first becomes actualized as a standing within the unity of the reciprocal counter-turning of the powers of blessed enmity. It is not just that the one power opposes itself to the other in their striving against one another, however. Rather, each power seeks to disempower the other in wanting to displace the other, and sets itself before the other, dissimulating and concealing it. The enmity is thus a reciprocal concealing, the happening of a concealment that prevails within itself. We release ourselves into such concealment when we hold fast to what is counter-turning and hostile in its blessedness—that is, its unity— instead of resolving it into determinate parts and then indeed wanting in the end to calculate it in terms of something. Yet this unity of the inimical is not that vacuous and superficial kind, where we merely weld together the unruly parts into a comprehensive amalgam. Such unity remains forever outside of what is unified and is incidental to it.

Originary unity, by contrast, is that which unites in letting spring forth, and as such letting spring forth, and, at the same time, holds apart that which has sprung forth in the hostility of its essential powers. Such originary and thus singular unifying is that prevailing unity that Hölderlin, when he tells of it, names by the word "intimacy," *Innigkeit*. For us, the word "intimacy" signifies merely an individual tonality of feeling, along the lines of a particularly cherished fondness of the heart. For Hölderlin, this word is the foundational metaphysical word, and therefore altogether removed from all romantic sentimentality, even where it is used to name the attunement of existence [*Dasein*]. Hölderlin on one occasion names the Greeks "the intimate people" ("The Archipelago," IV, 91, line 90). In an earlier context (p. 105ff.) we already pointed, by way of anticipation, to the word "intimacy" and what it refers to, and related its significance to the ἕν and ἁρμονία of Heraclitus (p. 111) To this alone is it comparable, and yet only comparable, by no means to be equated with it, and not only, for instance, because Hölderlin stands in another era. What he calls "intimacy" is, despite everything, fundamentally different too from what is thought by his contemporaries—say, from Hegel's concept of the Absolute. What Hölderlin names by this newly said word, intimacy, is named in a poetic naming or, better, nominated to what it is. Intimacy is that originary unity of the enmity of the powers of what has purely sprung forth. It is the mystery belonging to such beyng. What has purely sprung forth is never simply inexplicable in some respect, in *one* particular level of its beyng; it remains enigma through and through. Intimacy has the nature of a mystery, not because others fail to penetrate it; rather, in itself it prevails in essence as mystery. There is mystery only where intimacy holds sway. When, however, this mystery is named and told of as such, then it thereby becomes manifest. Yet the unveiling of its manifestness is precisely a not wanting to explain, but rather understanding it as self-concealing concealment. Bringing the mystery to understanding is indeed an unveiling, but it is that unveiling that may be accomplished only in song, in the poetizing.

How does poetizing, then, in its essence relate to this task? What is its relation to the mystery, to what has purely sprung forth? The poetic unveiling of this mystery can surely only be one particular task for poetizing; yet it has to take on this task when it itself arrives at its own limits and thus takes on itself in what it is capable of. Thus we come to the third question, that concerning the essence of song, of poetizing.

c) Poetizing as Founding Beyng in the Grounding
Opening Up of Intimacy

In one respect, the answer to this question already lies within what was said regarding the first and second points: Unveiling the mystery of what has purely sprung forth is the singular and authentic mandate for poetizing as such in general. The mystery is not just any enigma: The mystery is intimacy; yet the latter is beyng itself, the blessed enmity of conflicting powers, in which hostility there arises a decision concerning the gods and the Earth, human beings and all that they make. As the founding of beyng, poetizing is the grounding opening up of intimacy, which means nothing other than this: Poetizing is essentially a scarcely being allowed to unveil the mystery. This unveiling is not a special mandate for particular poets, in the sense that these poets would select a particular object for themselves. Rather, this mandate of scarcely being allowed to unveil the mystery of that which has purely sprung forth is *the* poetic mandate pure and simple—the only one. For this reason, everything else that calls itself poetry, and that in some sense also is this, always is so only in constantly remaining back behind this founding telling. If the essence of poetizing is to be determined, then poetizing, as with every essential creating of history, must always be comprehended in terms of its most extreme limit. The standards for determining its essence are to be found only where the creators exceed themselves beyond their ability. At such limits, the creators—and thus the poets too—know that there is no object for them, and that they must first found beyng. This is why the very question of what the object of art, poetizing, or philosophy is, is fundamentally inappropriate and the source of endless confusion. On the same grounds, not only can one not 'fabricate' the creators, one cannot set them any tasks either, nor even suggest such. One may not even expect of them that they 'bring the psychic import of our time into poetic form,' because this is an unpoetic suggestion to the poets, and poses no danger only because whoever is a poet will not listen to this and will leave to mere authors the task of fulfilling such assignments.

For this reason too, one can never directly say, on the basis of whatever is in each case contemporary, whether someone is a creator. At most, one can say that he is not. In any case, he who—today—does something like 'putting into verse the psychic import of our time' is not a poet: not because such content would supposedly be something indifferent, nor because the poetic form and the mastery thereof would be insufficient, but because such poetic composition is not a founding, but rather—as poetic reporting—differs from the activity of a newspaper journalist only by degree. In the case of such reportage, it is always what is presently at hand, and not the historical, that provides an otherwise missing anchor point and ground for those who are without that necessity that comes only from that beyng that is to be founded.

In other words, the scarcely being allowed to unveil the mystery is precisely a continually growing *necessity* to unveil that which has purely sprung forth. Why? We shall find the answer only if we now take a decisive step in our illumination of the essence of poetizing— that is, if we once again question, and indeed pose the following question: In what, then, is poetizing for its part grounded as a founding of beyng? By way of anticipation, and in a formulaic manner, we may answer: Because poetizing, as a founding of beyng, is of the same origin as that which it properly founds, for this reason, and for this reason alone, is poetizing also capable of telling of beyng, and even must do so.

We are unfolding the question concerning the origin and ground of poetizing as a founding of beyng here, however, not in its metaphysical context pertaining purely to thinking, but from out of the poetizing of Hölderlin as the poet of the poet, and this only within the limits of the interpretation of our poetic work "The Rhine." In so doing, we must indeed go beyond the bounds of the poem into the broader domain of this poetizing. Here, we wish above all to return to that poem that has, from the beginning, provided us with hints concerning the essence of the poet and of poetizing, that poem that is without a title and begins: "As when on feast day, to see the field / A countryman goes." If, in what follows, we shall also attempt a more essential elucidation than in our remarks hitherto, still this all remains far removed from a thoughtfully and poetically configured interpretation that would thus alone let this poetic work resonate. The first three strophes (IV, 151f.) read:

Wie wenn am Feiertage, das Feld zu sehn
Ein Landmann geht, des Morgens, wenn
Aus heisser Nacht die kühlenden Blize fielen
Die ganze Zeit und fern noch tönet der Donner,
In sein Gestade wieder tritt der Strom,
Und frisch der Boden grünt
Und von des Himmels erfreuendem Reegen
Der Weinstok trauft und glänzend
In stiller Sonne stehn die Bäume des Haines:

10   So steht ihr unter günstiger Witterung
Ihr die kein Meister allein, die wunderbar
Allgegenwärtig erziehet in leichtem Umfangen
Die mächtige, die göttlichschöne Natur.
Drum wenn zu schlafen sie scheint zu Zeiten des Jahrs
Am Himmel oder unter den Pflanzen oder den Völkern,
So trauert der Dichter Angesicht auch,
Sie scheinen allein zu seyn, doch ahnen sie immer.
Denn ahnend ruhet sie selbst auch.

Jezt aber tagts! Ich harrt und sah es kommen,
20   Und was ich sah, das Heilige sei mein Wort.
Denn sie, sie selbst, die älter denn die Zeiten
Und über die Götter des Abends und Orients ist,
Die Natur ist jezt mit Waffenklang erwacht,
Und hoch vom Äther bis zum Abgrund nieder
Nach vestem Geseze, wie einst, aus heiligem Chaos gezeugt,
Fühlt neu die Begeisterung sich,
Die Allerschaffende wieder.

As when on feast day, to see the field
A countryman goes, in morning, when
From sultry night the cooling lightning flashes fell
The entire time and far off the thunder still sounds,
The river returns to its banks,
And the soil becomes verdant afresh
And with the heavens' cheering rain
The grapevine is soaked and glistening
In tranquil sunlight stand the trees of the grove:

10   So you stand under favorable weather
You, who are taught by no master alone, but
Miraculously all-present, in gentle embrace,
The magnificent one, divinely beautiful Nature.

Thus when she seems to sleep at certain times of year
In the heavens or among the plants or peoples,
Then the poets' faces are mournful too,
They seem to be alone, yet they intimate always.
For resting she is intimative too.

But now day breaks! I waited and saw it coming,
20   And what I saw, may the Holy be my word.
For she, she herself, more ancient than the times
And beyond the gods of Occident and Orient,
Nature is now awakened with the clang of arms,
And from the Aether on high down into the abyss
According to solid law, as in times past, born of holy chaos
The inspiration feels itself anew,
All-creating once again.

The first strophe is a pure miracle of the purest simplicity of poetic say-ing. Even the most gentle attempt at an elucidation at once appears as a mistake and as superfluous. Nevertheless, here as nowhere else, not even for what seem at first sight to be Hölderlin's most obscure poems, an interpretation is needed. When it shall be destined to be provided for the Germans, we do not know. What we offer here is merely a hint, a tentative probing, and, above all, a warding off.

From this orientation, we may say this: The first strophe does not give the poetic depiction of a process of nature, nor the description of the atmosphere of a landscape. For this reason, it is also not some-thing like a graphic introduction to the subsequent poetizing of non-intuitable, abstract thoughts. What is said is not even a comparison—an 'image,' for instance, or 'metaphor'—even though the poem begins with the words "As when . . ." and strophe II continues "So they stand. . . ." Yet what, then, in all the world is a 'poetic comparison' meant to be, if not this, where surely psychic lived experiences within the mind of the poet are compared with the material circumstances out-side in nature?

We ask in response, initially and as an aside: Who, then, guarantees us that the concept of a 'poetic comparison' is not already the result of a misunderstanding of poetic telling, and that traditional poetics, just like logic and grammar, has not arisen from an inability to come to terms with the essence of poetizing? Let us just look at the dubious apparatus of contemporary literary theory, where all the components of ancient poetics are at work in a corruption of their essence and in all sorts of guises, even if the orientation of their content changes. Until recently one was still searching for the psychoanalytic underpinnings of poetizing; now, everything is dripping with [talk of] national tradition [*Volkstum*] and blood and soil, but everything remains wedded to the old.

'Poetic comparison'—what an unpoetic concept that is in the end! Yet people are so occupied with writing books, with founding new journals, with organizing compilations of literary works, and with not missing the boat that they have no time for such questions. An entire life could be spent on such things, even the effort of an entire generation. Indeed! So long as we fail to devote ourselves to such questions, talk of the 'heroic science' that is supposedly now coming is idle talk.

Poetic comparison for . . . What is being compared to what? A process in nature to a lived experience in the spirit. What does 'nature' mean here, and what does 'spirit' mean? Today we think both in a Christian manner, even if the terms have long since acquired a secularized sense. Yet in whatever way we wish to think these concepts, of what use is comparison, if the poet says that nature herself teaches the poet? The nature of which Hölderlin tells here and in his poetic work as a whole is not the nature of landscape; nature is also not the opposing domain to spirit or to history. Nature is here, as we might say quite vaguely and vacuously, the 'universal'—and yet not the primal soup or primal swamp and the bubbling over with which the biological-organic worldview ends and begins. Nature is the all-embracing. Yet this telling is far removed from every naturalism, and is just as remote from every spiritualism. "Nature"—what does Hölderlin say of her? See strophe III, lines 21f. (IV, 151):

> Denn sie [die Natur], sie selbst, die älter denn die Zciten
> Und über die Götter des Abends und Orients ist,

> For she [nature], she herself, more ancient than the times
> And beyond the gods of Occident and Orient,

We might think of the φύσις of the Greeks. And we may do so too, granted that we have a sufficient understanding and intimation of this φύσις. And yet—even this is not sufficient. Hölderlin is not the Greek world, but the future of the Germans. No one can help us get there if we do not rouse ourselves and, in so doing, first experience and concede that we still lack everything necessary for the departure on this journey.

The first strophe of our poem, and the poem itself, is no depiction of nature, no comparison. Here, nothing is said at all about something else. The saying of this poetizing is in itself the jubilation of beyng, the jubilant calm of beyng in awaiting its storm. This saying is not a layer of words referring to some meaning or hidden meaning; rather, it itself, just as it is said, is the prevailing of beyng. To our initial and habitual view, this saying is admittedly just a poem—printed, copied on many pages, something that can be read here or there. All this is an illusion, and indeed a necessary illusion of beyng itself, of the saying that is said here—said and yet stands unsaid among the people. This saying is not something merely at hand in their libraries or their bookstores or printing shops, but is right in the innermost midst of their language, in that language that is only a shell of communication and veiling, and can be such only because it is the core of historical Dasein—that language which each day in the depth of its flowing can splash over and roar over its own saying only because, in what is concealed, it remains a river in which and as which beyng founds itself.

Remaining quite extrinsically focused on the appearance of the poem as yet, let us simply heed those features we can point to in a formulaic manner: the sultry night (line 3); the tranquil sunlight (line 9); the lightning flashes that fall (line 3); the trees that stand (line 9); the vital, enriching freshness of the soil; and the far-receding thunder. What prevails in essence here, if not birth and the ray of light, the Earth and the Thunderer, the powers of the origin, and indeed in that temporary harmony that releases everything by binding it into its own prevailing, a blessedness that is yet only and properly enmity: intimacy itself, beyng. These powers are the "favorable weather" (line 10) of the origin for that which springs forth, powers to which need and discipline also belong, yet "are taught by no master alone . . ." (lines 11f.). All teaching is grounded in a relational being drawn into the origin. Everything *is* only within the conflict of powers itself, within the intimacy of nature. The latter, however, is herself counter-turning *as* the poetic saying, not simply *within* this saying, for the saying arises from the "storms" (line 39) that "drift between heaven and Earth and among the peoples" (line 42). The saying of the poetizing arises from beyng, yet only so as to preserve such beyng within itself and thus "bear witness to both" (line 49), to the gods and to humans, as whose midst there prevails in its essence what has purely sprung forth: the mystery, intimacy.

The saying of the poetizing, as a happening, is that which frees gods and humans for their vocation. Without this saying, everything would necessarily become confused in the darkness of the holy wilderness and be "consumed" in the 'searing excess of the heavenly fire.' (Cf. "The Titans," IV, 208, lines 23ff.) Poetizing is the opening up of the 'enmity of the powers of beyng': "Nature is now awakened with the clang of arms" (line 23). The enmity of beyng breaks out, and indeed out of the most far-ranging conflicts: "from the Aether on high down into the abyss" (line 24). In this conflictual turning of both, however, the all-creating, the founding, 'feels itself again' and comes once more to itself and into its unity. Within and as such founding, there prevails the intimacy of beyng itself.

Poetizing is the fundamental event of beyng as such. It founds beyng, and has to found it, because, as founding, it is nothing other than the clang of arms of nature herself, beyng that brings itself to itself in the word. Poetizing as founding—as that creating that has no object and that never merely sings about what lies at hand—is always an intimating, a waiting, a seeing come. Poetizing is the word of this that has been intimated; it is, as word, this that has been intimated itself. Because beyng prevails in essence as enmity, it appears to be sleeping at times and among the peoples. Blessedness looks like tranquil calm, and calm is the semblance of absence of movement—in this case of the movement of those that turn against one another, the swords that cross in the clang of arms. Yet as blessedness, this calm is in truth enmity. The as-yet inaccessible knowledge concerning it is therefore, with regard to the conflicts and their unity, at times more prepared, at times more interpretive and discerning, and at other times as though entirely absent. Yet beyng itself, nature, as this intimacy, is always "intimative" (line 18). Intimation is that arousing-restrained attunement in which the mystery opens itself as such, spreading out in its entire expanses and yet folding itself together into one, where the unharnessed announces itself in its being harnessed.

Because the poets are not directed toward nature as an object, for instance; because, rather, "nature" as beyng founds itself in saying, the saying of the poets as the self-saying of nature is of the same essence as the latter. This is why it is said of the poets that they 'intimate always.' Their saying is not the unfettered creating of an isolated individual; it is not oriented toward productions, nor does it evaluate productions with respect to whether and to what extent the 'personality' of the poet finds its fulfillment in what is created. The poets 'intimate always.' Therein lies a delimitation of the essence of poetizing, and it means: being originarily enjoined into the intimacy of beyng as such. This intimating is not some free-floating conjecture or mere trying out of ideas that occur to one, but rather "According to solid law, as in times past" (line 25). That the poets intimate always does not mean that they are poets and in addition they also intimate. It means, rather, that only insofar as they are those who steadfastly intimate—intimate together with beyng itself—do they become, and are they, poets. Poetizing as the founding of beyng is original law-giving, in such a way that laws as such do not emerge at all, and yet everything enjoins itself to such order.

These hints must here suffice to shed light on our third question concerning the origin of poetizing in its relation to the beyng that founds itself in it. In the essence of beyng itself, understood as "nature" (intimacy), is grounded the possibility and necessity of poetizing. The struggle for the essence of poetizing and its 'locale' within beyng finds fulfillment in the period of Hölderlin's greatest creativity. We must from the outset include in the sphere of this struggle those poetic attempts in which Hölderlin seeks to poetize the poet and thinker in the figure of "Empedocles" in order to establish a new commencement for the poetizing of our people. The poetizing of *Empedocles* has indeed remained a fragment; yet we always forget that what the poetizing of *Empedocles* sought to accomplish is configured to supreme purity in such poetic works as "Germania" and "The Rhine." We must only comprehend the purity of the standing within themselves of these poetic works from the outset as *said intimacy*. And this means as supreme enmity and as counter-turning that stands over against us like a 'holy confusion.' Such confusion can be undone if we bring with us the right measure for essential simplicity, and do not conflate this with an easy and straightforward comprehensibility.

Our task now is to pursue the poetizing itself as a scarcely being allowed to unveil the mystery of what has purely sprung forth.

d) River and Poet in Their Original Belonging to the Essence of Beyng. Poetizing as Scarcely Being Allowed to Unveil the Mystery

Before we set forth on this path, we shall once more recall some essential points. The saying concerns the river Rhine. This saying is the poetic thinking of demigods. Their essence is to inhabit and sustain the middle of beyng between gods and humans: that middle in which and for which the whole of beings opens itself up. To these demigods belong the creators themselves, and to these the poets. The beyng of the poet is grounded in "nature" (beyng as such), which says itself originarily in the poetizing.

The river, however, is not a symbol for the demigods; rather, it is itself, as it founds the land as land and as homeland of the people. This dwelling and Dasein of the people, however, insofar as it is, is poetic. In poetizing it originally sets paths and limits for its history. That is the essence of the river. The river's flowing, as having sprung forth from the origin, is that which has purely sprung forth.

The river is river, the demigod is demigod, the poet is poet. Yet river and poet both belong in their essence to the founding of dwelling and of the Dasein of a historical people. River and poet are the same in their originary belonging to the essence of beyng, insofar as it appears as history and thus also as nature in the narrower sense. Yet here, where Hölderlin is entrusted with the task of the founding of our beyng, that which has purely sprung forth, the originary essence of river and demigod must be said before all else. This saying is a scarcely being allowed to unveil. We know: The innermost essence of what has purely sprung forth is the intrinsically counter-turning doubling of origin as springing forth and having sprung forth. For this reason, the saying of the river cannot from the outset be a straightforward progression narrating its emergence, its subsequent course, and finally its flowing out into the sea. That would be a poetic depiction of a natural phenomenon, but not the poetizing that is here entrusted to Hölderlin as his task.

If we have some intimation of this poetizing, we must instead expect that what has purely sprung forth will unfold itself in the counter-turning relation between springing forth and having sprung forth. The sequence of strophes is in itself counter-turning, yet not only this: The emergence of this counter-turning relation as such becomes an intensification into the supreme strife of both; and in this strife the most intimate intimacy must finally open itself up. In this *telling opening up of intimacy,* however, the beyng of what has purely sprung forth of the demigods, the middle of beyng itself, is poetically founded.

We shall now—within this perspective on the whole—attempt an outline of the following strophes, not as a hasty indication of content as we pass over the strophes, but quite the contrary: We seek to bring ourselves closer to the fundamental trait of the poetizing, this saying of intimacy. For our interpretation, this means that we shall follow the blessed enmity of the strophes as it intensifies itself and drives itself to a peak from both sides. To this end, we may recall the articulation of the strophes that was indicated earlier: I, II to IX, X to XIII, XIV, and XV. This is merely a makeshift assistance, however. Whoever is capable of standing within the wrought simplicity of this poetizing has no need of such 'numbering.' We shall follow the strophes up to the next major break, strophe X.

§20. Strophes V to IX: Unfolding the Essence of What Has Purely Sprung Forth in the Conflict between Springing Forth and Having Sprung Forth

a) Strophe V: The Having Sprung Forth of What Has Purely Sprung Forth. The Coming to Be of the Original Landscape out of the Spirit of the River

Already in the fourth strophe, where we are told of what has purely sprung forth as a whole, and of the saying thereof, this saying itself begins at line 54:

Wo aber ist einer,
Um frei zu bleiben
Sein Leben lang, und des Herzens Wunsch
Allein zu erfüllen, so
Aus günstigen Höhn, wie der Rhein.
Und so aus heiligem Schoose
60   Glüklich geboren, wie jener?

Yet where is one,
To free remain
His whole life long, and his heart's wish
Alone to fulfill, from
Such favorable heights as the Rhine,
And from so holy a womb
60   Born happy, as that one?

Praising the good fortune of such an origin, the "favorable heights" (line 58), pure freedom and the blessedness of good fortune, from which everything here must turn out well—where it cannot properly be asked at all whether, given this supreme favor where such an origin withholds nothing, something could ever result in misfortune or in adversity. For this reason, such favor pertaining to the origin of what has purely sprung forth is accompanied, in harmonious counterplay, by the having sprung forth of what has purely sprung forth, of which we are told in strophe V (IV, 174):

V   Drum ist ein Jauchzen sein Wort.
Nicht liebt er, wie andere Kinder,
In Wikelbanden zu weinen;
Denn wo die Ufer zuerst
An die Seit ihm schleichen, die krummen,
Und durstig umwindend ihn,
Den Unbedachten, zu ziehn
Und wohl zu behüten begehren
Im eigenen Zahne, lachend
70   Zerreisst er die Schlangen und stürzt
Mit der Beut und wenn in der Eil'
Ein Grösserer ihn nicht zähmt,
Ihn wachsen lässt, wie der Bliz, muss er
Die Erde spalten, und wie Bezauberte fliehn
Die Wälder ihm nach und zusammensinkend die Berge.

V   Thus a jubilance is his word.
Not like other children does he love

To wail in swaddling wraps;
For where the banks at first
Creep to his side, the winding ones,
And thirstily entwining him desire
To steer the impudent one,
And presumably to protect him,
With his own tooth, laughing
70   He rips apart the serpents and rushes off
With his prey and if in his hurry
Someone greater does not tame him,
Lets him grow, like lightning must he
Split the Earth, and as though enchanted flee
After him the woods and mountains collapsing.

There is a "jubilance" (line 61) on the part of what has sprung forth—in its beyng, an overflowing breaking loose, high-spirited tearing apart and splitting the Earth, enchanting the Earth, the first untamed forming of the banks; the river draws the woods into its wake and the mountains as they collapse. Here the coming to be of the original landscape happens proceeding from the spirit of the river.

b) Strophe VI: The Harnessing of the Demigods and Creators by the God. The River as Grounder of the Dwellings of Humans

And yet, in this fortunate, jubilant beyng of what has purely sprung forth there now comes the first "however." See strophe VI (IV, 174f.):

VI   Ein Gott will aber sparen den Söhnen
Das eilende Leben und lächelt,
Wenn unenthaltsam, aber gehemmt
Von heiligen Alpen, ihm
80   In der Tiefe, wie jener, zürnen die Ströme.
In solcher Esse wird dann
Auch alles Lautre geschmiedet,
Und schön ists, wie er drauf,
Nachdem er die Berge verlassen,
Stillwandelnd sich im deutschen Lande
Begnüget und das Sehnen stillt
Im guten Geschäffte, wenn er das Land baut
Der Vater Rhein und liebe Kinder nährt
In Städten, die er gegründet.

VI   A god however wishes to spare his sons
A hurried life and smiles,
When unrelentingly, yet restrained

> By holy Alps, down
> 80   In the depths, the rivers rage at him, as does that one.
> In such a forge too is
> Everything pure then wrought,
> And beautiful it is, how then,
> Abandoning the mountains,
> And tranquilly wandering, he contents himself
> In the German land and stills his longing
> In good trade, as he builds the land,
> Does Father Rhine, and nourishes dear children
> In towns that he has founded.

"A god however wishes to spare his sons / A hurried life and smiles," "A god"—not just any god, rather: Where the origin is a divine one, as here, there the God has already preempted matters, and he wishes to spare all hurry. This preemptive intervention on the part of the God is the power of the origin in the form of an inhibition that restrains.

This "sparing" [sparen] is an essential word of Hölderlin's. It is ambivalent, and means on the one hand as much as 'to spare' [er-sparen] someone something, thus to exempt and protect them. For having one's origin from the divine constantly brings one in danger of excess, of untamed streaming away, and thus of desolation. Such desolation is spared through the God at the same time sparing in the sense of conserving and preserving within the original, divine vocation. The God casts a delay into the impetuousness of self-willing on the part of the one springing forth. The power of the origin in this way throws itself counter to the unrestrained release of what has sprung forth; it is spared its hurry. Through such sparingness, a domain is sparingly opened in having sprung forth within which that which has sprung forth is itself set into its limit and finds a hold and is hammered into its wrought shape. This sparing, as a protective sparing that preserves, belongs to the essence of the relation of the God to the demigods and creators. We hear directly of this relation in the poem "Conciliator, you who never believed . . ." (IV, 163, lines 28ff.):

> Zuvorbestimmt wars. Und es lächelt Gott
> Wenn unaufhaltsam aber von seinen Bergen gehemmt
> 30   Ihm zürnend in den ehernen Ufern brausen die Ströme,
> Tief wo kein Tag die begrabenen nennt.
> Und o, dass immer, allerhaltender, du auch mich
> So haltest und leichtentfliegende Seele mir sparest,

> Preordained it was. And God smiles
> When unceasingly yet constrained by his mountains

30   Raging at him the rivers thunder within their banks of ore,
        Deep where no day names the buried ones.
        And O, may you always, all-sustaining one, thus
        Preserve me too and spare my soul that readily takes flight,

Discipline, as this harnessing restraint, thus enters into the idiosyncratic force of that which has sprung forth, yet in such a way that this discipline itself, which is creative, effects limit and measure and constancy. This is why we read in strophe VI, line 83, "And beautiful it is, how then. . . ." The river now creates for the land a forged space and delimited locale for settlement and commerce, and for the people, land that can be cultivated and the sustaining of their immediate Dasein. The river is not a body of water that simply flows past the locale of human beings; rather, its flowing, as land-forming, first creates the possibility of grounding the dwellings of humans. The river is a founder and poet, not just metaphorically, but as itself.

That which has purely sprung forth thus now appears as inhibited, and as keeping to itself in being thus inhibited, and in this way first appears creative in a disciplined manner. What has purely sprung forth is brought to fulfillment in turning counter to the fortunate, wild jubilation characterizing its commencement, and to its tearing away. The river's 'contenting himself in the German land' appears as the fulfilled harmony of origin and having sprung forth.

c) Strophe VII: Inherence of Beyng in the Origin
as Condition for Creative Self-Restriction.
The Counter-Turning within the Beyng of the Demigods

Then begins strophe VII, forcefully set off against it (IV, 175):

90 VII Doch nimmer, nimmer vergisst ers.
         Denn eher muss die Wohnung vergehn,
         Und die Sazung, und zum Unbild werden
         Der Tag der Menschen, ehe vergessen
         Ein solcher dürfte den Ursprung
         Und die reine Stimme der Jugend.
         Wer war es, der zuerst
         Die Liebesbande verderbt
         Und Strike von ihnen gemacht hat?
         Dann haben des eigenen Rechts
100   Und gewiss des himmlischen Feuers
         Gespottet die Trozigen, dann erst
         Die sterblichen Pfade verachtend
         Verwegnes erwählt
         Und den Göttern gleich zu werden getrachtet.

90 VII Yet never, never does he forget it.
           For sooner must habitation pass away,
           And order and the human day
           Become deformed, before such as he
           Might forget the origin
           And the pure voice of youth.
           Who was it, who first
           Spoiled the bonds of love
           And made them into ropes?
           Then of their own right
100   Certain and of the heavenly fire
           Did they defiant mock, then first
           Despising mortal paths
           Chose reckless
           And endeavored to be equal to the gods.

Precisely now, in this harmony, the being of what has sprung forth turns against itself and leaps back into the origin. Having sprung forth would not be that pertaining to what has purely sprung forth if it were able to forget its origin. How should the river be a river—that is, flow— if it did not constantly spring forth before all else? Such flowing is above all in each case a creative one—building, nourishing, grounding. In such work there occurs restriction. This contentment with itself is not a return to some general appeasement or carefreeness. Nor is it a mere coming to an end of what has been once ordained and is now simply accepted as inalterable. Destiny in this fatalistic sense has no place within the sphere of such beyng of what has purely sprung forth. Harnessing the will that overflows in its commencement does not suffocate such a will, and is so far from doing so that what has been harnessed, precisely because it is now thrown back upon itself, must now properly interiorize its provenance. It lies in the essence of creative self-restriction to take over the restriction *as* restriction and to set it for itself, namely as a restriction of its own essence. Thus the restriction, in harnessing, precisely draws forth what is unharnessed—not simply in general, but as that which must indeed be preserved and laid claim to as the constant condition of restrictability pertaining to commencement. The inherence of beyng in the origin must beforehand want to outlast everything, and must do so even if all that has been grounded and built were to pass away through this wanting to go back into the origin. That which has been grounded and built would especially have to shatter if it were deprived of the origin and wished to carry on merely as the detached result of some rootless making.

We know from what has been said earlier (pp. 34, 167, 198) that
". . . poetically / Humans dwell upon this Earth."[1] The poetic remains
in power only if it itself always essentially prevails only in the origin
and "never forgets" the origin (line 90).

Thus, that which has purely sprung forth, from out of its having sprung forth—now harnessed, and without relinquishing this—
always drives itself back into its origin, and thus unfolds a counter-
turning within itself. The blessedness of contenting itself in the land,
precisely when it remains the river's streaming from its source, is
fundamentally enmity driven to the extreme. Yet as the river as an
undercurrent thus desires to go back into the origin, it simultaneously
turns away from its vocation once more—it becomes inimical toward
it. Desiring the origin, it even turns against the powers of the origin
in such enmity. And yet on the other hand, it is precisely these powers of the origin—the Earth and the God—that have let it spring forth
and determined the vocation of its having sprung forth. It is they who
have fundamentally inserted such enmity into the essence of what
has purely sprung forth, an enmity that now turns against them—
against them, who as powers of the origin bind their offspring into the
most intimate bonds. Whence in strophe VII, lines 96ff., the seemingly abrupt yet, as we now see, unavoidable question:

> Wer war es, der zuerst
> Die Liebesbande verderbt
> Und Strike von ihnen gemacht hat?

> Who was it, who first
> Spoiled the bonds of love
> And made them into ropes?

This is the question that opens up for us the entire enigmatic character of what has purely sprung forth, the question that must come
up against the fact that it is enmity that creates and that strife alone
accomplishes what is great. Thus we encounter the equally abrupt
and almost mutinous question arising in the poem "Peace" (IV, 137,
lines 24ff.):

> Wer hub es an? wer brachte den Fluch? von heut
>   Ists nicht und nicht von gestern, und die zuerst
>   Das Maas verloren, unsre Väter
>   Wussten es nicht, und es trieb ihr Geist sie.

---

1. "In beautiful blue . . . ," VI, 25, lines 32f.

> Who started it? who brought the curse? from today
>   It is not, and not from yesterday, and those who first
>   Lost the measure, our fathers
>   Knew it not, and their spirit drove them.

What has purely sprung forth must, for the sake of its having *sprung forth,* will the origin. This will becomes a counter-will against the powers of the origin, who will the vocation of *having* sprung forth. This counter-will against the powers of the origin, however, is the will to transgress the limit of the original inequality (cf. lines 104 and 120). The enmity that essentially prevails within what has purely sprung forth itself drives it into recklessness, defiance of the gods, and abhorrence of the paths of human beings. Such is the beyng of the demigods. This is how the middle of beyng appears—counter-turning on both sides, yet solely in order to preserve in an originary manner the relation to the gods and to humans, to the origin and to that which is created in having sprung forth.

We may now intimate to what extent these demigods are the blindest—because they have the will to see as no other creature sees, because they have an eye too many: the eye for the origin. Such an eye is not a non-binding regarding and looking back, but rather the accomplishment of an originary binding. This enmity of its essence, grounded within the origin itself, which drives into recklessness solely for the sake of safeguarding the origin—this is lack.

d) Strophe VIII: The Blessedness of the Gods as Concealed Ground for the Enmity within the Beyng of the Demigods

We might think that this is now enough regarding the enigmatic character of what has purely sprung forth. Yet only now does the poet venture to say what is most mysterious, and to tarry a moment in scarcely being allowed to unveil (IV, 175f.):

> VIII   Es haben aber an eigner
>   Unsterblichkeit die Götter genug und bedürfen
>   Die Himmlischen eines Dings,
>   So sinds Heroën und Menschen
>   Und Sterbliche sonst. Denn weil
> 110   Die Seeligsten nichts fühlen von selbst,
>   Muss wohl, wenn solches zu sagen
>   Erlaubt ist, in der Götter Nahmen
>   Theilnehmend fühlen ein Andrer,
>   Den brauchen sie; jedoch ihr Gericht
>   Ist, dass sein eigenes Haus

Zerbreche der und das Liebste
Wie den Feind schelt' und sich Vater und Kind
Begrabe unter den Trümmern,
Wenn einer, wie sie, seyn will und nicht
120   Ungleiches dulden, der Schwärmer.

VIII   Yet of their own
Immortality the gods have enough, and if one thing
The Heavenly require,
Then heroes and humans it is
And otherwise mortals. For since
110   The most blessed feel nothing of themselves,
There must presumably, if to say such a thing
Is allowed, in the name of the gods
Another participate in feeling,
Him they need; yet their own ordinance
Is that he his own house
Shatter and his most beloved
Chide like the enemy and bury his father
And child beneath the ruins,
If someone wants to be like them and not
120   Tolerate unequals, the impassioned one.

Here stand those almost prosaic words: "if to say such a thing / Is allowed" (lines 111f.). Yet these words, which may otherwise be a turn of phrase from the most superficial social interaction, are purely poetic. They are poetic because they are said from out of a supreme degree of fundamental poetic attunement.

Where are we within our river poem? Not in the presence of the river that has long since sprung forth, or better: there too, and therefore at the same time in the origin as well. This saying of what has purely sprung forth tears us beyond the origin and back—into the saying of the origin of the origin and thereby first face-to-face with the full mystery.

The strophe begins in an altogether exalted manner—entirely Hölderlin, and as though nothing had preceded it—with the telling of the gods. Because the gods, in their blessedness, of themselves feel nothing, an Other must partake in feeling so that, in such feeling, beings as such can be opened up in general. These Others are the demigods. The blessedness of the gods is the concealed ground for the necessity of the beyng of the demigods. Such beyng, however, is enmity—indeed recklessness toward the gods. The origin of this uprising is the blessedness of the gods. With this, the poet's saying attains the most intimate counter-turning within the essence of beings as a whole.

We can also surmise from this, at the same time, the inner belonging together of strophe VIII with the preceding strophes. Strophe IV: springing forth; Strophe V: having sprung forth in its being unleashed; Strophe VI: by contrast, having sprung forth in its being harnessed and in its self-contentment. Strophe VII: the necessary return, on the part of what has sprung forth, to itself as springing forth—to the origin—thus, within itself, enmity, not only within itself, but on account of this even against the origin and its powers. Strophe VIII: the powers of the origin themselves, the beyng of supreme blessedness in itself requiring supreme enmity.

With strophe VIII, the poet's thinking scales one of the most towering and solitary peaks of Western thinking, and at the same time of beyng. We know that upon such peaks the creators dwell close by one another, each on his own mountain and yet separated by abysses. On the peak now attained, Hölderlin dwells in proximity to the thinkers of the commencement of our Western history, not because Hölderlin is dependent on them, but because he is a beginner in the manner of commencement—a beginner of that commencement that still today, and for a long time now, as yet to commence, awaits empowerment.

What Hölderlin thinks poetically in strophe VIII is the supreme question-worthiness within the essence of beyng as it opened itself up within our history, though more frequently and continually it was buried. The paths of metaphysics hitherto—their manner of questioning, their concepts—are not sufficient to ask this question. Even a historiographical recollection of the commencement of Western thinking and poetizing is merely a makeshift, so long as we fail to ask the question of beyng as our own and as the question to come, and to venture ourselves forth in general into the strangeness of that which is question-worthy.

It would also be an error, were we to presume that Hölderlin himself, with an effortless poetic flourish, had vaulted up into the summit of the saying in this strophe, and thereby in the entire poetic work. Fortunately, we possess the draft that went into shaping the essential content of this strophe. By comparing the draft and the final version we are able to surmise something of the steepness of the ascent to the supreme necessity of this poetic saying. With regard to their form, we find a similar relationship between different versions, as, for instance, in the case of the first strophe of "Patmos" (cf. p. 51f.). As in that instance, here too our look into the workshop is not undertaken out of curiosity, but rather so as not to measure the inner violence of poetic creation by standards that are too meager, and to intimate something of the strangeness and rarity of such strophes. We may compare strophe VIII, lines 105 to 114, with the draft that follows (IV, 349):

> Denn irrlos gehn, geradeblikend die
> Vom Anfang an zum vorbestimmten End'
> Und immer siegerisch und immerhin ist gleich
> Die That und der Wille bei diesen.
> Drum fühlen es die Seeligen selbst nicht,
> Doch ihr Freude ist
> Die Sag und die Rede der Menschen.
> Unruhig geboren, sänftigen die
> Fernahnend das Herz am Glüke der Hohen.
> Diss lieben die Götter; jedoch ihr Gericht . . .

> For unerringly, looking straight ahead they go
> From the very beginning to the preordained end
> And always victorious and in any case the same
> Is deed and will for them.
> Thus the blessed ones feel it not themselves,
> But their joy is
> The saying and the talk of humans.
> Born restlessly, these soothe
> Their hearts, intimating afar, by the happiness of those on high.
> This the gods love; yet their ordinance . . .

In both versions, the issue is the beyng of the gods and their relationship to the beyng of humans. The great—that is, essential—divergence between the two versions is immediately striking. The draft still maintains itself entirely within the realm of an empathetic, human description of divine beyng, to which the beyng of humans is simply juxtaposed, as it were, as something in which the gods take pleasure, while humans soothe their hearts in the beyng of the gods. In the final version, everything is different, entirely exposed to what is strange and counter-turning. More explicit pointers will clarify the difference between the two versions, specifically (1) in relation to how the beyng of the gods is characterized, and (2) with regard to the relation of gods to humans.

Regarding 1: The draft describes more precisely the beyng of the gods—blessedness. This description is a kind of explanation. Blessedness is something like a consequence of the harmony of will and deed; blessed means unerring, always victorious and the same. By contrast, the final version says concisely and dismissively that they have enough of their own immortality. Such beyng is not described; quite the contrary: through the naming of their immortality as that of which they have more than enough, such beyng is directed entirely back into it-self—it is concealed and, in this concealment and closedness, the lack of need on the part of the blessed ones that prevails in essence within itself comes to light. Here blessedness appears, not as an inner conse-quence of harmony, but as the *ground* of an extreme counter-turning. Thereby, the relationship of the blessed ones to humans is also con-ceived entirely differently than in the draft. We are indeed told in both versions that the blessed ones do not feel their own beyng; yet even here there is a difference. The draft is purely descriptive: The blessed ones are so in harmony in terms of will and deed that they themselves do not feel this. This is simply the noting of a fact, and not feeling is a consequence of complete harmony. The final version says rigorously and essentially: 'they feel nothing of themselves.' Excessive fullness even closes them off from beings. Yet this supreme self-contentment and this closedness on account of excessive fullness is the ground for the fact that they need an Other.

Regarding 2: Accordingly, the relationship of gods to humans is also grasped differently. The draft, in continuing the description, as it were, says only "But their joy is / The saying and the talk of humans." With this feeble "But," the result is merely a superficial tacking on. Now the gods feel once again, namely joy—whereas in the poem itself there is no talk of such feelings, for of themselves they feel precisely nothing. Nor, therefore, can any such feeling determine their rela-tion to humans. Rather, it is now that the necessity of the relation to the Others is first grounded, and indeed the ground for the need and exigency is shifted to the excess of needlessness and to the inability to feel. It is not a merely descriptive "But" that leads over to humans, but a "For because" that furnishes the grounds. Cf. "Colombus" (IV, 264, lines 47ff.):

> Nemlich öfters, wenn
> Den Himmlischen zu einsam
> Es wird, dass sie
> Allein zusammenhalten . . .

> For often, when
> It becomes too lonely for the heavenly,
> That they remain
> Alone together . . .

Yet this thought is so monumental that the poet interjects: "if to say such a thing / Is allowed" (lines 111f.). This corresponds to how the relationship between gods and humans too is seen from the perspective of humans: In the draft we likewise find a harmony—humans soothe their hearts. The final version, on the other hand, makes necessary the existence [*Dasein*] of the demigods, who bear enmity within their essence and are driven to presumptuousness.

If we heed all this, then the transition in line 114 is not at all abrupt, as von Hellingrath thinks (IV, 347), since strictly speaking there is no transition here to something else at all. That which has already been said is simply thought through to its end—namely, that which is itself contained within the essence of those who are needed in this way, the demigods, who in wanting to return into the origin thereby want to "not / Tolerate unequals" (lines 119f.), do not want to tolerate inequality with the gods. For this reason, the demigods, on account of their divine origin, must shatter in their presumptuousness, and the gods themselves must smash those whom they need.

Thus, in the greatest severity of saying, *strife* is shifted into the ground of beyng itself. Yet this originary enmity is the truest intimacy, which we are admittedly unable—and above all, not permitted—to assess by the standards of human feelings. For this origin of what has purely sprung forth is the mystery, pure and simple. This mystery remains, even where that which has purely sprung forth contents itself and makes do with its having sprung forth.

This is something we must heed if we want to correctly understand how the next strophe (strophe IX) follows, and that means: understand it in its connection with the preceding strophe.

e) Strophe IX: Delimitation as Remaining within the Unharnessed Character of the Origin

IX Drum wohl ihm, welcher fand
      Ein wohlbeschiedenes Schiksaal,
      Wo noch der Wanderungen
      Und süss der Leiden Erinnerung
      Aufrauscht am sichern Gestade,
      Dass da und dorthin gern
      Er sehn mag bis an die Grenzen,
      Die bei der Geburt ihm Gott
      Zum Aufenthalte gezeichnet.
130   Dann ruht er, seeligbescheiden,
      Denn alles, was er gewollt,
      Das Himmlische, von selber umfängt
      Es unbezwungen, lächelnd
      Jezt, da er ruhet, den Kühnen.

IX And so presumably for him, who found
      A well-apportioned destiny,

Where recollection of his wanderings still
And, sweetly, of his sufferings
Washes up upon safe shores,
That there and fondly away
He may look to the boundaries
Which at his birth God
Drew for his stay.
130   Then he rests, blissfully humble,
For everything that he wanted,
That is heavenly, of its own accord surrounds
Him uncompelled, smiling
Now that he rests, the bold one.

It merely corresponds to the innermost will of the poetic telling if now, where what has purely sprung forth is named in terms of its most concealed origin, having sprung forth is once again and definitively, in the widest-ranging perspective, set over against it as that beyng that is content with itself (cf. the second part of strophe VI). If we wished to hear this strophe only as saying that everything had, after all, now dissolved into mere blessedness and tranquility, then this would be a collapse into a hopeless misinterpretation of the whole. With the aid of strophe IX, we would determine the beyng of the river in a purely calculative manner in terms of what has become of it. We would forget, moreover, that what carries and determines this having become as such in its essence, constantly prevailing within it, is precisely the origin. Let us only heed the fact that the last words of the strophe name the thus contented river the "bold one" (line 134). Its passion is not extinguished or even denied, but only harnessed. The origin is not forgotten, but preserved in the work. This well-apportioned destiny does not mean that now the beyng of the demigod has found salvation in some finitude, in the sense of finding comfort and rest in what has been attained. For what is finite in the habitual sense is distinguished from what is truly finite in that the former utterly fails to see its limits and, within its unseen limits, loses itself in what is average and without ground, in order then to finally cease somewhere by chance. True delimiting, however, constantly experiences restriction *as* restriction, and *is* what it is only within a harnessing; it enjoins itself to the limit as remaining in the unharnessed character pertaining to the origin. Indeed, the 'shores' are 'safe,' with everything in harmony, but only because the heavenly is "uncompelled" (line 133). Indeed, discipline and need have become so compelling that even the harnessing of what is unharnessed is taken on in the attunement of blessed contentment. That is genuine setting of limits.

Genuine limit and shaping, that which is originarily built and grounded, essentially prevails in its greatness and simplicity only as *restrained recklessness,* as a keeping to itself of the presumptuousness of leaping over the origin. Intimacy—the essence of that which has purely sprung forth—is restraint within the most inimical strife. In such strife, an inhering within the middle of being, between gods and humans, is fought for and attained and, at the same time, suffered. Beyng as destiny is only where such suffering attunes our passion and becomes the fundamental attunement of Dasein.

In strophes IV through IX, that which has purely sprung forth, the beyng of the demigods, is said in its essence. It prevails in essence as the conflict between springing forth and having sprung forth. Being a river means unfolding this conflict into supreme enmity and preserving the latter as intimacy, inhering within such intimacy. Strophe IX is to be grasped from here.

§21. Strophes X through XIII: Thinking the Beyng of the Demigods Starting from the Gods and from Humans

"Demigods now I think" (line 135)—now that all of this has been thought through and thought back into the unity of the essence of that which has purely sprung forth, and thinking has arrived at the thought, only now are the demigods thought. The poet says that he really must know such beyng as is thought here (line 136). Why? Because his longing is directed toward it, because his vocation as poet is nothing other than thrownness into this Dasein of the creators who stand between gods and humans. The beyng of the demigods is now truly projected, poetically founded.

Yet the poetizing is not yet at its end. For this reason we said at the start of our interpretation that the word that introduces strophe X is the pivot of the entire poem. This means that it is just as wrong to be of the view that the thinking of the demigods first starts with strophe X as it is to be of the view that this thinking comes to a stop with strophe X, where the thought has been achieved. Rather, now that the poet has poetically disclosed for himself the essence of being demigods, he can let this essence come to full presence. For our interpretation, the question arises of how this thinking of the beyng of the demigods that has come into its own will now attain its complete fulfillment. Manifestly, what follows does not bring a repetition of what has preceded, but rather something else. However, what other possibility now still remains of thinking this in-between being of the demigods? Basically, the answer is simple: if not from the middle of the between itself, then from that which it lies between—from the ends, as it were. This cannot, however, mean that now the gods are to be thought by themselves and humans by themselves; in the poetic work "The Rhine" as a whole, it is only ever demigods that are to be thought. And yet the possibility remains of thinking their beyng in a still more fulfilled manner: first, starting only from the gods, and then, starting only from humans. What is thought in this manner in turn enters into a counter-play within itself. This entire counter-play ultimately comes to play the counterpart to strophes II through IX. If we comprehend the following four strophes (X through XIII) in this manner, this also sheds light on strophes XIV and XV.

a) Strophe X: The Question Concerning the Stranger Who Remains within the Divine Origin

X   Halbgötter denk' ich jezt
     Und kennen muss ich die Theuern,
     Weil oft ihr Leben so
     Die sehnende Brust mir beweget.
     Wem aber, wie, Rousseau, dir,
140 Unüberwindlich die Seele,
     Die starkausdauernde ward,
     Und sicherer Sinn
     Und süsse Gaabe zu hören,
     Zu reden so, dass er aus heiliger Fülle
     Wie der Weingott, thörig göttlich
     Und gesezlos sie die Sprache der Reinesten giebt
     Verständlich den Guten, aber mit Recht
     Die Achtungslosen mit Blindheit schlägt
     Die entweihenden Knechte, wie nenn ich den Fremden?

X   Demigods now I think
     And the dear ones I must know,
     For often does their life
     So move my longing breast.
     Yet he whose soul, like yours,
140 Rousseau, became invincible,
     Enduring ever strong,
     And in its sense assured
     And sweet in its gift of hearing,
     Of talking thus, that out of holy fullness he
     Like the wine god, foolishly divine
     And lawlessly bestows this, the language of the purest,

Understandable for the good, yet rightly strikes
With blindness those who fail to heed
The unrevering slaves, how shall I name the stranger?

With strophe X, the thinking of the beyng of the demigods begins, as the thought of their essence that has now been achieved is unfolded in the direction of what they are not, yet how they could appear to be. Their proper essence, being between, thus first becomes visible indirectly through such contrasting, and the mystery is unveiled in its entire incomparability.

In terms of its linguistic configuration, strophe X—from line 139 to the end of the strophe, line 149—is a singular hinge in the shape of a singular question. At its end stands a question mark. It is all the more important to heed this because Hölderlin proceeds quite 'arbitrarily' in his placing of punctuation marks—arbitrarily, that is, from the perspective of some unpoetic theory of punctuation that may be valid for ordinary language. Hölderlin's arbitrariness, by contrast, is bound by the unspoken law of his poetic saying. Of the fifteen strophes of the poem, only one other strophe ends with a question mark. Tellingly, it is strophe IV, where the questioning concerning that which has purely sprung forth is initiated and begins with a hint regarding the favor of the origin. But this question is, properly speaking, a rhetorical one, as grammar calls it, and this because the answer lies within that to which the question is directed, within the essence of what has purely sprung forth, and because this essence is unfolded in strophes V through IX that immediately follow. By contrast, the genuine question, which is said as strophe X, remains unanswered. What this strophe tells of is only a question, and remains only a question: namely, that concerning the stranger. Who is this stranger, this one who remains strange? In this strophe we find the name "Rousseau." We know that his name was inserted only later, in place of the name of Hölderlin's friend, Heinse. In strophe XI, line 163, the words "by the Bielersee" are likewise a later addition that, in reference to the naming of Rousseau, mentions his place of residence. An original interpretation of the strophe must therefore be kept clear of reference to Rousseau; conversely, it is only in terms of the meaning of the strophe that we can instead come to understand why the poet can also name Rousseau here.

"[H]ow shall I name the stranger?" (line 149)—naming, once again, in the sense of the originary founding of that beyng that is asked after here. The poet names that which, "foolishly divine" (line 145), 'hears and talks' and is "lawless" (line 146)—that is, not against the law, but not needing any law, "out of holy fullness" (line 144), speaking "the language of the purest" (line 146), "understandable for the good" (line 147), and striking down "the unrevering slaves" (line 149).

The being that is named there in the manner of questioning is not the gods, but something divine, "foolishly divine" only out of such fullness, something that has its origin in the divine and, simply remaining in this origin, streams forth this, the divine origin. Yet it is not something that has properly sprung forth—that is, escaped from this beyng of the gods and even rebelled against them. It is not a proper demigod, not a between whose essence is counter-turning, but rather constant, uninterrupted harmony with the gods and with beyng in general—*nature*.

The essence of such a primordial beyng, uninterrupted in its naturalness, suggests the thought of Rousseau and his teaching, although here we must still ponder the fact that that particular era—roughly, that of Kant and German Idealism—regarded Rousseau quite differently from how we do today. Yet none of this is of primary importance here, rather simply this: The poet is approached—precisely in thinking the beyng of the demigods—by the *possibility* of such a beyng purely intimate with the God, but it remains a question, and that means: The beyng of the demigods and thereby the beyng of the poet himself remain excluded from it. The one being asked after is a stranger, whereas the poet precisely is familiar with the demigods (start of the strophe).

Von Hellingrath engages in a misinterpretation of this part. The stranger is neither identified at all, nor indeed is what directly follows, the "sons of the Earth" (line 150), the answer. Nor, above all, are "the stranger," the "sons of the Earth," and the demigods the same. Quite the contrary: The task is precisely to say the *divergence* of these three. Von Hellingrath fails to appreciate the fundamental content of the entire poem.

b) Strophe XI: The Beyng of the Demigods in Its Relation to the Care-freeness of Humans

150 XI   Die Söhne der Erde sind, wie die Mutter,
         Allliebend, so empfangen sie auch
         Mühlos, die Glüklichen, Alles.
         Drum überraschet es auch
         Und schrökt den sterblichen Mann,
         Wenn er den Himmel, den
         Er mit den liebenden Armen
         Sich auf die Schultern gehäufft,

Und die Last der Freude bedenket;
Dann scheint ihm oft das Beste
160   Fast ganz vergessen da,
Wo der Stral nicht brennt,
Im Schatten des Walds
Am Bielersee in frischer Grüne zu seyn,
Und sorglosarm an Tönen,
Anfängern gleich, bei Nachtigallen zu lernen.

150 XI The sons of the Earth are, like the Mother,
All-loving, so too they receive
Effortlessly, those fortunate ones, everything.
Thus it surprises too
And terrifies the mortal man,
In pondering the heaven, which
He with loving arms
Has heaped upon his shoulders,
And the burden of his joy;
Then often it seems best to him,
160   To be almost entirely forgotten,
Where the ray does not burn,
In the shade of the woods
There by the Bielersee amid the fresh green leaves,
And careless-free of tones,
Like beginners, to learn with nightingales.

In sharp contrast to the questioning strophe X, the start of strophe XI names the "sons of the Earth" by simply saying this without any question. They are the humans: That is, the in-between being of the demigods is now being viewed from its other 'end.' We are not, for instance, given a description of the existence [*Dasein*] of human beings in themselves, which in any case is never possible; rather, it is named with constant guiding regard for, and in contrast to, the frightfulness of the beyng of the demigods. Seen from this perspective, humans are the 'effortless' ones; more precisely, they "too" (line 151) are effortless, as is in his own way that stranger who with 'sense assured' (line 142) simply streams forth the divine, and in streaming it forth nevertheless remains precisely within it. This stranger and the humans too carry a relation to the gods within their own beyng, each in a different way, even the "sons of the Earth," for the Earth is, after all, a goddess.

Yet these divine ones, who are in each case different—the stranger and the humans—are never themselves gods. Just as little, however, are they demigods, for the beyng of the demigods is determined in terms of the between; they are this between, whereas those ones in each case stand only on one side and thus simply retain a relation to the divine. Thereby they give rise to the illusion of demigod-beyng, and for this reason the poet must name them. That is to say: They are not simply introduced only as counter-possibilities, as possibilities that are of no concern to the beyng of the demigods and can do them no harm. Rather, because being a demigod means between-beyng, the latter for this reason itself stands constantly in danger of wanting to be one or the other of those between which the demigods are. The demigods themselves are chased from one end to the other, and indeed through themselves, so as not to have to be what is frightful about this between, and yet at the same time in so doing to preserve the vocation of the divine and their relation to it. Yet as this between, they are, after all, always the Others. To be the always Other is their essence—the always Other in an ambiguous sense: on the one hand, the Other (line 113) that the gods need; then, as this Other, nevertheless other than that stranger; finally, also other than human beings.

"Thus it surprises too / And terrifies the mortal man" (lines 153f.). When it comes over the mortal man that he is indeed a human being and yet the Other, who bears the burden of the heavens, then a profound anxiety befalls him; he is agitated by terror. Yet where should he go, so as to preserve his vocation? Where else than to that locale "Where the ray does not burn" (line 161), where the lightning flashes of the gods do not strike and flatten (cf. "As when on feast day . . . ," IV, 153, lines 56ff.), and on the other hand to the place where the divine streams forth, yet without question, foolishly and in pure abundance—by the Bielersee—that is, into the beyng of that stranger: Not the between—but "careless-free" (line 164), not having to create, but being allowed simply to learn, like beginners. Cf. IV, 240:

O dass ich lieber wäre, wie Kinder sind!
    Dass ich, wie Nachtigallen, ein sorglos Lied
        Von meiner Wonne sänge!

O, that I would rather be, as children are!
    That I, like nightingales, might sing a carefree song
        Of my delight!

See also IV, 278:

Wo bist du? Himmelsbotin! umsonst erwacht
    Mein Auge mir des Morgens nur, mich weht kalt

Die Zukunft an, und ach! gesanglos
Birgt sich das schaudernde Herz im Busen.

Where are you? Messenger of the heavens! in vain
    Does my eye awaken in the morning, the future
        Blows coldly toward me, and alas! songless
            My quivering heart buries itself within my breast.

It seems to the demigod that the best thing is to forget himself in care-freeness: away free from care—that is, from the essential ground of Dasein—in accordance with which existence is thrown into beyngs, so as to open them up in projection and set them into the work and thus assume beyng. This word 'care' [*Sorge*] is for us the name for the fundamental metaphysical essence of Dasein. What this word means is equally far removed from gloom and busyness as it is from the 'forceful assertiveness' of the heroic petty bourgeois that is apparently superior to care. Everydayness is properly care-freeness, in that it only diverts care into concern [*Besorgen*] and solicitude [*Für-sorge*] and thus conceals it in its essence. Because Dasein is in essence care, its everydayness, despite all its worries, indeed *as* these, must be care-freeness.

Because the demigods have to be the between in the sense of that which has purely sprung forth, it suggests itself precisely to them to seek salvation in the magnificence of that beyng of the stranger and likewise in the happily busy, carefree beyng of humans, where "lovers are / What they always were" (lines 186f.), where no ropes are made from the bonds of love, as happens in the between (lines 97f.), where "destiny is / Evened out for a while" (lines 182f.), and where, unlike in the between and as the between, destiny is not what it fundamentally is: the beyng of what has purely sprung forth—as the intimacy of enmity.

c) Strophes XII and XIII: The Bridal Festival of Humans and Gods and the Inevitability of Night

Yet this magnificence—'the bridal festival of humans and gods'—that unity of the counter-possibilities of the between, this it is not. It is only a fleeting while,

Bevor das freundliche Licht
Hinuntergeht und die Nacht kommt.

Before the friendly light
Goes down and night arrives.

(Lines 193f.)

Strophes XII and XIII may now follow (IV, 178f):

XII   Und herrlich ists, aus heiligem Schlafe dann
      Erstehen und aus Waldes Kühle
      Erwachend, Abends nun
      Dem milderen Licht entgegenzugehn,
170   Wenn, der die Berge gebaut
      Und den Pfad der Ströme gezeichnet,
      Nachdem er lächelnd auch
      Der Menschen geschäfftiges Leben
      Das othemarme, wie Seegel
      Mit seinen Lüften gelenkt hat,
      Auch ruht und zu der Schülerin jezt,
      Der Bildner, gutes mehr
      Denn böses findend,
      Zur heutigen Erde der Tag sich neiget.

180 XIII Dann feiern das Brautfest Menschen und Götter
      Es feiern die Lebenden all,
      Und ausgeglichen
      Ist eine Weile das Schiksaal.
      Und die Flüchtlinge suchen die Heerberg,
      Und süssen Schlummer die Tapfern,
      Die Liebenden aber
      Sind, was sie waren; sie sind
      Zu Hausse, wo die Blume sich freuet
      Unschädlicher Gluth und die finsteren Bäume
190   Der Geist umsäuselt, aber die Unversöhnten
      Sind umgewandelt und eilen
      Die Hände sich ehe zu reichen,
      Bevor das freundliche Licht
      Hinuntergeht und die Nacht kommt.

XII   And glorious it is, then from holy sleep
      To arise and from the coolness of the woods
      Awakening, at evening now
      To go towards more mellow light,
170   When he, who built the mountains
      And drew the rivers' path,
      Having directed with a smile
      The busy lives of humans,
      Short of breath, guiding their sails
      With his breezes too,

Now rests and to her, the pupil,
The creator, finding
More good than evil,
To the present Earth the day inclines.

180 XIII Then humans and gods the bridal festival celebrate,
All the living celebrate,
And destiny is
Evened out for a while.
And those in flight seek asylum,
And sweet slumber the courageous,
But lovers are
What they always were, they are
At home, where the flower enjoys
Benevolent warmth and spirit caresses
190   The darkling trees, but those unreconciled
Are now turned around and hasten
To extend hands to one another,
Before the friendly light
Goes down and night arrives.

With this inevitability, the section we have identified, strophes X through XIII, comes to a close. Night is there once more: the necessity of being the between, of catching the ray of lightning and of transforming the dazzling and piercing quality of its light into a gentle and tranquil lucidity, in which humans can accomplish their Dasein. In this between, there is no equalizing, for every equalizing seeks to fill in the inner fissure of the between, to dissolve enmity into a mere blessedness, whether in the foolishness of that stranger, or in the comfortable reassurance of human beings. Mere blessedness, however, robs all possibility of intimacy, for the latter prevails in essence only as the counter-turning of the highest and most extreme strife.

Only now does the entire fullness of the mystery of what has purely sprung forth lie open before us—only now where, as the between, it is directed into those possibilities that swirl around it, in which it seeks to save itself time and again from its own frightfulness for a while.

The demigods have now been thought, scarcely unveiled in the song, and the beyng of the demigods—destiny—has been poetically founded. What has thus been said has been placed into the midst of the language of the people. Only a historical people is truly a people. It is historical, however, only when it happens out of the ground of the middle of beyng, when the between is there and when the demigods—the creators—effect happening as history. A historical people, as a people, is community only when the community knows—and that means, wills—the fact that community can be as historical only if those Others as Others venture and sustain their being Other. This necessity for the Others to be Other is certainly not a license for all those stubborn and vain, those irksome and unproductive types who think their mere standing on the periphery is itself an accomplishment. The necessity of being the Other is such only out of the need and for the need of those who actually create—that is, on the grounds of the work that is effected.

§22. Strophe XIV: Retaining the Mystery. The Thinking of the Poet Grounded in the Poetizing of the Thinker

XIV   Doch einigen eilt
      Diss schnell vorüber, andere
      Behalten es länger.
      Die ewigen Götter sind
      Voll Lebens allzeit; bis in den Tod
200   Kann aber ein Mensch auch
      Im Gedächtniss doch das Beste behalten,
      Und dann erlebt er das Höchste.
      Nur hat ein jeder sein Maas.
      Denn schwer ist zu tragen
      Das Unglük, aber schwerer das Glük.
      Ein Weiser aber vermocht es
      Vom Mittag bis in die Mitternacht
      Und bis der Morgen erglänzte
      Beim Gastmahl helle zu bleiben.

XIV   Yet this hurries
      Quickly by for some, others
      Retain it longer.
      The eternal gods are
      At all times full of life; yet until death
200   Can a human being too
      In memory retain what is best,
      And then he experiences the highest.
      Only each one has his measure.
      For difficult to bear is misfortune,
      But fortune more difficult still.
      A wise man, however, was able,
      From midday unto midnight,

> And until the morning shone forth,
> To stay lucid at the banquet.

"Yet this hurries / Quickly by for some, others / Retain it longer." Because the beyng of the demigods is concealed in mystery, and is thus essentially something concealed, it remains difficult to grasp, even when it is named and said—indeed especially then, and still more difficult to retain. Yet because the mystery, as something said, must stand within the Dasein of the historical people, if such Dasein is to determine itself from out of the middle of beyng, a retaining belongs for this reason to the mysterious character of the mystery itself. Accordingly, the saying of the river, of the grounding beyng of the demigods, first finds its conclusion in strophe XIV.

The mystery, the middle of beyng, is nothing arbitrary and therefore also not something that can be grasped by everyone in the same manner. In retaining the unconcealment of what is concealed as such, "each one has his measure" (line 203). Not only is each person distinct from every other in degree of removal from the mystery, for instance; rather, what is proper to the essential measure consists in the fact that here in general the orientations of our habitual estimating are wrong. In our habitual judgment, misfortune is always what is difficult and most difficult, whereas good fortune, by contrast, is easiest to bear, because one seemingly does not have to bear it at all. Rather, it bears us. In truth, however, 'fortune is more difficult to bear.' In truth—that is, assessed from the middle and the essence of beyng—good fortune, if it succeeds, lies in being something purely sprung forth, bringing about blessedness as enmity and enduring it to the point of intimacy.

Just as our habitual judgment fails to understand that it is harder to bear fortune than misfortune, so our habitual willing is equally misdirected when the issue is blessedness. It asks: What must I do to become blessed? The answer to this question, however, if it is to hit upon what is true, must be such as to reject this question as mistaken. At the same time, however, this answer also remains disconcerting for our habitual judgment. Nietzsche on one occasion touches upon this relation when, to the question "What must I do in order to become blessed?," he responds: "That I do not know, but I say to you: be blessed and then do what you feel like."[1] Be blessed! That is it, and that reveals the entirely unsupported and unconditional character of that beyng that is the *between* between the intoxication of sultry nights and the solid configuration of day. In order to endure both in one, in

---

1. Nietzsche, *Werke*, Bd. XII. *Nachgelassene Werke,* Leipzig 1919 (3rd edition), 285.

their belonging together, the task is "to stay lucid" (line 209). "A wise man, however, was able" (line 206). This lucidity is itself created solely in genuine knowing, in essential thinking. The ring has closed. The poet demands the thinker. The thinking of the poet—demigods now I think—is grounded in the poetizing of the thinker.

§23. Strophe XV: The Poet as the Other

210   XV   Dir mag auf heissem Pfade unter Tannen oder
            Im Dunkel des Eichwalds gehüllt
            In Stahl, mein Sinklair! Gott erscheinen oder
            In Wolken, du kennst ihn, da du kennest, jugendlich,
            Des Guten Kraft und nimmer ist dir
            Verborgen das Lächeln des Herrschers
            Bei Tage, wenn
            Es fieberhaft und angekettet das
            Lebendige scheinet oder auch
            Bei Nacht, wenn alles gemischt
220   Ist ordnungslos und wiederkehrt
            Uralte Verwirrung.

210   XV   To you on sultry paths beneath the firs or
            Shrouded in the dark of oak woods
            In steel, my Sinclair! may God appear or
            In clouds, you know him, for, in your youth, you know
            The force of good, and never is from you
            Concealed the smiling of the lord
            By day, when
            Feverish and chained down the
            Living all appear or indeed
            By night, when all is mixed
220   Disorderedly and there returns
            Primordial confusion.

The intimacy of poetic-thoughtful knowing is bestowed by that familiarity with beyng that remains strong enough to be a site for the encounters with the God, whether he appears on sultry paths and in the darkness of the Earth, or in clouds, in lightning flashes; whether he appears by day, when everything is chained down, or by night where there returns "primordial confusion" (line 221).

This is said by the concluding strophe. It directly addresses the friend of the poet. In strophes II through XIII, it transpires that the poet must apprehend a destiny—that of the river—and indeed in such a way that he must think poetically what being a destiny signifies. Strophe XIV steps out of this thinking and back into immediate historical Dasein, which poses the question concerning the manner of preservation of a beyng that has been opened up in this way. The concluding strophe, however, enters the yet narrower and most intimate circle of the poetic Dasein itself. It speaks to the friend. It praises him as one of those coming ones and knowing ones. This praising is a cautiously reticent thinking of one who knows that he is one of those who know not where to, and to whom lack is given in his soul, because it is his vocation to be a mortal man and yet the Other.

In the concluding strophe, the poet seeks salvation in the secure and evened-out Dasein of the friend, and thus indirectly and reticently says who he himself is—the Other.

§24. The Metaphysical Locale of Hölderlin's Poetizing

a) The Historical Vocation of Germania

Our engagement with Hölderlin's poetic work "Germania" was deflected to the poem "The Rhine" at that point of the poem "Germania" where we are told of the man who is moved by many transformations (strophe III, line 38). We now know who this man is: He is such a one who must hold out in the middle of beyng in order to embrace the encounters with the gods at this locale, and thus to found the dwelling of human beings upon the Earth and their history. History, however, is always the singular history of this people in each instance—here, of the people of this poet, the history of Germania. In our knowing, and insofar as we know who the man is in terms of his essence, we have arrived at what we were seeking: *the metaphysical locale of Hölderlin's poetizing*. This is the middle of being itself, the beyng of the demigods, the beyng of the man, of our poet. We may recall what this poet says of himself ("As when on feast day . . . ," IV, 151, lines 19f.):

Jezt aber tagts! Ich harrt und sah es kommen,
Und was ich sah, das Heilige sei mein Wort.

But now day breaks! I waited and saw it coming,
And what I saw, may the Holy be my word.

What he saw and apprehended and shaped into the word is the poem "Germania," as well as the entire compass of poetic works to which we repeatedly returned. The man in the poem "Germania," the poet as such, sees the eagle:

> Weil an den Adler
> Sich halten müssen, damit sie nicht
> Mit eigenem Sinne zornig deuten
> Die Dichter,

> Since the poets
> Must stay with the eagle, so that they
> Do not interpret angrily
> Using their own sense,
> (Fragment from the period of "The Titans," IV, 217, lines 60ff.)

The eagle is the messenger of the God. The poet sees the girl "hidden in the woods and flowering poppy" ("Germania," line 65); she is the daughter of Mother Earth; a land—the German land. The poet sees how the eagle seeks out the girl, and the poet hears how the eagle, quickly recognizing her, calls loudly to her (IV, 183, lines 62ff.):

> "Du bist es, auserwählt
> "Allliebend und ein schweres Glük
> "Bist du zu tragen stark geworden.

> "You it is, the chosen one,
> "All-loving and a grave good fortune
> "Have you become strong to bear.

That hard-to-bear good fortune is assigned as a task to the people of this land: to be a between, a middle, out of which and in which history is grounded. This can only happen in such a way, however, that this people itself grounds and founds its Dasein—that is, first names beyng in an originary manner once again, poetically and thoughtfully founds it. The mandate and message from the eagle thus culminates in the demand for that threefold naming that must be accomplished by this land and its people, and that means in the first instance by its creators. What is to be named—to be once more opened up in an originarily founding saying and knowing—is, on the one hand, the Mother, the Earth herself. But in this naming, as poetic, there resonates the "divinity of old" (line 100) together with that which is to come: History arises. Only from out of these two does Dasein attain the "middle of time" (line 103)—the true counter-turning. The latter is not what lies nearest, the mere present day and contemporaneous that we always come upon; rather, the middle of time is that which comes last, that which is only insofar as it comes to be in founding and grounding. It is that historical Dasein within which and as which the essence of this land finds and completes itself. Then, if only for a while, there is that harmony of the "needless" (lines 107 and 108), of those who have had enough of their own blessedness, the gods (Earth and heavens), together with the needless (that is, the people), insofar as it has once again created the feast days where humans and gods celebrate the bridal festival.

This land, its people—that is, the historical Dasein of the Germans—is then of such a kind as to "defenselessly" give "counsel" "Around the kings and peoples" (lines 111f.) As we already indicated earlier (p. 19ff.), this defenselessness does not mean the laying down of weapons, weakness, or the avoidance of struggle. "Defenseless" means that historical greatness that no longer requires defense or resistance, that is victorious through Da-sein, insofar as the latter brings beings to appearance as they are, through the standing-in-themselves effected through the work. It is not some counseling or offering of prescriptions that speaks in a didactic or schoolmasterish manner—but rather that most powerful and direct pointing of the ways, which brings itself about through these paths being *taken,* Dasein grounding itself.

The poet is not referring to a Germany of poets and thinkers as the rest of the world imagines them and wishes them to be: mere clueless dreamers who are then easy to persuade in decisive matters and are meant to become the fools of everyone else. Rather, he means the poetizing and thinking that break into the abysses of beyng, and are not content with the shallow waters of some universal world reason—the poetizing and thinking that bring beings to appearance and to stand in the work anew and in the manner of a commencement.

b) The Opposition in Essence of Greek and German Dasein.
The Conflictual Intimacy of What Is Given as
Endowment and What Is Allotted as Task

Yet the poet also knows this: This "middle of time" (line 103), this presence, first springs forth from out of genuine provenance and from the future that has been creatively taken hold of on the ground of the Earth. This middle of time first comes about, and it comes to be, only if the freedom and inherence of the German essence is fought for.

The poet knows in addition and above all that this is what is most difficult: "the free use of" (as he puts it) the "national." Hölderlin speaks about this in that letter to which we have already had recourse on several occasions, the letter to his friend Böhlendorff of December 4, 1801, shortly before his journey to France, from where he returned to his homeland half a year later as one struck by Apollo—smitten by the excess of light. The two poetic works, "Germania" as well as "The Rhine," however, also date from the year of this letter. The relevant section reads (V, 319f.):

> We learn nothing with greater difficulty than the free use of the national. And, as I believe, precisely the clarity of presentation is originally so natural to us as the fire from the heavens was to the Greeks. For this very reason the Greeks will have to be *surpassed* more in beautiful passion, which you also have preserved for yourself, than in that Homeric presence of mind and gift for presentation.
>
> It sounds paradoxical. Yet I assert it once more and place it at your disposal to test and to use, namely that in the progression of culture, the properly national will always have the lesser advantage. For this reason, the Greeks are less masters of the holy pathos, because it was innate to them, whereas they excel in their gift of presentation, from Homer on, because this extraordinary human being was soulful enough to capture Occidental, *Junonian sobriety* for his Apollonian kingdom, and thus to truly appropriate the foreign. With us it is the reverse. For this reason it is also so dangerous to abstract artistic rules for oneself solely and uniquely from Greek excellence. I have labored long over this, and now know that, with the exception of what must be the highest for the Greeks and for us, namely, the living relationship and skill, we are presumably not allowed to have anything *identical* with them. Yet one's own must be learned just as well as the foreign. This is why the Greeks are indispensable to us. Only we shall not come close to them precisely in what is our own, our national, because, as mentioned, the *free* use of one's *own* is what is most difficult.

We must here forgo a detailed interpretation. Yet there are three things that we cannot pass over, which we shall mention briefly:

1. The poet's eye for the essence sees the essence of Greek Dasein in its essential opposition to the Dasein of the Germans. The poet has an eye for these essential relations because he experiences beyng as a whole from out of the ground of need. To the essence of historical Dasein belongs: first, being struck by beyng as a whole; second, being able to grasp beyng in an effectual presentation of beyngs. Being struck: "the fire from the heavens"; being able to grasp: "the clarity of presentation."

Both are apportioned differently: in each instance to a people with historical vocation, yet always in such a way that one is native (endowment), the other given as a task—to be struggled for. Our historical vocation is always to transform our given endowment, the "national," into what is given us as a task: "the free use of the national"—that is, the creating of a space of play within which the national can freely transform itself into history. The national by itself is nothing present at hand, not merely something at hand, not a history, but the national—what is given as endowment—is the necessary, though not sufficient condition for historical Dasein, that is, for the free use of the national. This, however, is "what is most difficult." Cf. IV, 264:

>   meinest du   zum Dämon
> Es solle gehen,
> Wie damals? Nemlich sie wollten stiften
> Ein Reich der Kunst. Dabei ward aber
> Das Väterländische von ihnen
> Versäumet und erbärmlich gieng
> Das Griechenland, das schönste, zu Grunde.
> Wohl hat es andere
> Bewandtniss jezt.

>   you say   to the demon
> Things should go,
> As back then? For they wanted to found
> A kingdom of art. Yet in so doing
> They missed the mark
> Of the fatherland and pitifully did
> Greece, the most beautiful, perish.
> Presumably things
> Stand differently now.

The Greeks are given as their endowment: a rousing proximity to the fire from the heavens, being struck by the violence of beyng. Given to them as a task is harnessing the unharnessed in the struggle for the work—grasping, bringing to a stand.

The Germans are given as their endowment: the ability to grasp, the preparation and planning of domains and calculating, setting in order to the point of organization. It is given to them as a task to come to be struck by beyng.

What is on each occasion most difficult for a people—the 'national in its free usage'—can be won, however, only through the struggle for what is on each occasion given as a task—that is, for effecting the conditions for the possibility of free usage. In this struggle, and only in it, does a historical people attain its highest. Because the task given to the Greeks was the free use of their passion for the overwhelming, there fell to them, from out of this struggle, their highest achievement: the enjoining of beyng into the jointure of the work (cf. summer semester 1936: enjoining and system[1]). Conversely, our highest achievement will come about for us if we set to work the endowment of being able to grasp, in such a way that this grasping binds and determines itself and enjoins itself to the jointure of beyng, if our ability to grasp does not become perverted into an end in itself and merely dissipate within the exercise of our own capacity. Only that which has been struggled for and is to be attained through struggle—not that which is merely one's own—provides the guarantee and granting of the highest. Because what is given as endowment and task are in each case differently apportioned to the Greeks and the Germans, the Germans, precisely in what is their own, will never surpass the highest achievement of the Greeks. That is what is 'paradoxical.' In fighting the battle of the Greeks, but on the reverse front, we become not Greeks, but Germans.

2. This letter therefore shows unequivocally how things stand with the Greek world of this most profound and intimate German harbinger of Greek Dasein: nothing of Humanism or Classicism, nothing of Romanticism or infatuation. The supreme freedom of the creator places him in the most extreme oppositionality. Yet this is also the sole true way of being bound to the originality of that commencement with the Greeks.

Genuine repetition springs forth from originary transformation. Mere imitation or attempts at renewal only ever achieve the blind absolutizing of a dependency that has not been mastered.

3. What Hölderlin here sees as the essence of historical Dasein—the conflictual intimacy of endowment and task—was discovered again by Nietzsche under the titles of the Dionysian and the Apollonian, but not with such purity and simplicity as in Hölderlin; for in the meantime Nietzsche had to make his way through all those fateful steps signaled by the names Schopenhauer, Darwin, Wagner, *Gründerjahre.*[12] Not to mention the most fateful thing of all: namely, what subsequent and contemporary interpretations of Nietzsche have made of this in their many approaches.

The hour of our history has struck. We must first take what has been given us as endowment into pure safekeeping once again, yet only so as to comprehend and take hold of what has been given as our task—that is, to question our way forward and through it. The violence of beyng must first and actually become a question again for our ability to grasp.

---

1. *Schellings Abhandlung über das Wesen der menschlichen Freiheit (1809).* Ed. H. Feick. Tübingen, 1971. Translated as *Schelling's Treatise on the Essence of Human Freedom* by Joan Stambaugh. Athens: Ohio University Press, 1985.

This engagement with Hölderlin's poetizing began with his word:

Vom Höchsten will ich schweigen.
Verbotene Frucht, wie der Lorbeer, ist aber
Am meisten das Vaterland. Die aber kost'
Ein jeder zulezt.

Concerning what is highest, I will be silent.
Forbidden fruit, like the laurel, is, however,
Above all the fatherland. Such, however, each
Shall taste last.

Let this engagement conclude with Hölderlin's word:

"We learn nothing with greater difficulty than the free use of the national."

Editor's Epilogue

The lecture course reproduced here was held in the winter semester of 1934–35 in two-hour sessions at the University of Freiburg. An initial typescript had been prepared by Herr Fritz Heidegger at the request of Martin Heidegger, who subsequently helped with the process of collation. In keeping with the guidelines established by Heidegger for the *Gesamtausgabe*, the typescript and manuscript were collated anew by the editor and, in the process, passages that had not been incorporated in the typescript were inserted into the text. The passages in question are parenthetical remarks, additions located on the right-hand side of the manuscript, and notes on separate sheets.

The text of the lecture course had been fully elaborated by Heidegger. In keeping with his instructions, some abbreviated formulations had to be expanded into complete sentences, fillers were deleted, and all reviews and summaries were preserved. Particular care was taken to reproduce accurately Heidegger's spelling of "beyng" [*Seyn*] and "being" [*Sein*]. As things stand, however, it appears that the author did not consistently maintain the distinction, so that misspellings, with "y" instead of "i" and vice-versa, are possible. Forward and back references in the text are for the most part contributed by the editor.

In accordance with Heidegger's instructions for the second division of the *Gesamtausgabe*, the text, which was written as a continuous body, was furnished with a detailed structure, including paragraphs and sections with headings. This structuring is intended as an aid for scholarly engagement with the text. It does not spare the reader the effort of working out the lecture course as a whole, which has a rigorous, cohesive flow of thought.

Double quotation marks (" . . .") are used for titles and word-for-word text citation. Single quotation marks (' . . . ') are used for highlighting words (concepts and expressions) as well as for altered citations. Elucidations of Heidegger's within quotations are placed in square brackets.

In preparing the text for typesetting, I have been helped by Herr Professor Dr. Friedrich-W. von Herrmann and Herr Dr. Hartmut Tietjen. I thank them sincerely for this. I thank Herr Klaus Neugebauer for his help in reading the proofs.

October 1979
Susanne Ziegler

Translators' Notes

[1.] A *Privatdozent* is an unsalaried private lecturer who holds a doctorate and habilitation.

[2.] The Latin, from Terence, means: "I am a human being; nothing human can be alien to me."

[3.] In the following excerpt, the numerals within the brackets indicate the version being referenced.

[4.] The German word for boredom, *Langeweile*, literally means the "long while"; *kurzweilig machen*, to make for entertainment or diversion, literally means to make "short [in] while." For an extended analysis of boredom and its temporal character, see Heidegger, *Gesamtausgabe* volume 29/30, *Die Grundbegriffe der Metaphysik: Welt—Endlichkeit—Einsamkeit.* Frankfurt: Klostermann, 1983. Translated as *The Fundamental Concepts of Metaphysics: World, Finitude, Solitude* by William McNeill and Nicholas Walker. Bloomington: Indiana University Press, 1993.

[5.] Translation adapted from Michael Hamburger, *Friedrich Hölderlin: Poems and Fragments*, 653. New York: Cambridge University Press, 1980.

[6.] Adapted from *Phenomenology of Spirit,* translated by A. V. Miller. Oxford: Oxford University Press, 1977, 19.

[7.] Adapted from *Phenomenology of Spirit,* translated by A. V. Miller. Oxford: Oxford University Press, 1977, 41.

[8.] Heidegger here differentiates *Mit-leiden*, "suffering-with," from *Mitleid*, mere "pity," and distinguishes *Leid*, "pain" in the sense of affliction or sorrow, from the *Leiden* or "suffering" that lies at the root of *Leidenschaft*, "passion." The German here reads, "Das Seyn der Halbgötter ist ein Leiden des Seyns, und Leiden kann nur wieder im Leiden erfahren werden, in einem Mit-leiden, das freilich von einem bloßen Mitleid als schwächlichem Nachgeben und Bedauern ebensoweit entfernt ist wie das bloße Leid von jenem Leiden, dem die Leidenschaft entspringt."

[9.] Here we read *Beistand* in place of *Bestand*.

[10.] The German *Notwendigkeit*, "necessity," literally means the turning of "need," *Not*.

[11.] The reference is to paragraph 163 of the *Phenomenology of Spirit*.

[12.] The term *Gründerjahre*, "founders' years," refers to the period of rapid industrial expansion in Germany from 1871–1873, following the Franco-Prussian war of 1870.

German–English Glossary

das Abendland	Western world
der Abgrund	abyss
die Absage	refusal
abwesen; die Abwesenheit	to absence; absence
ahnen; die Ahnung	to intimate; intimation
andenken; das Andenken	to remember; remembrance
der Andere	the other
der Andrang	pressure, approach
der Anfang	commencement
die Ankunft	arrival
anschaulich	intuitable, vivid, graphic
das Ansehen	appearance
der Anspruch	claim
anwesen; die Anwesenheit	to presence; presence
aufbewahren	to preserve
die Aufgabe; das Aufgegebene	task; what is allotted as a task
der Auftrag	mandate
der Augenblick	moment
die Ausdruckserscheinung	outwardly manifest expression
die Auseinandersetzung;	encounter, confrontation;
die Aus-einander-setzung	confrontational setting apart
aussetzen; die Ausgesetztheit	to expose; exposure
die Bedrängnis	distress
der Beginn	beginning, start
die Be-grenzung	the placing of limits
begründen	to ground, to found
beherrschen	to govern
die Berechnung; berechenbar	calculation; calculable
der Bereich	realm
die Bereitschaft; bereit	readiness; readied
bergen	to shelter
der Beruf; die Berufung	calling; calling
bestimmen; be-stimmen	to determine; to determine and attune
die Bestimmung	vocation, determination
bewahren; die Bewahrung	to preserve; preservation
das Bild	image
die Bindung	binding
bleiben	to remain
der Blitz	lightning flash
der Boden	soil

brauchen	to need, to use
die Bresche	breach
die Darstellung	presentation
das Dasein	existence
denken; denkerisch	to think; thoughtful
dichten; dichterisch	to poetize; poetic
die Dichtung	poetry, poetizing, poetic work
drängen	to press, to thrust
dürfen	to permit, to allow
eigentlich	proper, properly, authentic
der Eigenwille	self-will
der Einklang	harmony
einrücken	to be displaced into, to be transported into
die Einsamkeit; einsam	solitude; solitary
die Einschränkung	restrictive limitation
die Empfindung	sentiment
das Entbehrenwollen	to be willing to be deprived
enthüllen; die Enthüllung	to unveil; unveiling
entrücken; die Entrückung	to transport, to transport out; transport, rapture
die Ent-schränkung	delimiting
die Entschiedenheit	resolve
die Entscheidung; entscheidend	decision; decisive
entsprechen; die Ent-sprechung	to co-respond to; co-respondence
entspringen; das Entspringende	to spring forth, to spring from; that which springs forth
entwerfen; der Entwurf	to project; projection
erbarmen; die Erbarmung	to pity; pity
die Erde; die heimatliche Erde	the Earth; the Earth as homeland
sich ereignen	to come to pass, to occur
das Ereignis	the event
die Erfahrung	experience
erharren	to await
das Erhören	acquiescent hearing
die Erinnerung	recollection
erkämpfen	to struggle for
das Erkennen	cognition
das Erlebnis	lived experience
das Er-leiden	the suffering that sustains
der Ernst	seriousness
eröffnen	to open up
die Erscheinung	appearance
erschüttern; die Erschütterung	to unsettle; unsettling

erschweigen	to keep silent
der Erstling	the first-born
erwarten; die Erwartung	to await; expectation
erzittern	to quiver
der Fehl	lack
der Feiertag	feast day
die Feindseligkeit; die Feind-seligkeit	enmity; blessed enmity
die Ferne	distance, remoteness
die Freude; freudig	joy; joyful
fügen; der Fug	to configure, to enjoin; order, jointure
das Gedicht	poem
die Gefahr; die Gefährlichkeit	danger; dangerousness
das Gefüge	configuration
die Gegenstimmung	counter-attunement
die Gegenstrebigkeit	counter-striving
die Gegenwart; gegenwärtig	the present; present
die Gegenwendigkeit	counter-turning
der Gegenwille	counter-will
das Geheimnis	mystery
der Geist; geistig	spirit; spiritual
die Gemeinschaft	community
das Gepräge	stamp
das Gerede	idle talk
das Gesagte	what is said
geschehen; das Geschehen	to occur; occurrence, event
der Geschehenszusammenhang	nexus of occurrence
das Geschehnis	event, occurrence
die Geschichte; geschichtlich	history, historical
die Geschichtlichkeit	historicality
das Geschick	destiny
das Geschlecht	race
das Gesetz	law
das Gespräch	dialogue
die Gewalt; gewaltig; gewaltsam	force, power; mighty; violent
die Gewaltsamkeit	violence
die Gewesenheit	having been
die Geworfenheit	thrownness
gleichursprünglich	equiprimordial
die Götterlosigkeit	the absence of the gods
die Göttlichkeit	divinity
die Grenze	border, limit, threshold
gründen; die Gründung	to ground, grounding

das Grundgefüge	fundamental configuration
das Grundgeschehen; das Grundgeschehnis	fundamental occurrence; fundamental event
die Grundstellung	fundamental orientation
die Grundstimmung	fundamental attunement
das Grundverhältnis	fundamental relation
der Halbgott	demigod
die Haltung	stance, composure, disposition
das Harmonischentgegengesetzte	the harmoniously opposed
harren	to await
heilig	sacred, holy
die heilig trauernde, bereite Bedrängnis	holy mourning in readied distress
die Heimat; heimatlich	homeland; of the homeland
hell	lucid
das Heraufkommen	emergence
die Herkunft	provenance
herrschen; die Herrschaft	to reign, to govern; domination
herstellen	to produce
der Hinweis	pointer
hören; hörenkönnen	to hear; to able to hear
hüllen	to shroud, to veil
die Innigkeit; innig	intimacy; intimately
die Inständigkeit	inherence
irren	to wander in errancy
die Kameradschaft	comradeship
der Kampf	struggle, battle
das Kaum-Enthüllen-Dürfen	scarcely being allowed to unveil
klagen; die Klage	to have plaint; plaint
künftig	futural, to come
die Langeweile	boredom
leiden; das Leiden	to suffer; suffering
die Leidenschaft; die Leidenschaftlichkeit	passion; impassioned character
der Lichtblick	illuminating look
der Lichtstrahl	ray of light
die Macht	power
der Machtbereich der Dichtung	the domain in which poetry unfolds its power
das Maß	measure
das Miteinandersein	being with one another

das Mitgegebene; die Mitgift	what is given as endowment; endowment
mithören	to accompany the hearing
mitleiden	to suffer with
mitsagen	to follow the telling
die Mitte	middle
das Mögliche; die Möglichkeit	the possible; possibility
die Nähe	proximity, nearness
nennen	to name
das Nichthörenwollen	not wanting to hear
das Nichtsein	non-being
das Nichttreffenkönnen	not being able to hit the mark
das Nicht-wirkliche	the non-real
die Not	need
nötigen	to compel
die Notlösigkeit	needlessness
die Notwendigkeit	necessity
offenbar; offenbar machen; die Offenbarkeit	manifest; to make manifest; manifestness
die Offenbarung	revelation
die Offenheit	openness
opfern	to sacrifice
der Ort; die Örtlichkeit	locale; locality
die Pforte	portal
prägen; das Gepräge	to stamp, to coin; stamp
das Rätsel	enigma
der Raum	space
rechnen	to reckon
reißen	to tear
retten	to save
die Rückfügung	being enjoined back
rufen; das Rufen	to call; calling
die Sage	legend, myth
sagen	to say, to tell
schaffen	to create
der Schein	semblance
die Scheu	reticence
scheitern	to fall short
schicken; das Schickliche	to fit; what is fitting
das Schicksal	destiny
die Schickung	sending

der Schmerz	pain
schweben	to hover
schweigen	to keep silent
schwingen	to oscillate, to resonate
das Schwingungsgefüge	overarching resonance
seelig	blessed
des Seiende, das Seyende	beings, beyngs
das Sein, das Seyn	being, beyng
das Seinsgefüge	configuration of being
die Seinsmacht	power of being
die Selbstständigkeit	self-steadfastness
die Seligkeit; selig	blessedness, bliss; blessed
die Sendung	mission
die Seynsbedrohung	threatening of beyng
der Sinn	meaning
das Sinnbild	sensuous image
die Sorge	care
die Sorg-losigkeit	care-freeness
sparen	to spare
das Sprachgebilde	linguistic construction
das Sprachgefüge	configuring of language
das Sprachgeschehnis	event of language
sprechen	to speak
der Spruch	saying
der Sprung	leap
der Staat	state
die Stelle	point, place; excerpt
stiften; die Stiftung	to found; founding
die Stimme	voice
stimmen; durchstimmen	to attune; to attune through and through
die Stimmung	attunement
der Streit	strife
teilnehmen	to partake
das Tor	gate, gateway
trauern; die Trauer	to mourn; mourning
die Treue	fidelity
überantworten	to be delivered over
überfallen	to befall
überhören; das Überhören	to fail to hear; the failure to hear
die Überlegenkeit	superiority
die Übermacht	overwhelming power
das Übermaß	excess
der Übermensch; übermenschlich	overhuman; what exceeds the human
überspringen	to leap over

das Überwaltigende	the overwhelming
der Überwille	excess of will
der Umschlag	sudden turnaround
umstimmen	to change attunement
unangebunden	untethered
uneigennützig	disinterested
uneigentlich	inauthentic
unerfahren	untraveled
das Unerschöpfliche	the inexhaustible
das Ungesagte	what is unsaid
ungesprochen	unspoken
das Unschickliche	what is unfitting
unschuldig	innocent
unsinnlich	non-sensuous
der Untergang	decline
untergehen	to perish
der Untergott	undergod
das Un-vermutete	something unsuspected
das Unwesen	corrupted essence
das Unwirkliche	the unreal
die Unzeit	inopportune time
der Urbereich	primordial realm
die Ursprache	originary language
der Ursprung; ursprünglich	origin; originary
das Vaterland	fatherland
verantworten	to take responsibility
verbergen	to conceal
der Verdienst	merit
die Verendlichung	tending toward self-limitation
der Verfall	decline
die Vergangenheit	what is past
vergehen; das Vergehen	to pass; dissolution
das Verhalten	comportment
verhören	to mishear
die Verhüllung	veiling
die Verlassenheit	abandonment
verlegen	to locate, to transfer
die Verleugnung	denial
vermitteln	to mediate
vernehmen	to apprehend
versagen	to refuse
versetzen; das Versetztsein	to transpose; transposition
versinnbildlichen	to symbolize
der Verstand	intellect
verzichten; der Verzicht	to renounce; renunciation
das Volk	people

vorbeigehen	to pass by
der Vor-bruch	breakthrough
der Vorgang	process
vorhanden	present at hand
das Vor-leiden	to suffer in advance
vor-springen	to leap ahead
die Vorstellung	representation
das Wahre; die Wahrheit	the true; truth
walten; durchwalten	to prevail; to prevail throughout
die Wandlung	transformation
der Weg	path
weisen; die Weisung	to point; pointer
werden	to come into being, become
werfen	to throw
das Werk	work
wesen; das Wesen	to prevail in essence, to come to presence; essence
das Wesende	what is still present, what still presences
die Wesensbestimmung	essential determination
der Widerstreit	conflict
der Wink	beckoning
der Wirbel	turbulence
das Wirkliche	the real
das Wirkungsfeld; die Wirkungsmacht	effective domain; effective power
das Wissen; wissend	knowing; knowingly
die Wissenschaft	science
wohnen	to dwell
wollen	to will, to want
das Zeichen	sign
zeigen	to show
die Zeit; die Zeitentscheidung	time; temporal decision
zeitigen; die Zeitigung	to temporalize; temporalizing
die Zeitlichkeit	temporality
zerklüften	to cleave
zeugen; der Zeuge	to witness, to bear witness, to engender; witness
die Zucht	discipline
die Zukunft; zukünftig	future; futural, of the future
die Zweideutigkeit	ambiguity
der Zweifelende	he who doubts
zwingen	to compel
das Zwischenwesen	in-between being

English–German Glossary

abandonment	die Verlassenheit
to absence; absence	abwesen; die Abwesenheit
the absence of the gods	die Götterlosigkeit
abyss	der Abgrund
to accompany the hearing	mithören
acquiescent hearing	das Erhören
to be allowed	dürfen
ambiguity	die Zweideutigkeit
appearance	das Ansehen; die Erscheinung
to apprehend	vernehmen
approach	der Andrang
arrival	die Ankunft
to attune; to attune through and through	stimmen; durchstimmen
attunement	die Stimmung
authentic	eigentlich
to await	erwarten, erharren, harren
battle	der Kampf
beckoning	der Wink
to become	werden
to befall	überfallen
beginning	der Beginn
being; beyng	das Sein; das Seyn
beings, beyngs	das Seiende, das Seyende
being with one another	das Miteinandersein
binding	die Bindung
blessedness; blessed enmity	die Seligkeit; die Feind-seligkeit
bliss; blissful	die Seligkeit; glükseelig
border	die Grenze
boredom	die Langeweile
breach	die Bresche
breakthrough	der Vor-bruch
calculation; calculable	die Berechnung; berechenbar
to call; calling	rufen; die Berufung, der Beruf, das Rufen
care	die Sorge
care-freeness	die Sorg-losigkeit
to change in attunement	umstimmen
claim	der Anspruch
to cleave	zerklüften

cognition	das Erkennen
to coin	prägen
what is to come	künftig
to come to be	werden
to come to pass	sich ereignen
to come to presence	wesen
commencement	der Anfang
community	die Gemeinschaft
comportment	das Verhalten
comradeship	die Kameradschaft
to compel	nötigen; zwingen
composure	die Haltung
configuration of being	das Seinsgefüge
to configure; configuration	fügen; das Gefüge
configuring the ground	das Grundgefüge
configuring of language	das Sprachgefüge
conflict	der Widerstreit
confrontation; confrontational setting apart	die Auseinandersetzung; die Aus-einander–setzung
to conserve	verwahren
to correspond to; co-respondence	entsprechen; die Ent-sprechung
corrupted essence	das Unwesen
counter-attunement	die Gegenstimmung
counter-striving	die Gegenstrebigkeit
counter-turning	die Gegenwendigkeit
counter-will	der Gegenwille
to create	schaffen
danger; dangerousness	die Gefahr; die Gefährlicheit
decision; decisive	die Entscheidung; entscheidend
decline	der Verfall; der Untergang
delimiting	die Ent-schränkung
to be delivered over	überantworten
demigod	der Halbgott
denial	die Verleugnung
deprivation	das Entbehren
destiny	das Geschick; das Schicksal
determination	die Bestimmung
to determine; to determine and attune	bestimmen; be-stimmen
dialogue	das Gespräch
discipline	die Zucht
disinterested	uneigennützig
to be displaced, to be displaced into	einrücken
disposition	die Haltung
dissolution	das Vergehen

distance	die Ferne
distress	die Bedrängnis
divinity	die Göttlichkeit
the domain in which poetry unfolds its power	der Machtbereich der Dichtung
domination	die Herrschaft
doubt; he who doubts	der Zweifel; der Zweifelnde
to dwell	wohnen
the Earth; the Earth as homeland	die Erde; die heimatliche Erde
effective domain; effective power	das Wirkungsfeld; die Wirkungsmacht
emergence	das Heraufkommen
endowment; what is given as endowment	die Mitgift; das Mitgegebene
to engender	zeugen
enigma	das Rätsel
to enjoin; being enjoined back	fügen; die Rückfügung
enmity; blessed enmity	die Feindseligkeit; die Feind-seligkeit
enraptured	entrückt
equiprimordial	gleichursprünglich
essence	das Wesen
essential determination	die Wesensbestimmung
event	das Geschehen, das Geschehnis, das Ereignis
event of language	das Sprachgeschenis
exceeding the human	übermenschlich
excerpt	die Stelle
excess	der Übermaß
excess of will	der Überwille
existence	das Dasein
expectation	die Erwartung
experience	die Erfahrung
to expose; exposure	aussetzen; die Ausgesetztheit
the failure to hear	das Überhören
to fall short	scheitern
fatherland	das Vaterland
fidelity	die Treue
the first-born	der Erstling
to fit	schicken
fitting	das Schickliche
force	die Gewalt
to found; founding	begründen, stiften; die Stiftung
fundamental attunement	die Grundstimmung
fundamental configuration	das Grundgefüge

fundamental event	das Grundgeschehnis
fundamental occurrence	das Grundgeschehen
fundamental orientation	die Grundstellung
fundamental relation	das Gründverhältnis
futural, of the future	zukünftig
future	die Zukunft
gate, gateway	das Tor
to govern	beherrschen, herrschen
graphic	anschaulich
to ground; grounding	begründen, gründen; die Gründung
the harmoniously opposed	das Harmonischentgegengesetzte
harmony	der Einklang
having been	die Gewesenheit
to hear; to be able to hear	hören; hörenkönnen
historicality	die Geschichtlichkeit
history; historical	die Geschichte; geschichtlich
holy	heilig
holy mourning in readied distress	die heilig trauernde, bereite Bedrängnis
homeland; of the homeland	die Heimat; heimatlich
idle talk	das Gerede
illuminating look	der Lichtblick
image	das Bild
inauthentic	uneigentlich
the inexhaustible	das Unerschöpfliche
inherence	die Inständigkeit
inopportune time	die Unzeit
instruction	der Auftrag
intellect	der Verstand
intimacy; intimately	die Innigkeit; innig
to intimate; intimation	ahnen; die Ahnung
intuitable	anschaulich
jointure	der Fug
joy; joyful	die Freude; freudig
knowing; knowingly	das Wissen; wissend
lack	der Fehl
law	das Gesetz
leap	der Sprung
to leap ahead; to leap over	vor-springen; überspringen
legend	die Sage

lightning flash	der Blitz
limit; the placing of limits	die Grenze; die Be-grenzung
linguistic construction	das Sprachgebilde
lived experience	das Erlebnis
locale; locality	der Ort, die Örtlichkeit
to locate	verlegen
lucid	hell
mandate	der Auftrag
manifest; to make manifest	offenbar; offenbar machen
manifestness	die Offenbarkeit
meaning	der Sinn
measure	das Maß
to mediate	vermitteln
merit	der Verdienst
middle	die Mitte
to mishear	verhören
mission	die Sendung
moment	der Augenblick
to mourn; mourning	trauern; die Trauer
mystery	das Geheimnis
myth	die Sage
to name	nennen
nearness	die Nähe
necessity	die Notwendigkeit
need	die Not
to need	brauchen
needlessness	die Notlösigkeit
nexus of occurrence	der Geschehenszusammenhang
non-being	das Nichtsein
the non-real	das Nicht-wirkliche
non-sensuous	unsinnlich
not being able to hit the mark	das Nichttreffenkönnen
not wanting to hear	das Nichthörenwollen
to occur; occurrence	geschehen, sich ereignen; das Geschehen
openness	die Offenheit
to open up	eröffnen
order	der Fug
origin; originary	der Ursprung; ursprünglich
originary language	die Ursprache
to oscillate	schwingen
the Other	der Andere
outwardly manifest expression	die Ausdruckserscheinung
overarching resonance	das Schwingungsgefüge

overhuman	der Übermensch
the overwhelming	das Überwältigende
overwhelming power	die Übermacht
pain	der Schmerz
to partake	teilnehmen
to pass; to pass by	vergehen; vorbeigehen
passion; impassioned character	die Leidenschaft; die Leidenschaftlichkeit
past; what is past	die Vergangenheit; das Vergangene
people	das Volk
to perish	untergehen
to permeate with attunement	durchstimmen
to permit	dürfen
to pity; pity	erbarmen; die Erbarmung
to have plaint; plaint	klagen; die Klage
poem	die Dichtung, das Gedicht
to poetize	dichten
poetry, poetic work, poetizing	die Dichtung
point	die Stelle
to point; pointer	weisen; die Weisung
pointer	der Hinweis
portal	die Pforte
the possible; possibility	das Mögliche; die Möglichkeit
power	die Macht; die Gewalt
power of being	die Seinsmacht
to presence; present	anwesen; die Anwesenheit
present	die Gegenwart
what is still present, what still presences	das Wesende
present at hand	vorhanden
presentation	die Darstellung
to preserve; preservation	aufbewahren, bewahren; die Bewahrung
to press; pressure	drängen; der Andrang
to prevail; to prevail throughout	walten; durchwalten
to prevail in its essence	wesen
primordial realm	der Urbereich
process	der Vorgang
to produce	herstellen
to project; projection	entwerfen; der Entwurf
proper, properly	eigentlich
provenance	die Herkunft
proximity	die Nähe
question-worthiness	die Fragwürdigkeit
to quiver	erzittern

race	das Geschlecht
rapture	die Entrückung
ray of light	der Lichtstrahl
readiness; readied	die Bereitschaft; bereit
the real	das Wirkliche
realm	der Bereich
to reckon	rechnen
recollection	die Erinnerung
to refuse; refusal	versagen; die Absage
to reign	herrschen
to remain	bleiben
to remember; remembrance	andenken; das Andenken
remoteness	die Ferne
to renounce; renunciation	verzichten; der Verzicht
representation	die Vorstellung
resolve	die Entschiedenheit
to resonate	schwingen
restrictive limitation	die Einschänkung
reticence	die Scheu
revelation	die Offenbarung
sacred	heilig
to sacrifice	opfern
to save	retten
to say; what is said	sagen; das Gesagte
saying	das Sagen, der Spruch
science	die Wissenschaft
self-limitation, tending toward	die Verendlichung
self-steadfastness	die Selbstständigkeit
self-will	der Eigenwille
semblance	der Schein
sending	die Schickung
sensuous image	das Sinnbild
sentiment	die Empfindung
seriousness	der Ernst
to show	zeigen
to shroud	hüllen
sign	das Zeichen
silence; to keep silent	das Schweigen; erschweigen, schweigen
soil	der Boden
solitude; solitary	die Einsamkeit; einsam
space	der Raum
to speak	sprechen
spirit; spiritual	der Geist; geistig
to spring forth; that which springs forth	entspringen; das Entspringende

to stamp; stamp	prägen; das Gepräge
stance	die Haltung
to stand firm	standhalten
start	der Beginn
state	der Staat
strife	der Streit
to struggle; struggle	erkämpfen; der Kampf
sudden turnaround	der Umschlag
to suffer; suffering	leiden; das Leiden
suffering in advance	das Vor-leiden
suffering that sustains	das Er-leiden
to suffer with	mitleiden
superiority	die Überlegenheit
to symbolize	versinnbildlichen
to take on	übernehmen
to take responsibility	verantworten
task; what is allotted as a task	die Aufgabe; das Aufgegebene
to tear	reißen
to tell; the telling	sagen; das Sagen
to follow the telling	mitsagen
temporality	die Zeitlichkeit
to temporalize; temporalizing	zeitigen; die Zeitigung
to think; thoughtful	denken; denkerisch
threatening of beyng	die Seynsbedrohung
threshold	die Grenze
to throw; thrownness	werfen; die Geworfenheit
to thrust	drängen
time	die Zeit
to transfer	verlegen
transformation	die Wandlung
to transport; transport	entrücken; die Entrückung
to transport into	einrücken
to transpose; transposition	versetzen; das Versetztsein
the true; truth	das Wahre; die Wahrheit
turbulence	der Wirbel
turnaround	der Umschlag
undergod	der Untergott
un-essence	das Un-wesen
unfitting	unschicklich
the unreal	das Unwirkliche
unsaid; the unsaid	ungesagt, das Ungesagte
to unsettle; unsettling	erschüttern; die Erschütterung
unspoken	ungesprochen
something un-suspected	das Un-vermutete
untethered	unangebunden

untraveled	unerfahren
to unveil; unveiling	enthüllen; die Enthüllung
scarcely being allowed to unveil	das Kaum-Enthüllen-Dürfen
to use	brauchen
to veil; veiling	hüllen; die Verhüllung
violence	die Gewaltsamkeit
violent	gewaltig, gewaltsam
vivid	anschaulich
vocation	die Bestimmung
voice	die Stimme
to wander in errancy	irren
to want	wollen
Western world	das Abendland
to will	wollen
to witness, to bear witness; witness	zeugen; der Zeuge
work	das Werk